How to Build M&E Systems to Support Better Government

Keith Mackay

http://www.worldbank.org/ieg
http://www.worldbank.org/ieg/ecd

2007
The World Bank
Washington, D.C.

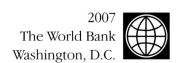

Cover photo credits: Upper left, Egyptian planners, by Ray Witlin, World Bank Photo Library; upper right, road repairs in South Africa, by Trevor Samson, World Bank Photo Library; lower left, picture courtesy of Leica Geosystems; lower right, Egyptian railway worker, by Ray Witlin, World Bank Photo Library.

ISBN: 978-0-8213-7191-6
e-ISBN: 978-0-8213-7192-3
DOI: 10.1596/978-0-8213-7191-6

Library of Congress Cataloging-in-Publication Data have been applied for.

World Bank InfoShop
E-mail: pic@worldbank.org
Telephone: 202-458-5454
Facsimile: 202-522-1500

Independent Evaluation Group
Knowledge Programs and Evaluation Capacity
Development (IEGKE)
E-mail: eline@worldbank.org
Telephone: 202-458-4497
Facsimile: 202-522-3125

 Printed on Recycled Paper

Contents

Foreword

Since its creation in 1973, the World Bank's Independent Evaluation Group (IEG)—formerly known as the Operations Evaluation Department—has supported the efforts of governments in developing countries to strengthen their monitoring and evaluation (M&E) systems and capacities. Over this period, IEG has accumulated considerable experience in this topic in a wide range of countries and public sector environments.

In 1998, IEG initiated a series of working papers and other publications on this topic to document and to help disseminate these lessons. These publications are available on the IEG Web site: http://www.worldbank.org/ieg/ecd. The very high interest in this topic is reflected in the high level of readership of these publications—the Web site alone attracts more than 110,000 visitors each year, and it accounts for a substantial proportion of IEG's total readership.

IEG's publications on this topic document good practice and promising practice country systems for M&E. They also include diagnostic guides, country diagnoses, examples of highly influential evaluations, and didactic material on M&E tools and impact evaluation, among other things. In this context, the purpose of this volume is to synthesize and digest for readers this body of knowledge.

Part I of this volume starts by focusing on exactly what monitoring and evaluation has to offer to governments. It endeavors to clarify the sub-stance underlying the rhetoric. A brief primer on M&E is provided (chapter 2), together with a discussion of the specific ways in which monitoring information and evaluation findings can and have been used to improve government performance, such as in support of budget decision making (chapter 3). It is argued that utilization of M&E information is a necessary condition for the effective management of public expenditures for poverty reduction—in other words, that M&E is necessary to achieve evidence-based policy making, evidence-based management, and evidence-based accountability. This is why most of the member countries of the Organisation for Economic Cooperation and Development—the richest countries in the world—place considerable emphasis on having and using M&E information in support of sound governance. Some of the key trends influencing countries to give higher priority to M&E are also discussed (chapter 4).

Part II focuses on the experience of several countries that have succeeded in building a well-functioning government M&E system. Chapter 5 examines what exactly a "successful" M&E system looks like. Several country examples—including Chile (chapter 6), Colombia (chapter 7), and Australia (chapter 8)—illustrate such a system. However, note that a special theme of this volume is that there is no "best" model of what a government or sectoral M&E system should look like. In relatively weak countries, a more cautious focus on incremental changes can be appropriate if they have the potential to demonstrate that M&E is cost effective. Africa, where there are many severe capacity constraints, is examined (chapter 9) in that light.

Part III analyzes the lessons from building government M&E systems in these and many other countries, both developing and developed. Thirteen key lessons are emphasized (chapter 10); these are also consistent with international experience in other types of public sector capacity building. The lessons include, for example, the prerequisite of substantive government demand for monitoring information and evaluation findings and the central role of incentives. They also include the value of conducting a diagnosis of M&E in a country and of having a powerful champion for M&E. Weak government demand for M&E is common and is often perceived as an insuperable barrier to efforts to build an M&E system. This is not the case, however; there exist a number of ways to create demand for M&E, using a mix of carrots, sticks, and sermons (chapter 11).

Ways to strengthen a government M&E system are presented in Part IV. Particular attention is paid to the benefits from conducting a country diagnosis (chapter 12). Such a diagnosis can provide a sound understanding of current M&E efforts in a country, the civil service environment, and the opportunities to use M&E information for core government functions such as budget decision making and ongoing management of programs and projects. A diagnosis would naturally lead to an action plan that identifies the main options for strengthening a government's M&E system (chapter 13).

Part V maps out those issues where international experience with government M&E systems is not well understood or well documented. These include frontier, cutting-edge issues such as the cost-effectiveness of alternative approaches to strengthening government systems and good practice models of M&E at the sector and subnational levels (chapter 14). Answers are provided to a number of questions that are frequently raised on the topic of government M&E systems (chapter 15). These include a list of the main dangers and pitfalls to avoid when trying to strengthen M&E in a country, such as the mistaken belief that M&E has intrinsic merit, or taking a technocratic approach to capacity building.

Finally, Part VI provides a series of commonly asked questions on M&E—and their answers.

Acknowledgments

This volume was written by Keith Mackay, who initiated the series of IEG working papers and other publications on this topic in 1998. It has benefited from peer review comments provided by Harry Hatry and David Shand. Heather Dittbrenner edited the volume. However, the views expressed in this volume are solely those of the author and do not necessarily represent the views of the World Bank or the IEG. The generous financial support of the Norwegian Agency for Development Cooperation (Norad) is gratefully acknowledged.

ABBREVIATIONS

AfrEA	African Evaluation Association
ANAO	Australian National Audit Office
COINFO	Data Coordination Committee (Colombia)
CONPES	National Council for Economic and Social Policy (Colombia)
CRC	Citizen report card
DAC	Development Assistance Committee (OECD)
DANE	National Statistical Office (Colombia)
DDTS	Directorate for Sustainable Territorial Development (Colombia)
DEPP	Directorate for Evaluation of Public Policy (Colombia)
DFID	Department for International Development (United Kingdom)
DIFP	Directorate for Investment and Public Finance (part of DNP)
DNP	Department of National Planning (Colombia)
DoF	Department of Finance (Australia)
ECD	Evaluation capacity development
GAO	Government Accountability Office (United States)
HMN	Health Metrics Network
IADB	Inter-American Development Bank
ICBF	Colombian Institute for Family Welfare
IDEAS	International Development Evaluation Association
IEG	Independent Evaluation Group
M&E	Monitoring and evaluation
MEN	Ministry of Education (Colombia)
MDGs	Millennium Development Goals
MoF	Ministry of Finance (Chile)
NGO	Nongovernmental organization
NIMES	National Integrated Monitoring and Evaluation System (Uganda)
OECD	Organisation for Economic Co-operation and Development
OMB	Office of Management and Budget (United States)
PART	Program Assessment Rating Tool (United States)
PBB	Performance-based budgeting
PEAP	Poverty Eradication Action Plan (Uganda)
PEP	Portfolio Evaluation Plan (Australia)
PETS	Public Expenditure Tracking Survey (Uganda)
PRSP	Poverty reduction strategy paper
SEDESOL	Secretariat for Social Development (Mexico)
SENA	Vocational Training Institute (Colombia)
SIGOB	Sistema de Programación y Gestión por Objetivos y Resultados (System of Programming and Management by Objectives and Results, Colombia)
SINERGIA	Sistema Nacional de Evaluación de Resultados de la Gestión Pública (National System for Evaluation of Public Sector Performance, Colombia)
SIIF	Financial management information system (Colombia)
ToRs	Terms of reference

1

Introduction

A growing number of governments are working to improve their performance by creating systems to measure and help them understand their performance. These systems for monitoring and evaluation (M&E) are used to measure the quantity, quality, and targeting of the goods and services—the outputs—that the state provides and to measure the outcomes and impacts resulting from these outputs. These systems are also a vehicle to facilitate understanding of the causes of good and poor performance.

There are many reasons for the increasing efforts to strengthen government M&E systems. Fiscal pressures and ever-rising expectations from ordinary citizens provide a continuing impetus for governments to provide more government services and with higher standards of quality. These pressures are also reason enough to find more cost-effective ways of operating so that governments can do more with less. Countries in the developing world often look to the richest countries—the members of the Organisation for Economic Cooperation and Development (OECD)—and adopt the public sector management tools that these countries typically employ, such as M&E and performance budgeting. Civil society and parliaments are also putting accountability pressures on governments to publicly report and explain their performances. And international donors are being pressed to demonstrate the results of the large volumes of aid spending for which they are responsible; they in turn are working to persuade and support developing countries to strengthen their own M&E systems.

In recent years, donor support has particularly focused on poorer countries, that is, those that prepare poverty-reduction strategies as part of debt-relief initiatives. These countries are trying to achieve the Millennium Development Goals (MDGs). Donors are also starting to appreciate that country M&E systems can play a role in anti-corruption efforts; these systems help identify "leakages" in government funding, as well as some of the possible consequences of corruption—such as when government spending is not reflected in the physical quality of infrastructure or in the volume and quality of services provided.

M&E, and systems for M&E, are often viewed in narrow, technocratic terms, akin to developing a financial management or a procurement system. There are indeed technical aspects of M&E and M&E systems that need to be managed carefully. But a technocratic emphasis is highly inadequate if it ignores the factors that determine the extent to which M&E information is actually used. Where an M&E system is underutilized, this not only constitutes a waste of resources, but it is also likely to seriously undermine the quality of the information the system produces. It also throws into question the sustainability of the system itself.

Evaluation specialists often argue that M&E and M&E systems are a "good thing" and have intrinsic merit. Management improvement experts often appear to argue that results-based management or other ways of using M&E information offer some sort of panacea for improving government performance. Weak advocacy arguments of this kind are unconvincing to skeptical or overstressed governments in the developing world. However, highly convincing examples do exist of governments that have devoted the necessary effort to building an M&E system. These governments heavily utilize the M&E information the systems produce and have used this information to significantly improve the performance of their policies, programs, and projects.

The purpose of this volume is to help governments in their efforts to build, strengthen, and fully institutionalize their M&E systems, not as an end in itself but in support of improved government performance—in other words, sound governance. The volume brings together the considerable experience accumulated by the World Bank's Independent Evaluation Group (IEG) in its longstanding program of support for governments and Bank staff in their efforts to build M&E systems. It also draws on the growing body of literature from other sources on this issue.

There is currently a great deal of emphasis on *results* and on being able to demonstrate performance. Part I focuses on exactly what M&E has to offer governments; it endeavors to clarify the substance underlying the rhetoric. Chapter 2 provides a brief primer on monitoring and evaluation. Annex E is a continuation of that discussion, presenting the glossary of key terms in evaluation and results-based management developed by the Development Assistance Committee (DAC) of the OECD. To some senior officials and donor staff, M&E can appear to be a highly technical topic with techniques that are difficult for nonspecialists to understand. This chapter endeavors to demystify

M&E by providing an eagle's-eye view of a range of different types and methods of M&E.

Chapter 3 follows with a discussion of the specific ways M&E can and has been used to improve government performance. The focus here is on ways governments have used M&E, such as in support of budget decision making. Examples are provided to show civil society's use of M&E to measure and prompt governments to improve their performance. A number of examples of influential evaluations are also provided, and these confirm that M&E can be highly cost-effective for governments. Key trends that are influencing countries to build M&E systems are considered briefly in chapter 4.

Part II focuses on the experience of several countries that have succeeded in building a well-functioning M&E system. Chapter 5 outlines what a "successful" government M&E system looks like; three dimensions of success are proposed. A common question is whether there are actually any countries that have successfully created a national M&E system. The answer to this question is an unambiguous "yes." Many developed and a small but growing number of developing countries have succeeded in building well-performing, whole-of-government M&E systems. Case studies of three such countries—Chile, Colombia, and Australia—are presented in chapters 6, 7, and 8.

The special case of Africa is discussed in chapter 9. Africa is clearly a high priority for the international community, and it has been the focus of a considerable amount of development assistance, including capacity building. Efforts to strengthen M&E have been made in the context of preparation of poverty-reduction strategies. This chapter considers some of the difficulties and opportunities faced by poor countries in these efforts.

Many developed and developing countries have accumulated substantive experience in building monitoring and evaluation systems. As with any form of capacity building, there are a number of hard-won lessons about what works best and what does not, and these are discussed in Part III.

The consistency of these lessons across different countries and Regions is not surprising; the experiences are in accord with international experience with other types of capacity building in the area of public sector management, such as budget systems or civil service reform (chapter 10). As noted earlier, the issue of utilization of M&E information is central to the performance and sustainability of an M&E system. Utilization depends on the nature and strength of demand for M&E information—which depends, in turn, on the incentives to use M&E. Countries whose demand for M&E is low or only lukewarm may be perceived as facing an insuperable barrier to building M&E systems. But this perspective is far too pessimistic; there are ways to increase demand by strengthening incentives, and these are discussed in chapter 11, which focuses on carrots, sticks, and sermons to ensure utilization of M&E information.

Ways that a government M&E system can be strengthened are presented in Part IV. One of the lessons for building an M&E system is the importance of conducting a country diagnosis (chapter 12). That diagnosis provides a sound understanding of the current M&E efforts, the public sector environment, and opportunities for strengthening M&E systems and using M&E information. The information can be used for core government functions such as budget decision making and ongoing management of programs and projects. Perhaps equally important, a diagnosis helps focus key stakeholders within government and the donor community on the strengths and weaknesses of current M&E arrangements. Such a diagnosis can also ensure that these stakeholders share a common awareness of the issues. A diagnosis naturally leads to an action plan that identifies the main options for strengthening a government M&E system (chapter 13).

This volume cannot and does not attempt to address all the issues that can arise when seeking to build a government M&E system or to strengthen an existing system. Part V maps out some issues about which international experience is not well understood or documented. These frontier, cutting-edge issues are topics that are important for

the institutionalization of M&E but where current knowledge appears to be insufficient (chapter 14). They include good practice models of M&E at the subnational and sectoral levels; ways governments can effectively and credibly work to support civil society on issues of M&E of government performance; and the cost-effectiveness of alternative models of donor support for the institutionalization of M&E.

Some concluding remarks are provided in chapter 15.

Part VI provides answers to a number of questions that commonly arise at national and international conferences on the topic of this volume. The frequency with which similar questions are raised helps us identify key issues that have to be addressed when seeking to institutionalize an M&E system.

One challenge faced by government and donor evaluation offices alike is to ensure that the evaluations they produce are used intensively. It is now well understood that it is not enough to complete an evaluation report, make it publicly available, and assume that utilization will somehow take care of itself. Instead, individual evaluators and their evaluation offices need to be highly proactive in implementing a detailed strategy for dissemination of not just the evaluation report but its findings as well—to encourage acceptance of the evaluation's findings and implementation of its recommendations. Various lessons and tips for ensuring evaluations are influential are presented in annex A.

Annex B includes an example of a country diagnosis for Colombia. Illustrative terms of reference (ToRs) for a more in-depth diagnosis of Colombia's M&E system are presented in annex C. The findings of a self-evaluation of IEG's support for institutionalizing M&E systems are shown in annex D. This evaluation provides one possible model for donors and governments seeking to evaluate their own efforts to build or strengthen a country's M&E system. Finally, a glossary of key M&E terms is provided in annex E.

PART I

WHAT DO MONITORING AND EVALUATION HAVE TO OFFER GOVERNMENTS?

Part I focuses on what exactly M&E has to offer to governments; it endeavors to clarify the substance underlying the rhetoric. Chapter 2 provides a brief primer on monitoring and evaluation. It addresses the question of what exactly M&E is and discusses some of the main tools, methods, and approaches governments and international donors commonly use. This is followed in chapter 3 by a discussion of the specific ways M&E can be and has been used to improve government performance. Key trends influencing countries to build M&E systems are then considered briefly in chapter 4.

What Is M&E?
An M&E Primer

There are many related terms and concepts in the field of M&E. These can be confusing. Moreover, different countries and different development agencies often use varying definitions of similar concepts. DAC has developed a glossary of key terms and concepts in an effort to reduce this confusion and achieve some harmonization (DAC 2002). Annex E provides that text. This chapter offers a broader overview discussion.

Performance indicators are measures of inputs, activities, outputs, outcomes, and impacts of government activities. Indicators can be very high level, in terms of measuring the government's performance relative to the MDGs or the national development plan, or in terms of ministry and agency activities and outputs. They are useful for setting performance targets, for assessing progress toward achieving them, and for comparing the performance of different organizations. They are a relatively inexpensive means of measuring government performance on a frequent basis.

Although performance indicators can be used to identify problems, thus allowing corrective action to be taken, a limitation is that they do not usually reveal whether government actions led to improved performance. They can, however, be used to flag the need for a follow-up review or evaluation of an issue. A common danger with performance indicator systems is overengineering the system by including too many underutilized indicators; this can lead to poor-quality data.

Rapid appraisal methods are quick, low-cost ways to gather the views and feedback of beneficiaries and other stakeholders. These views provide rapid information for management decision making, especially at the activity or program level. Methods include interviews, focus group discussions, direct observation, and mini-surveys. It can be difficult to generalize the findings from these qualitative methods. They are also less valid, reliable, and credible than formal surveys.

Rapid evaluation involves a formal review of a government activity or program. In Chile, for example, rapid evaluations entail desk reviews by external consultants of a program's objectives and preparation of a logframe analysis (which maps the causal links between government activities and desired outcomes and impacts). Any available data (including performance indicators) are analyzed to assess the efficiency and effectiveness of the activity. The World Bank uses this approach in many of its ex ante and ex post project evaluations. The Bank also uses a range of additional information in its ex post evaluations, including the findings of supervision missions, key informant interviews, and any primary or secondary data that have been collected.

The main strengths of rapid evaluations are their speed and relatively low cost. Their main disadvantages—compared with more rigorous approaches—are their weaker empirical evidence and much weaker data-analysis techniques. They also face difficulty in identifying possible causal relationships between government actions and subsequent improvements in performance.

Impact evaluation focuses on the outcomes and impacts of government activities. Rapid evaluation methods can be used to estimate impact, but more sophisticated methods of impact evaluation can provide much more reliable and persuasive findings. Such methods entail the comparison of program beneficiaries with control or comparison groups at two or more points in time. Advanced statistical techniques are used to identify the precise impacts of the program on beneficiaries. This type of evaluation is highly demanding in terms of data and can be very expensive; however, there are ways this cost can be reduced significantly. It is necessary to plan such evaluations well in advance of when their findings will be needed, as it is usually not possible to conduct them quickly. Although sophisticated evaluations are often expensive, they can be highly cost-effective when they lead to even marginal improvements in program performance.

Comprehensive spending reviews are a type of policy evaluation. Chile's finance ministry uses these to review all programs within a particular functional area, such as schools. These entail desk reviews of issues of inefficiency and program duplication. The United Kingdom's biennial spending reviews investigate these issues, as well as program outcomes and government priorities.

The advantages and disadvantages, costs, skills, and time needed to use these M&E tools are discussed in *Monitoring and Evaluation: Some Tools, Methods and Approaches* (IEG 2004b). See also DAC's evaluation glossary (2002) and annex E.

Contribution of M&E to Sound Governance

3

M&E can provide unique information about the performance of government policies, programs, and projects. It can identify what works, what does not, and the reasons why. M&E also provides information about the performance of a government, of individual ministries and agencies, and of managers and their staff. And it provides information on the performance of donors that support the work of governments.

It is tempting—but dangerous—to view M&E as having inherent value. The value of M&E does not come simply from conducting M&E or from having such information available; rather, the value comes from using the information to help improve government performance. As we shall see, there are many governments that systematically use M&E information to improve their performance. Ways M&E information can be highly useful to governments and to others include the following:

- To support **policy making—especially budget decision making—performance budgeting, and national planning.** These processes focus on government priorities among competing demands from citizens and groups in society. M&E information can support government's deliberations by providing evidence about the most cost-effective types of government activity, such as different types of employment programs, health interventions, or conditional cash transfer payments. Terms

that describe the use of M&E information in this manner include evidence-based policy making, results-based budgeting, and performance-informed budgeting (box 3.1).

- To help government ministries in their **policy development** and policy analysis work and in program development.
- To help government ministries and agencies **manage activities** at the sector, program, and project levels. This includes government service delivery and the management of staff. M&E identifies the most efficient use of available resources; it can be used to identify implementation difficulties, for example. Performance indicators can be used to make cost and performance comparisons—performance benchmarking—among different administrative units, regions, and districts. Comparisons can also be made over time that help identify good, bad, and promising practices, and this can prompt a search for the reasons for this performance. Evaluations or reviews are used to identify these reasons (see, for example,

Box 3.1: What Is Performance Budgeting?

The majority of countries in the OECD undertake some form of performance budgeting (Curristine 2005). Some other countries, such as Chile, have created a government M&E system to support performance budgeting, and a growing number of developing countries are following suit. M&E is widely viewed as a useful tool to help governments under fiscal stress reduce their total spending by identifying programs and activities that have relatively low cost-effectiveness. Performance budgeting also helps governments prioritize among competing spending proposals. In this way, it is a vehicle to help them achieve greater value for money from their spending.

Performance budgeting involves the use of monitoring information and evaluation findings. There are three main approaches to performance budgeting. The first is known as **direct performance budgeting**—where there is a direct, often formula-driven relationship so that the budget allocation for a program is based on its performance as measured by its results (that is, its outputs or outcomes). An example is university funding based on the number of students who graduate in each discipline, such as medicine or the arts.

The second approach is **indirect performance budgeting.** This is the most common form of performance budgeting. M&E infor-mation on program results is an input, but only one input, into decisions on the budget allocation for the program. Other information, as well as the government's policy priorities (including equity considerations), also influences budget allocations.

The third approach is **presentational performance budgeting.** The government uses M&E information to report the actual (past) or expected (future) performance in the budget documents it sends to the Parliament or Congress. This information may have no influence on budget decision making and is the weakest form of performance budgeting.

A common misconception is that evidence of poor performance should lead to a program either having its appropriations reduced or being abolished entirely. Although this might happen with a low-priority government activity, often more money will need to be spent on the program to fix it, at least in the short run. For example, an evaluation finding that primary education or public hospital spending is highly inefficient would not lead to these programs being abolished; they are too important. Instead, it would be necessary to identify the reasons for poor performance—which an evaluation should reveal—and to address them.

Wholey, Hatry, and Newcomer 2004). This is the learning function of M&E, and it is often termed results-based or results-oriented management.

- To **enhance transparency and support accountability relationships** by revealing the extent to which government has attained its desired objectives. M&E provides the essential evidence necessary to underpin strong accountability relationships, such as of government to the Parliament or Congress, to civil society, and to donors. M&E also supports the accountability relationships within government, such as between sector ministries and central ministries, among agencies and sector ministries, and among ministers, managers, and staff. Strong accountability, in turn, can provide the incentives necessary to improve performance.

These uses of M&E place it at the center of sound governance arrangements as a necessary condition for the effective management of public expenditures for poverty reduction. Thus M&E is necessary to achieve evidence-based policy making, evidence-based management, and evidence-based accountability. An emphasis on M&E is one means to achieve a results-oriented and accountable public sector, including a performance culture in the civil service. For this reason M&E should not be viewed as a narrow, technocratic activity.

Within the four broad categories of use of M&E information, there are many specific activities where it can be used. At the same time, M&E is closely related to other aspects of public sector management:

- Budgetary tracking systems and financial reporting
- Intergovernmental fiscal relations, including government decentralization, and the extent to which they encompass a focus on government performance[1]
- Accountability institutions such as national audit offices

- Commercialization and private sector (profit and nonprofit) delivery of public services, for example, by contracting out government functions.[2] Success in these activities requires a clear understanding of objectives and actual performance.
- Clarification and public reporting of program goals, objectives, and the strategies necessary for achieving them
- The setting of explicit customer service standards by service delivery agencies, and monitoring and publicizing the extent to which these are achieved
- Civil service reform that focuses on personnel performance, management, and appraisal, including merit-based hiring, promotion, and firing—recognizing the links between individual performance and project or program performance
- The quality of the civil service's policy advice and the extent to which this advice is evidence based (using M&E)
- Anticorruption efforts—M&E can be used to identify the "leakage" of government funds via, for example, public expenditure tracking surveys (PETS). Community monitoring of donor (or government) projects can also be an effective way to help curb corruption in the implementation of projects.
- Participation in civil society—M&E provides a vehicle to magnify the voice of civil society and to put additional pressure on government to achieve higher levels of performance.

Country Experiences

Most OECD governments place considerable emphasis on the four uses of M&E information—to support evidence-based policy making (especially performance budgeting), policy development, management, and accountability. OECD governments collectively possess a great deal of experience in this topic: there is a general understanding that for a government to improve its own performance it needs to devote substantial effort to measuring its performance. The OECD secretariat and others have published numerous surveys and analyses of the work of member countries to strengthen their performance orientation (for example, OECD 1995, 1997a, 2005; Curristine 2005; Shand 2006). These include an extensive re-

view of governments' evaluation practices and lessons on both capacity building and utilization of evaluation (OECD 1997a) and a review of performance budgeting practices and lessons:

The performance orientation of public managements is here to stay. It is essential for successful government. Societies are now too complex to be managed only by rules for input and process and a public-spirited culture. The performance movement has increased formalized planning, reporting, and control across many governments. This has improved the information available to managers and policy makers (OECD 2005, p. 81).

Over the past 15 years, the majority of OECD governments have sought to shift the emphasis of budgeting and management away from inputs towards a focus on results, measured in the form of outputs and/or outcomes. While the content, pace, and method of implementation of these reforms varies across countries and over time, they share a renewed focus on measurable results. . . . In the majority of OECD countries, efforts to assess the performance of programmes and ministries are now an accepted normal part of government. Countries follow a variety of different methods to assess performance, including performance measures, evaluations, and benchmarking (Curristine 2005, pp. 88–89).

The diversity of country approaches to M&E, and especially the ways M&E information is used, is striking. Examples from five countries whose M&E systems have been well documented and analyzed are shown in box 3.2.

These five country examples contain some common features, such as a whole-of-government approach to measuring government performance, a leading role by a powerful central ministry (such as the finance or planning ministry), and an emphasis on using M&E information to support the budget process. But the diversity of approaches is also evident. Some countries stress the budget

Box 3.2: Governments with Intensive Utilization of M&E Information

Australia

In the late 1980s, the government created a whole-of-government evaluation system, managed by the Department of Finance (DoF). All ministries were required to evaluate each of their programs every three to five years. They were also required to prepare *portfolio evaluation plans*. These detailed the evaluations planned over the following three years and indicated the programs to be evaluated, the issues to be addressed in each evaluation, and the evaluation methods to be used.

The evaluations were conducted by the line ministries themselves, but they were overviewed by the DoF and other central departments. As a result, the number of evaluations being conducted grew rapidly, and by the mid-1990s about 160 of these evaluations were under way. A main use of these evaluations was in the annual budget process. Each new spending proposal by line ministers was required to clearly specify the objectives of the proposal and to present any available evaluation findings on the actual or likely performance of the government activity. Similarly, *savings options*, which were proposals to cut government spending and which were prepared either by the DoF or by line ministries, were also required to report any available evaluation findings.

The DoF estimated that by 1994, almost 80 percent of new spending proposals relied on evaluation findings, usually to a significant degree. About two-thirds of savings options also relied on evaluation findings. DoF officials, who attended the Cabinet meetings that considered these budget proposals, judged that this information was highly influential on the Cabinet's budget decision making. The Australian National Audit Office found that line departments also used this information intensively, particularly to help themselves improve their operational efficiency (see chapter 8 for more about Australia.).

Chile

The Ministry of Finance (MoF) progressively developed a whole-of-government M&E system starting in 1994. It includes about 1,550 performance indicators, rapid evaluations (about 10–12 are completed each year), and rigorous impact evaluations (about four per year). The MoF commissions the evaluations externally to academics and consulting firms, and it uses standardized ToRs and methodologies for each type of evaluation. MoF officials use the monitoring information and evaluation findings intensively in their budget analysis of the performance of each ministry and agency as an input to the government's budget decision making. The ministry also uses the information to set performance targets for each agency and to impose management improvements on both ministries and agencies. The MoF carefully oversees the extent to which each ministry implements these management improvements (see chapter 6 for more about Chile).

Colombia

The government's M&E system, SINERGIA, is managed by the Department of National Planning (DNP). One of the system's main components is a performance information database containing about 500 performance indicators to track the government's performance against all of the 320 presidential goals.

For each performance indicator, the publicly available database records the objective, the strategy to achieve the objective, baseline performance, annual targets, and the amount spent by the government. Where performance targets are not met, the manager responsible for meeting the target is required to prepare a statement explaining this underperformance. The president uses this information, in his monthly management control meetings with each minister and in his weekly town hall meetings in municipalities around the country (see chapter 7 for more about Colombia).

United Kingdom

In 1998, the government created a system of performance targets, contained in Public Sector Agreements between the Treasury and each of the 18 main departments. The Public Sector Agreements state the department's overall goal, the priority objectives, and key performance targets.

There are currently 110 targets for the government as a whole, and they are heavily focused in the priority areas of education, health, transport, and criminal justice. The targets are mainly expressed in terms of the outcomes (rather than outputs) to be achieved. Twice a year departments report publicly on the number of evaluations, as an input to budget decision making. Spending priorities, expenditure ceilings, and the related performance targets are established in a system of three-year spending reviews. The U.K. National Audit Office reports that departments also use the performance information from the Public Sector Agreements for their internal planning and accountability; less use is made of this information for ongoing management, however.

United States

In 2002, the government created the Program Assessment Rating Tool (PART), building on earlier efforts to measure government performance. All 1,000 government programs are being rated using the PART methodology, which focuses on four aspects of program performance: (1) the clarity of program objectives and design;

Box 3.2: Governments with Intensive Utilization of M&E Information *(continued)*

(2) quality of the strategic planning and extent of focus on program targets; (3) effectiveness of program management; and (4) actual program results achieved. This last criterion accounts for 50 percent of the PART rating for each program.

All four criteria place heavy emphasis on having solid evidence of program performance, based on monitoring information and evaluation findings. The ratings are prepared jointly by the Office of Management and Budget (OMB), which is the finance ministry in the U.S. government, and by departments and agencies; however, OMB has the final say in deciding the ratings.

In fiscal 2005, 44 percent of programs were rated as effective or moderately effective; 24 percent were rated as results not demonstrated because of insufficient M&E information (this was a significant decline from fiscal 2002, when 50 percent of programs were rated results not demonstrated).

PART ratings are required to be used by departments in their annual budget funding requests to OMB. The requests must highlight the PART ratings, the recommendations for improvements in program performance, and performance targets. OMB, in turn, also uses the PART ratings as one input when it prepares the administration's funding requests to the Congress. And OMB uses the PART ratings to agree or to impose performance improvement requirements on departments.

The U.S. Government Accountability Office (GAO) has concluded that PART has helped OMB analyze M&E information on program performance as part of its budget analysis work. And it has also stimulated departments' interest in budget performance information. However, GAO concludes that the Congress continues to take a traditional approach to its budget deliberations, with relatively little emphasis on M&E information.

Sources: Australia—Mackay 1998a, 2004; Chile—Rojas and others 2005; Guzmán 2003, 2005, 2006; Colombia—Castro 2006a, 2006b; May and others 2006; United Kingdom—United Kingdom Treasury (undated); United Kingdom National Audit Office 2006; United States—OMB 2003; GAO 2004; Sandoli 2005.

process, and others stress planning. Some stress accountability, while others stress learning to support ongoing management. And some emphasize both monitoring and evaluation, while others stress only monitoring or only evaluation.

It is tempting to conclude that the differences between countries are greater than the similarities. But what is common among a growing number of countries is a systemic approach to M&E, usually involving a whole-of-government system, although sometimes—as with Mexico—involving only one particular agency (the social development agency, SEDESOL) that constitutes an "island" of good practice. A unique feature of Mexico's system is that, following the success of M&E in SEDESOL, a whole-of-government M&E system is now being created, with the support of the finance ministry, the comptroller's office, and the recently created national evaluation council (Hernandez 2007).

Many developing countries look to high-income countries—members of the OECD—to find best practice models of good governance, including M&E, but this can be a misleading and potentially

dangerous concept. The public sector environment of each country is unique, and OECD countries themselves exhibit a wide range of approaches to assessing government performance and making use of this information. So, although there are many common trends influencing governments to create M&E systems, and although there are many common tools for M&E across these countries, there also are wide differences in the emphasis given to each tool and to the types of use made of them.

Civil Society

In creating systems for monitoring and evaluating government performance, it can be tempting to focus only on government players, such as central ministries, sector ministries and agencies, subnational levels of government, and the Parliament or Congress. But this would ignore the important role civil society can play in the monitoring and evaluation of government performance. Civil society—nongovernment organizations (NGOs), universities, research institutes, think tanks, and the media—can play a role in M&E in several ways, including as both a user and producer of M&E information.[3]

Box 3.3: Citizen Report Cards—A Powerful Tool for Civil Society

The Bangalore Citizen Report Card (CRC) was pioneered by an independent NGO, the Public Affairs Centre, in 1994. The report cards involve surveys of random samples of households in Bangalore to assess their satisfaction levels with various dimensions of the quality of services provided by the municipal government and other public service agencies. The dimensions covered by these service delivery surveys include behavior of staff who serve them, quality of service, information provided by staff, and extent of corruption (speed money). The agencies that householders are asked to rank include water, power, other municipal services, transport, housing, telephones, banks, and hospitals.

The first report card found several problems: low levels of public satisfaction; public agencies that were not citizen friendly; a lack of customer orientation; corruption; and a high cost for the inefficiency of the public sector. The second CRC survey in 1999 revealed improvements in satisfaction levels but no improvement in the proportion of households paying bribes. The Public Affairs Centre disseminated the report card findings widely through the mass media—where the findings were front-page news—public meetings, and presentations to public service provider agencies.

The IEG commissioned an assessment of the impact of the first two report cards (1994 and 1999) based on interviews with a sample of agency heads, senior state officials, citizen action groups, and the media in Bangalore. The interviewees reported that they were generally appreciative of the report card as a tool to obtain feedback on services. Following the CRC findings, many of the agencies initiated reform measures. The report cards helped increase public awareness of the quality of services and stimulated citizen groups to demand better services. They influenced key officials in understanding the perceptions of ordinary citizens and the role of civil society in city governance. Bangalore has witnessed a number of improvements, particularly following the second report card. The state government and municipal public agencies launched a number of reforms to improve the city's infrastructure and services—including through property tax reform, the creation of the Bangalore Agenda Task Force, and streamlining of agencies' internal systems and procedures. There is now greater transparency in the operations of government agencies and better responsiveness to citizens' needs. Although a number of other factors have also contributed to this transformation of Bangalore, the report cards acted as a catalyst in the process.

The benefits to be derived from report cards appear to depend to a large extent on several factors. First is the use of such information by the media and by civil society. The media clearly play an important role in publicizing poor agency performance, and this in turn can provide a stimulus to civil society, to the agencies themselves, and to other key stakeholders within government. An active civil society can play an important role in continuing to press for needed reforms to agencies and in monitoring the extent to which reforms actually occur. In this way, report cards also perform a political function (World Bank 2003).

The responsiveness of government agencies, particularly their leadership, is very important. Where senior officials are concerned with the performance of their agencies and with serving ordinary citizens as well as possible, this is likely to provide a much more fertile ground for action on the basis of CRC findings. Of course, to the extent that the civil service culture is not customer oriented or concerned with achieving high levels of performance, there will be important constraints on what can be achieved even when the most senior officials are committed to reform. The Bangalore experience illustrates what can be achieved when a dynamic organization, the Public Affairs Centre, is able to (1) conduct rigorous surveys on citizen satisfaction with government performance, (2) ensure a high level of media coverage of the findings, and (3) both persuade and provide some support to government agencies to help them improve their performance.

Sources: Ravindra 2004; Bamberger, Mackay, and Ooi 2004. See also http://www.pacindia.org/.

One of the strongest examples to display both roles is the citizen report cards initiated by an NGO in Bangalore, India, in 1994; this model has since been replicated in many other cities in India and in countries such as Bangladesh, the Philippines, Uganda, Ukraine, and Vietnam. Report cards have been used by the Bangalore NGO to highlight good and bad performance of various departments of the municipal government and to successfully press the government to improve its performance (see box 3.3).

A similar example comes from Bogotá, Colombia, where a civil society initiative was developed independently of the national and municipal governments in 1997. Known as Bogotá Cómo Vamos (*Bogota, How Are We Doing?*), this initiative was created by a consortium of a private foundation, the main daily newspaper in Bogotá, and the Chamber of Commerce; it now appears to be a permanent feature of the social landscape.[4] Bogotá Cómo Vamos involves the expert analysis and widespread publication of data on municipal government performance, together with data from public opinion surveys on the quality and availability of municipal services. The initiative has successfully put pressure on the municipal government to improve its performance; it has also stimulated the government to collect and publish a broader range of reliable information on its own performance.

Another role of civil society is in the conduct of evaluations. Some governments, such as Chile and Colombia, contract out to academia or consulting firms all the evaluations conducted as part of the government M&E system.[5] One reason for contracting out these evaluations, rather having them conducted by government officials, is to help achieve a higher level of independence, objectivity, and credibility for the evaluations—and to avoid the potential or perceived conflict of interest that can arise from self-evaluation. Another reason can be the often-limited availability of evaluation expertise within the government itself. Contracting out evaluations can also help expand the pool of available evaluators in a country. And, as most governments disclose the evaluations conducted—both those that have been contracted out and those conducted internally, by ministries and agencies themselves—this opens up the quality of the evaluations to external scrutiny. This in turn would reduce incentives for governments to produce uncritical, self-serving, or dishonest evaluations.

Conclusions

Monitoring information and evaluation findings can contribute to sound governance in a number of ways: evidence-based policy making (including budget decision making), policy development, management, and accountability. Many governments around the world have realized much of this potential, including most OECD countries and a small but growing number of developing countries. This is illustrated by the five countries whose intensive use of M&E information is summarized in this chapter. These countries have all taken purposive steps to create and progressively refine M&E systems in support of core government functions. Various trends influencing governments and the lessons from international experience in building government M&E systems are discussed further in chapters 4 and 5, respectively.

The potentially important role of civil society should also be stressed, as both a producer and user of M&E information on government performance. One such example is the Bangalore report cards, which have been influential with state and municipal governments. The report card approach has been replicated in many other countries.

4

Key Trends Influencing Countries—Why Countries Are Building M&E Systems

Research by OECD suggests that there are cycles or trends in the types of public sector reform countries adopt (for example, OECD 1995, 1997a, 1997b, 1998b, 2004, 2005). Reform priorities that developed countries emphasized during the 1990s included privatization, customer service standards, results-based management, contracting out, performance pay, decentralization, and performance budgeting.

Similar trends influence developing countries, some of which consciously look to adopt world best practice approaches. As noted earlier, this can be a dangerous concept for M&E systems because of the need to tailor them closely to country circumstances and priorities.

The influence of OECD trends on developing countries appears to operate with a delay of a number of years. The significant benefit from this is that developing countries can learn about the successes and failures of implementation elsewhere.

Thus, in Latin America, for example, it is evident that a growing number of countries—as many as 20—are currently working to strengthen their government M&E systems (May and others 2006). A second explanation of this trend is the demonstration effect provided by the leading countries, including Chile, Colombia, Mexico, and Brazil. Third, a common set of economic and social pressures are perhaps more important in Latin America: continuing macroeconomic and budgetary constraints; dissatisfaction that growth in government spending in the social sectors has not been matched by commensurate increases in the quality or quantity of services provided; continuing pressures to improve and extend government service delivery and income transfers; and growing pressures for government accountability and for "social control"—that is, clearer accountability of governments to ordinary citizens and to the congress.

In Eastern Europe an additional influence is seen. Countries that have joined the European Union or are candidate countries are required to strengthen their M&E systems, and this is providing further impetus to the trend (Boyle 2005).

The initiatives of international donors such as the World Bank are also having a strong influence on borrower countries, particularly those that are more dependent on international aid. The Bank's debt relief initiative for heavily indebted poor countries has required—as a form of donor conditionality—the preparation of poverty reduction strategy papers (PRSPs) by the countries, including measures of the extent of the country's success in poverty-reduction efforts (IEG 2002). Donor emphasis on achievement of the MDGs is necessitating a similar focus. PRSPs have required an analysis of each country's M&E system, particularly the adequacy of available performance indicators. However, most poor countries have found it difficult to strengthen their monitoring systems, in terms of data production and especially in terms of data utilization (World Bank and International Monetary Fund 2004; Bedi and others 2006).

There are also strong accountability pressures on international donors themselves to demonstrate results from the billions of dollars in aid spent each year and to place more emphasis on M&E. For the World Bank, these pressures have led to its results agenda, which entails among other things the requirement that the Bank's country assistance strategies be focused firmly on the extent to which results are actually achieved and the Bank's contribution to them (World Bank 2004a, IEG 2006).

This movement is leading to a considerably greater focus on the availability of M&E information about the performance of Bank projects in countries, as well as on broader issues of country performance in relation to development objectives. This in turn necessitates a greater reliance on country monitoring systems and the information they produce.[1] And weaknesses in these systems are prompting the Bank to put more effort into providing support to strengthen them through Bank loans, grants, and technical assistance.

At the same time, there is a somewhat changing emphasis in the loans made by the Bank and other donors, away from narrowly defined projects and toward programmatic lending. This entails provision of block funding (in effect, broad budget support). The absence of clearly defined project activities and outputs from such lending also requires a focus on big-picture results or outcomes of development assistance. This in turn requires a greater reliance on country systems for national statistics and for M&E of government programs.

Similar accountability pressures on other donors have led to both their greater involvement in these issues and greater collaboration. One vehicle that allows donors to share experience in this topic is the Managing for Development Results Initiative, which promotes better measurement, monitoring, and management for results by donors and governments. This initiative was established at a meeting of the multilateral development banks in Monterrey, Mexico, in 2002 and has led to an ambitious program of activities, including high-level conferences in Marrakech (2004), Paris (2005), and Hanoi (2007). The initiative has also included the preparation of a growing collection of resource materials and case studies from developing countries concerning the application of M&E and performance management at the national, sector, program, and project levels.[2]

These factors have combined to increase the level of donor involvement in building or strengthening developing countries' M&E systems. Part of this effort is focused on national statistical systems that measure *country* progress against the MDGs. Part is focused on the government systems for M&E of *government* performance. (The importance of this distinction is discussed in chapter 9.)

IEG has estimated that, by 2002, the World Bank was already working with more than 30 countries on the latter type of system building (IEG 2002); the number has increased substantially since that time. The World Bank has a Regional program to support building M&E systems in Latin America, and this includes the creation of a high-level community of practice for M&E system managers and others. The Asian Development Bank also created a similar community of practice,[3] and the African Development Bank has announced a similar community for Africa. The Inter-American Development Bank in 2005 initiated a program of support to help countries in the Latin America and Caribbean Region build their M&E systems; about 20 countries have received grant support via this program. Other donors, such as the United Kingdom's Department for International Development (DFID), are also increasingly active in this area. DFID, for example, has had a particular focus on poverty monitoring systems and on the use of performance information to support the budget process (for example, Booth and Lucas 2001a, 2001b; Roberts 2003).

One final trend that is influencing the focus on M&E is the growth in the number and membership of national, regional, and global evaluation associations. In Africa, for example, there are now 16 national associations, and some of these (such as in Niger, Rwanda, Kenya, and South Africa) have been particularly active in recent years. Sustaining their level of activity is a continuing challenge, however, as it depends very much on the presence and energy of local champions.

There are also several regional associations, such as the African Evaluation Association (AfrEA) and, in Latin America, Preval and the new regional association, ReLAC (Red de Seguimiento, Evaluación y Sistematización en América Latina y el Caribe—Latin America and Caribbean Evaluation Network). At the global level there is the International Development Evaluation Association (IDEAS) and the International Organisation for Cooperation in Evaluation; the latter association comprises the heads of regional and national evaluation associations.[4] Multilateral and bilateral donors, including the World Bank, have provided funding and other support for a number of these evaluation associations.

These associations reflect, in part, the growing interest in M&E and the growing number of individuals working in the field. Such communities of practice have the potential to influence the quality of M&E work and thus to facilitate the efforts of governments to strengthen their M&E systems. Some national associations, such as the one in Niger (RenSE), have involved close collaboration among academics, consultants, government officials, and donor officials; the major conferences of regional and global evaluation associations, such as AfrEA and IDEAS, are also bringing these constituencies together. This growth has the potential to spread awareness and knowledge of M&E among government officials—and thus to increase demand for it.

PART II
SOME COUNTRY EXPERIENCE

Part II focuses on the experience of several countries that have successfully built well-functioning M&E systems, and on Africa. A common question asked by skeptical government ministers and officials is whether there are actually any countries that have successfully created a national M&E system. The answer to this question is an unambiguous "yes." Many developed, and a small but growing number of developing, countries have succeeded in building well-performing, whole-of-government M&E systems. Chapter 5 outlines what a "successful" government M&E system looks like; three dimensions of success are proposed. Three such countries—Chile, Colombia, and Australia—are presented in chapters 6, 7, and 8. The special case of M&E in Africa, where there are many severe capacity constraints, is considered in chapter 9.

Good Practice Countries— What Does "Success" Look Like?

Officials in many developing countries are interested in the experiences of governments with well-functioning M&E systems. Such governments have accumulated valuable lessons about how to set up and successfully manage an M&E system—what to do, how to do it, and the pitfalls to avoid. These governments also showcase the cost-effectiveness of M&E.

As noted in chapter 3, there are dangers in attempting to uncritically replicate another country's model. In Latin America, for example, many countries look to the case of Chile—which has a very strong and disciplined M&E system—and would like to apply it to their own country. However, Chile possesses a specific and rare combination of characteristics: a highly centralized budget system, a highly capable and extremely powerful finance ministry, sector ministries and agencies that closely follow the rules and procedures set down by the finance ministry, a disciplined civil service, and a highly capable academic community. These are all success factors for the Chilean government's M&E system. But there is only one Chile.

This is not to say that Chile's experience, or that of other countries with successful M&E systems, is irrelevant to other countries, even those with relatively weak public administrations. The very process of comparing any individual country with another that possesses a successful M&E system is illuminating; it helps reveal the reasons for that success, and it clarifies how easy or difficult it might be to replicate that success.

The concept of a successful M&E system also requires some examination. The definition applied throughout this volume is as follows:

> The successful institutionalization of M&E involves the creation of a sustainable, well-functioning M&E system within a government, where good quality M&E information is used intensively.

Three dimensions of success are stressed here:

1. **Utilization of M&E information.** The information is used in one or more of the four principal ways outlined in chapter 3, that is, to support government policy making, including performance budgeting or national planning; for policy development and analysis and program development; for program and project management; or for accountability purposes. Utilization of M&E information can, of course, range along a spectrum from zero or negligible to substantial (or intensive). Intensive utilization can be viewed as reflecting the mainstreaming of the M&E

function in the government. Most evaluators and evaluation offices in governments and donor organizations have a surprisingly poor understanding of the extent to which their evaluation findings are or are not used by others.

2. **Good quality M&E information.** Governments differ considerably in terms of what they conduct under the heading of "M&E." Some stress a system of performance indicators—focused on national development goals; ministry goals; and lower levels of ministry outputs, service delivery, and processes. Others focus on carrying out various types of evaluation, such as rapid reviews, rigorous impact evaluations, or other types and methods of evaluation. There are standards against which M&E can be compared to determine if it represents good quality or not.[1] Most evaluation offices have some sort of quality control mechanism in place. Most, however, do not appear to conduct or commission formal evaluations of the quality of their M&E work.

3. **Sustainability.** This relates to the likelihood that the M&E system will survive a change in administration or in government ministers or top officials. Where the utilization of M&E information is firmly embedded—that is, mainstreamed—in core government processes such as the budget cycle, it can be said to be institutionalized and thus is likely to be sustained over time. Conversely, where M&E has only a handful of key supporters or is little used, or if it is largely funded by donors rather than by the government itself, then sustainability would be seen as less likely.

Three case studies of countries with good practice government M&E systems are presented in the next chapters: Chile, Colombia, and Australia. In-depth reviews of their M&E systems are available (Rojas and others 2005; Mackay and others 2007; Mackay 2004). None of the three can be considered to constitute a "perfect" M&E system in terms of the three dimensions of success outlined above. Each has strengths and weaknesses, as is evident in the following discussions.

Chile

The government of Chile has progressively developed its M&E system over a number of years, with most of the development having occurred since 1994. The system has been largely designed, implemented, and managed by the powerful Ministry of Finance (MoF), with the overall objective of improving the quality of public spending.

The system's development has also been influenced by fiscal pressures and the need to rein in overall government spending. Another influence has been the changing landscape of public sector reforms. In this context, the system has—appropriately—been developed in an opportunistic manner.

Main Components of the M&E System

The system has six main components. The first, long-standing component is the ex ante cost-benefit analysis of all investment projects. This was first introduced in 1974. This work is undertaken by the planning ministry. All the other components of the government's M&E system are based in the MoF. As noted in chapter 5, Chile has a very powerful and capable MoF. It plays a dominant role in the annual budget process and in the M&E system; the MoF is significantly more powerful than the sector ministries and agencies.

The second component of Chile's M&E system is performance indicators, which were first piloted in 1994 (see box 6.1). The MoF currently collects about 1,550 performance indicators, for all sectors.

The third component—comprehensive management reports—was introduced in 1996. These reports are prepared annually by ministries and agencies and report on their objectives, spending, and performance.

The fourth component is the evaluations of government programs, initiated in 1996. These follow a standardized format and comprise rapid reviews, which include a logframe analysis of a program, a desk review, and an analysis of existing data. Rigorous impact evaluations are the fifth component. They were introduced in 2001, entailing primary data collection and analysis usually based on sophisticated statistical techniques.

The sixth and most recently introduced M&E component is comprehensive spending reviews (2002). These reviews analyze all programs within a particular functional area and address issues such as inefficiency and duplication of programs.

A commendable feature of Chile's system is its "graduated approach" to M&E. It regularly collects performance information for all programs and

Box 6.1: Chile's Whole-of-Government M&E System

The six main components of the M&E system are as follows:

Ex ante cost-benefit analysis is required for all government projects (since 1974). This component is managed by the ministry of planning; it is the only component not managed by the MoF.

Performance indicators are collected for all government programs. They were first introduced on a pilot basis in 1994. The number of performance indicators has increased rapidly in recent years, from 275 in 2001 to about 1,550 currently. Of these, 25 percent relate to process issues, 57 percent to government outputs (that is, goods and services produced), and 18 percent to outcomes. Each ministry and agency provides the information to the MoF; there are about 11 indicators per entity. Entities are expected to have management information systems in place to produce this information. The MoF undertakes some data checking and data audits, and it includes the performance information in the budget bills it prepares each year.

Comprehensive management reports (1996). Each ministry and agency prepares one of these reports annually, based on MoF guidelines. The reports are intended to be the main public disclosure document. They report spending, use of funds, and performance; the reports thus draw heavily on the performance information that entities are required to produce and on the evaluations commissioned by the MoF. The reports also describe the progress made by the entity in achieving the formal institutional

commitments it has agreed to with the MoF; these comprise specific actions the entity has promised to implement to improve its performance (discussed in the main text). The draft reports are reviewed by the MoF and the ministry of the presidency, and entities make any necessary revisions. The final versions of the reports are sent to the Congress.

Evaluations of government programs (1996). Some 185 of these rapid reviews have been conducted so far (that is, until the end of 2006). They entail the clarification and agreement (between the MoF and the ministry or agency whose program is being evaluated) of detailed program objectives. A logframe analysis and desk review of program performance is conducted, drawing on available performance information. Their average cost is about $11,000, and they usually take four to six months to complete.

Rigorous impact evaluations (2001). These evaluations involve primary data collection, sophisticated data analysis, and often the use of control groups. Eighteen have been completed so far, at an average cost of $88,000 and taking up to 18 months to finish. Excluding defense spending and income transfer payments, more than 60 percent of government spending has been evaluated so far.

Comprehensive spending reviews (2002). These reviews assess all programs within a particular functional area or ministry. They examine issues of inefficiency and duplication of programs. Eight of these desk reviews have been conducted so far, at an average cost of $48,000.

activities; these are also used in its evaluations. The evaluations of government programs are conducted selectively, particularly for newer programs. More in-depth impact evaluations are conducted later in the life of a program, especially where the impact is unknown or where the program is a government priority.

Performance Budgeting

A number of features of Chile's M&E system are important for its operation; they determine how much the M&E information the system produces is used. One feature is the close link between the system and the annual budget cycle. A danger

with any M&E system—whether it is a whole-of-government system or a sectoral system—is that it is managed by a stand-alone, specialist unit that operates separately from the mainstream activities of its host ministry. In Chile, the five components of the M&E system that are the responsibility of the MoF are managed by its management control division. This division works closely with the director of the budget, to whom it reports—and who has ministerial rank and is a member of the Cabinet—and also with the budget sections that have responsibility for overseeing the finances and performance of all sector ministries and agencies.

Indications of poor program performance are used in Chile as one trigger to warrant a more in-depth investigation of the causes, through a formal evaluation: either a rapid evaluation or a sophisticated impact evaluation. The MoF's budget directorate plays the main role in identifying government programs that should be evaluated. In preparing this evaluation agenda, the MoF endeavors to anticipate the information needs of the coming budget.

The agenda is also discussed with the ministries of the president and planning—indeed, these three central ministries comprise an interministerial committee that oversees all evaluations—and with the Congress, but it is clear that the main player is the MoF. The budget section heads in the MoF are also required to provide detailed comments on evaluation reports relating to the entities they oversee, and the evaluations are then discussed with MoF's budget director. Decisions concerning budget allocations may be taken at this stage.

During the budget process, the budget director meets with staff of the management control division and the budget sections to discuss each entity's budget proposals and the entity's overall performance. These meetings discuss the comprehensive management reports that each entity is required to provide[1]—they include the entity's objectives, financial and performance information, evaluation findings, and progress against the performance targets[2] that were set during previous budget rounds.

This M&E information constitutes an important input into budget decision making, but it is only one input among others. As noted in chapter 3, there is rarely any direct formulaic relationship between good or bad entity performance and budget allocations. Thus, in some cases, poor performance by an entity will lead to reduced budget funding or even the termination of the program. But in other cases, poor performance of a program considered a government priority might necessitate a short-run increase in budget funding to correct the problems identified.

Management Improvement

A notable feature of Chile is the way the MoF uses M&E information to improve the performance of ministries and agencies. It does this in two ways. First, the performance indicators provide baselines of program performance, and the MoF agrees on performance targets for the coming budget year with each organization. The MoF monitors the extent to which the targets are met. In 2003, for example, about three-quarters of these targets were met.[3] Second, when the MoF considers the recommendations made by the evaluations it has commissioned, it discusses them with the evaluated organizations and formally agrees on changes to the programs. In effect, the MoF imposes these agreements—known as formal commitments—on the organizations. It is quite unique for a MoF to systematically impose such management changes on ministries and agencies. Chile's MoF is able to do this because of its powerful role within the government.

Table 6.1 shows how the MoF uses the evaluations it has commissioned. These uses include minor changes to program management (for 24 percent of evaluated programs); major changes (38 percent); substantial program or organizational redesign (25 percent); institutional relocation of the program (5 percent); and program termination (8 percent).

Strengths and Weaknesses of Chile's M&E System

Chile's system can be assessed against the three criteria of a successful M&E system: high utilization, good quality M&E, and sustainability. As noted, M&E information is used intensively in budget analysis and decision making. It is also used intensively to impose program improvements on ministries and agencies. Last, it is used in reporting government performance to the Congress and to civil society.

What is missing from this list, however, is utilization of the M&E information by ministries and agencies themselves (other than those program changes that the MoF imposes on them). A recent World Bank evaluation of Chile's M&E system

Table 6.1: Utilization of Government Evaluations—2000–05[a]

Effect on program	Minor adjustment of program, for example, improved processes or information systems	Major adjustment of management processes, for example, changed targeting criteria, or new information systems	Substantial redesign of program or organizational structure	Institutional relocation of program	Program termination
Percent programs affected	24	38	25	5	8

Source: Guzman 2007.

a. Percentages relate to evaluated programs.

found that utilization was low (Rojas and others 2005).[4] The main reason for this is the low level of ownership—or acceptance—of the findings of the evaluations commissioned by the MoF. This weakness of Chile's M&E system arises from its centrally driven, force-fed nature.

Another limitation of Chile's centralized system is the apparent absence of incentives for ministries and agencies to conduct their own evaluations.

The available evidence on the quality of monitoring information and evaluations conducted by the M&E system indicates that the quality is broadly adequate and that the M&E information is thus broadly reliable—but no better than that. Although data verification and some data audits are conducted, there is no systematic approach to undertaking data audits of performance information.

The MoF contracts the evaluations out to academia and consultants to help ensure that they are conducted in an independent manner. Standardized ToRs are used for the evaluations, and this helps achieve some commonality in the issues evaluated and methods used; however, lack of data is sometimes a constraint on the quality of evaluations and the evaluation methods used. Evaluations are conducted within tight time constraints to ensure they can feed into the MoF's budget analysis and decision making. The MoF also ensures that the cost of evaluations is kept as low as possible. These tight time and cost constraints sometimes result in an inability to collect

the primary data necessary to conduct rigorous impact evaluations, for example.[5]

The likely sustainability of Chile's M&E system appears high. A series of budget directors in the MoF has worked to progressively develop the M&E system as an integral part of the budget process, and M&E is now embedded as a core function of the MoF. Given the preeminent role of the MoF, there do not appear to be any trends or pressures that would reduce the priority it gives to M&E. One weakness, already noted, is the low level of ownership of M&E by sector ministries and agencies. This constitutes, in part, a lost opportunity for the government as a whole to use M&E information more intensively; it also constitutes a lost opportunity to achieve a stronger performance culture within these sector entities.

The sustainability of the M&E system thus relies on the MoF's continuing willingness and ability to drive the system centrally. If the government should ever decide to reduce the central power of the MoF, then the strength and utilization of the MoF's M&E system might be called into question.

A more detailed list of the strengths and weaknesses of Chile's system is presented in table 6.2.

Conclusions

The government of Chile has succeeded in creating a system whose monitoring information and evaluation findings are utilized intensively, particularly during the budget process. It has also suc-

Table 6.2: Strengths and Weaknesses of Chile's M&E System

Strengths	Weaknesses
• "Graduated" approach to M&E. • Evaluations are conducted externally, in a fully transparent process, and are considered highly credible by other ministries and the Congress. • All M&E information is reported publicly and sent to the Congress. • The M&E system is closely linked to the information needs of the MoF, especially for the budget process. There is high utilization of M&E information in the budget. • Performance information is used to set performance targets for ministries and agencies; these are largely met. • The MoF uses evaluation findings to impose management changes on ministries and agencies. • The MoF closely monitors the extent of utilization of its evaluation findings.	• Unevenness exists in the quality of evaluations conducted; this is probably caused by cost and time constraints imposed by the MoF. • Chile is probably not spending enough on evaluations. • There is a low level of utilization—because of low ownership—of evaluation findings by sector ministries. • There is an apparent absence of incentives for ministries and agencies to conduct their own evaluations.

cessfully driven management improvements in sector ministries and agencies. The M&E system includes what is in effect an "evaluation factory" for planning, commissioning, managing, reporting, and using the evaluations. This approach keeps the cost of evaluations, and thus the overall cost of the evaluation system, low: the finance ministry annually spends a total of around $0.75 million on the M&E system,[6] which is a very modest figure compared with the total government budget of $20 billion.

This high utilization of M&E information is very impressive, and this alone makes Chile's M&E system the strongest in Latin America and one of the strongest in the world. Chile has demonstrated that a whole-of-government M&E system can be built and operated at a relatively low cost. Many other governments in the Region are looking to emulate Chile's M&E system, although a number of the success factors in Chile appear to be unique—such as the very powerful role of the MoF and the compliant nature of sector ministries and agencies.

Chile's M&E system appears to be highly cost-effective: the MoF extracts considerable use from

the M&E information produced and does so at relatively low cost. One issue for the government to consider is whether it is spending enough on its M&E system. Sophisticated, wide-ranging evaluations can cost much more than Chile has spent on any of its evaluations in the past.

In Mexico, for example, a series of rigorous impact evaluations of the *Progresa* conditional cash transfer program in the 1990s cost several million dollars—compared with total government spending on the program of $780 million in 1999. These evaluations thus constituted only a small fraction of total government spending on the program. The evaluations have been highly influential in persuading successive governments not only to retain the program but to scale it up significantly; by 2005 the government was spending about $6 billion on the program (renamed *Oportunidades*) annually, covering 21 million beneficiaries, or about one-fifth of the Mexican population.

A question for the Chilean government to consider is whether it would ever spend a large amount on an evaluation of one of its programs, even if the program were one of its major priorities. Failure to spend adequately on evaluations will limit the depth and reliability of evaluation findings, and this has probably been the cause of the quality problems of some of the evaluations commissioned by the MoF.

Finally, sector ministries' and agencies' low level of utilization of the system's evaluation findings constitutes an unexploited opportunity for the government. One way for the MoF to achieve greater ownership of evaluation findings and to encourage the development of a performance culture in the civil service as a whole would be to pursue a somewhat less centralized, more collegial approach to the planning and oversight of the evaluations conducted. A broader base of support for M&E within the government would also further increase the likely sustainability of Chile's M&E system.

Colombia

T he government of Colombia decided in 1991 to create an M&E system, which would be based initially on the World Bank's own approach to evaluation. A constitutional requirement for evaluation was introduced later that year, and the Bank and other donors quickly followed with a range of technical and financial support. The government also introduced a series of laws, decrees, and regulations to buttress the M&E system.

During its early years, the main emphasis of the system was on monitoring information rather than evaluation. The system has waxed and waned, however, and by 2000 Colombia even considered abolishing the system—because of the perception of difficulties with the system's management, and also because of doubts about its relevance to the government's public sector reform agenda.

A substantial change of fortune occurred with the election of a reformist president in 2002. The president had been dismayed to note that the large increases in government spending in areas such as schools and health care had not been matched by corresponding increased performance (outputs and outcomes) in these areas. At the same time, he was strongly committed to a new culture of public administration based on social accountability—or social control. The president recommitted the government to a rejuvenated M&E system, and this was followed by a fresh infusion of donor support. These steps quickly strengthened the system.

Main Components of the M&E System

There are two main components of the system—which is known by its Spanish acronym, SINERGIA (Sistema Nacional de Evaluación de Resultados de la Gestión Pública, or National System for Evaluation of Public Sector Performance)—as well as several other components that have been or are currently being piloted. The most visible and most heavily utilized component is the subsystem for monitoring progress against all 320 presidential goals and the country's development goals (as contained in the national development plan).

This subsystem (Sistema de Programación y Gestión por Objectivos y Resultados [SIGOB], or System of Programming and Management by Objectives and Results) records the goals, their strategies, baseline and target performance, and amounts spent by the government on them. Goal managers are also required to provide detailed explanations when goals are not met. All this information, including the contact details for each goal manager, is publicly available on a government Web

Box 7.1: Colombia's Whole-of-Government M&E System

The main components of the M&E system are as follows:

There are about 500 performance indicators relating to 320 presidential goals, and for each indicator, SIGOB records the objective, the strategies for achieving it, baseline performance, annual targets, actual performance against these targets, and imputed amounts spent by the government. Thus, SIGOB includes a large number of indicators on government performance. The information is disaggregated by region, including for the major cities.

In addition, where a target has not been met, the goal manager is required to prepare an explanation of the reasons for the shortfall. These exception reports are included in the SIGOB database, the core of which is publicly available on a real-time basis. The Web site also encourages accountability by identifying the goal manager and his or her ministry and formal position and e-mail address. It is the responsibility of ministries and agencies to supply the SIGOB data to the system's manager—the Department of National Planning (DNP)—which undertakes some data checking. However, there is no formal system of data audits, and some concerns have been raised about ministries gaming (that is, distorting) the data they provide.

About 15 rigorous impact evaluations and institutional and management evaluations are under way, and another 22 are planned. Their cost ranges from $15,000 to $2 million; most cost between $50,000 and $200,000.

These evaluations are contracted out to academia or consultants, with oversight by the planning department in close collaboration with both the evaluated agency and the donors funding the evaluation. Rapid evaluations are also being piloted, with a view to mainstreaming them in the budget and planning work of the finance and planning ministries. The rapid evaluation methodologies have drawn on Chile's approach and on the rating approach of the United States' PART system (see boxes 6.1 and 3.2). The pilots currently being conducted are expected to cost between $15,000 and $25,000 each.

site (http://www.sigob.gov.co/ini). The President uses the SIGOB information intensively for political and social control.[1]

SINERGIA's second main component is the series of evaluations it is conducting (see box 7.1). At the end of 2006, 15 evaluations were being conducted or had recently been completed, with another 22 planned for the following five years. The total cost of these evaluations is $11.1 million. Unlike in Chile, no standardized types of evaluation are conducted; Chile has standardized ToRs, evaluation approach, and cost limits for each type of evaluation the MoF commissions. The three main types of evaluation in Colombia are rigorous impact evaluations, "institutional" evaluations, and "management" evaluations—the latter two focus on management and process issues. The most expensive ($2 million) is a rigorous impact evaluation of a conditional cash transfer program.

These evaluations are collaborative exercises involving the planning department, the sector ministry or agency responsible for the program being evaluated, and donors. Most of the funding for these evaluations is provided through donor loans.

Most of the programs being evaluated are managed by the ministry of social protection, the family welfare institute, or the ministry of education.

A fourth type of evaluation is currently being piloted—rapid evaluations of those government programs that are either high priority or that have some suspected performance problems. The pilots are being conducted by the finance ministry and the planning ministry.[2] The intention is that rapid evaluations will eventually be mainstreamed in the core budget analysis and decision-making work of the two ministries. (In Colombia, there is a split budget: The finance ministry is responsible for recurrent spending; the planning ministry is responsible for the investment side, including education spending and cash transfers.)

The M&E system has other components, but they are weaker and much less fully institutionalized. One is an effort to partner with civil society—such as establishing consortia of NGOs and the media—in analyzing government performance. Another component is support for two municipalities that are undertaking performance monitoring and performance budgeting.

One final component is the preparation of performance budget reports to the Congress. These have been prepared by the planning ministry as an annex to the conventional budget documents. They present government spending on a programmatic basis and report the available M&E information on the performance of these programs. As noted in box 3.1, such performance reporting is a form of performance budgeting, albeit a weak type. It is particularly weak in Colombia because the Congress plays a weak role in the budget process, it has little technical support to enable congressmen to easily digest performance information and evaluation findings, and Congress' discussion of the annual budget tends to focus on narrower political issues (see annex B).

Accountability—Political and Social Control

A unique feature of Colombia has been President Uribe's strong commitment to the use of M&E information to enhance political control of the executive government and to support social control. The SIGOB database is loaded in his personal computer, and he uses this information in his monthly management control meetings with each minister and the DNP. During these meetings, the progress being made against each presidential goal is reviewed, and ministers are required to provide reasons for any shortfalls in performance. Performance indicators and ac-

tions to meet these targets are also agreed. The president uses this SIGOB information in his weekly town hall meetings in different municipalities around the country and also in an annual television presentation to citizens, in which he and his ministers discuss the government's performance and answer citizen questions on these issues.

This strong presidential commitment to using M&E information to monitor and report on the government's performance appears to be unique in Latin America—and perhaps in the world. It sends powerful signals to individual ministers and civil servants. However, there does not appear to have been a widespread adoption of M&E practices by ministries and subnational governments. Several ministries and agencies in the social sectors, as well as two municipalities, are currently working to strengthen their M&E systems with assistance from the DNP and donors.

Use of Evaluations to Support Government Decision Making

By early 2007 only three evaluations had been completed, so the opportunity to make use of evaluation findings to support government decision making in both the national budget and for national planning has been limited. But one notable example of an influential evaluation does exist (see box 7.2).

Box 7.2: An Influential Evaluation in Colombia

Familias en Acción is a government conditional cash transfer program that provides income support to poor families that commit to ensuring that their children receive preventive health care, enroll in school, and attend classes. The program was created in 1999 in response to an economic crisis.

A rigorous impact evaluation of the program was contracted out to external consultants, under the supervision of the planning department. The evaluation found that the program achieved impressive nutrition, education, and health impacts. These findings persuaded the government of President Uribe, who was elected

in 2002, not only to retain the previous government's program but to double its coverage, from 500,000 to 1 million poor families. In late 2006, the government decided to further increase the program's coverage, to 1.5 million families.

The *Familias en Acción* evaluation has cost $1.5 million so far. Although this is a large amount, it is relatively small when compared with total government spending on that program (around $100 million at the time of the evaluation). Because of its major influence on the government, this evaluation can be judged to have been highly cost-effective.

Source: Mackay and others 2007.

Strengths and Weaknesses of Colombia's M&E System

Colombia's system can also be assessed against the three criteria of a successful M&E system: high utilization, good quality M&E, and sustainability. The evidence base for such an assessment for Colombia is not as robust as it is for Chile, but some conclusions can nevertheless be drawn. Utilization by the president of the monitoring component (SIGOB) of the M&E system is notably high, for purposes of social and political control—that is, for accountability.

The quality of the monitoring data is unclear, but there are fears—held by some senior civil servants and by some influential members of civil society—that the data are not wholly reliable and that some of the information provided by sector ministries and agencies might be self-serving. The sustainability of this monitoring component seems highly likely, however, even after a change of administration and a new president. This is because of the usefulness of such data for the DNP and the president's office in their oversight of government performance.

The other main component of Colombia's M&E system is the ambitious program of rigorous impact evaluations, institutional evaluations, and management evaluations. Only a few evaluations have been completed, but one of them—*Familias en Acción,* one of the government's most important programs—has been highly influential and can be judged as having been very cost-effective. This is noteworthy because even a single, high-profile evaluation that influences a government's decisions can also influence more widespread acceptance of M&E by demonstrating its value.

The quality of Colombia's evaluations has not been formally reviewed, although there is some comfort concerning their likely quality and reliability: they have been contracted out to eminent academics, including some internationally renowned evaluators, and have had significant involvement from evaluators from the World Bank and other donors. The sustainability of the evaluation program is not entirely assured, however.

In the short term—that is, for the next five years—the evaluation agenda will be supported by a new World Bank loan; one feature of this agenda is a declining level of donor financial support for these evaluations, in the explicit expectation that the government will take up the slack by using its own budget funds to pay for them.[3] This is likely to happen if the government judges the evaluations produced as worth the time and effort; this in turn places the onus on the planning department to ensure that the evaluations are intensively utilized.

Comparison with Chile's M&E System

There are other notable issues, particularly if Colombia's M&E system is compared with that of Chile. One is that Chile's system is managed by the budget directorate, ensuring the close integration of M&E and budget work. But in Colombia the M&E system has been essentially managed as a stand-alone activity that almost coincidentally happens to be located within the planning department. Until now the M&E system has not been integrated with either the planning work or the budget responsibilities of the department; nor has there been collaboration with the finance ministry's budget work.

This scenario might be about to change. The rapid evaluations being piloted involve the M&E and budget directorates in the planning department, as well as the budget area of the finance ministry. If these pilots are judged successful—that is, as being cost-effective for purposes of performance budgeting—then it is likely that M&E will become mainstreamed in the core budget work of both ministries.

Some observers have argued that a major constraint on the use of M&E information to influence budget decision making in Colombia arises from the various rigidities in the national budget. These include a large number of earmarked expenditures that cannot easily be varied. As a result, between 90 and 95 percent of budget spending in Colombia cannot be changed in the short term. Various counterarguments can be made here (see annex B); but perhaps the most telling observation is the

Table 7.1: Strengths and Weaknesses of Colombia's M&E System

Strengths	Weaknesses
• Very high level of utilization of monitoring subsystem by the president and his office • Performance information used to set performance targets for ministers and their ministries and agencies. Public reporting of the extent to which performance targets are achieved; where they are not achieved, managers have to provide public explanations. • Evaluations conducted externally in a transparent process and considered highly credible by other ministries and the Congress • Evaluations planned and conducted in a collaborative approach involving the planning department and sector ministries and agencies • All M&E information reported publicly and sent to Congress.	• Low-level utilization of M&E information by the budget and planning directorates of the planning ministry, and by the finance ministry • Concerns about the reliability of monitoring data supplied by sector ministries and agencies • Excessive reliance on donor funding of the evaluation agenda

high level of influence of Colombia's *Familias en Acción* evaluation on the government's priorities and on its budget allocations (box 7.2).

One final point when comparing Colombia and Chile is the high level of collaboration between Colombia's M&E directorate in the planning department and the sector ministries and agencies whose programs are being evaluated. The DNP has shared its evaluation expertise and some funding with its sector partners, and none of the sometimes antagonistic relationships that can exist in other countries when the finance ministry plays an active role in the evaluation agenda appear to have arisen. This collaborative approach between the central ministry and the sector entities might change if and when Colombia adopts a more active form of performance budgeting.

However, if performance budgeting is to work well, there will need to be close collaboration among the M&E directorate within the planning department, the budget directorate of that department, and the budget directorate of the finance ministry. One way to foster close collaboration

between these central ministries and with sector entities would be to include all of them in the high-level government committee that has formal responsibility for oversight of SINERGIA. The government plans to move in this direction.

A summary list of the strengths and weaknesses of Colombia's M&E system is presented in table 7.1. The World Bank's diagnosis of Colombia's system is reproduced as annex B to this volume.

Conclusions

The government of Colombia has succeeded in creating a monitoring subsystem of government performance relative to all 320 presidential goals and the country's other development goals. It is notable that the president uses this subsystem intensively in his direct oversight of ministerial and ministry performance and in reporting to civil society.

The government has also embarked on an ambitious evaluation agenda; evaluation findings have already had some significant influence on government decisions and budget allocations.

A weakness in Colombia's system is that M&E information is not yet systematically used for the core budget and planning work of the two ministries responsible for the national budget. There is a good chance that mainstreaming of M&E into budget analysis and decision making will occur, but until it does there will be limits on the extent of utilization of monitoring information and evaluation findings. Such utilization would also considerably increase the probability of sustainability of the central M&E system.

Several ministries and agencies conduct M&E for their own internal purposes, to aid their own planning, analysis, and ongoing program management. These entities are the exception, however. With World Bank support, the government is currently examining options for mandating M&E more widely within all ministries, agencies, and subnational governments.

It would be fair to conclude that Colombia's M&E system is less well developed and mature than that of Chile. The Chilean system was progressively developed over more than a decade; and although Colombia's system has existed in some form since the early 1990s, it is only since 2002 that it has really blossomed. The Colombian M&E system currently costs around $2 million per annum, or almost three times the cost of the Chilean system ($0.75 million per annum).[4] The source of this cost difference is the particular emphasis on major impact evaluations in the Colombian system. Both countries' systems could be improved, but both—and particularly the Chilean—can be judged to be cost-effective.

Australia

Australia elected a reformist government in 1983. That government faced a very difficult macroeconomic situation. In response, it progressively reduced total government spending, from 30 percent of gross domestic product in 1984 to 23 percent in 1989—a very significant reduction by international standards.

At the same time, the government targeted its spending much more tightly toward the most disadvantaged in society. It was keen to obtain greater value for money from government spending, and with this goal in mind it introduced a series of innovative public sector reforms, particularly in the areas of financial management and budgetary reform. Collectively, these reforms placed Australia at the forefront of OECD countries in terms of public sector management.[1]

The reforms provided much greater autonomy to the heads of line departments to manage their budget appropriations—under a philosophy of letting the managers manage. Although it had initially been hoped that the reforms would encourage departments to closely manage and measure their performance, this expectation was not met. With the support of other central departments, the powerful Department of Finance (DoF) therefore developed a whole-of-government evaluation strategy. This strategy received the cabinet's strong endorsement through a formal cabinet decision. The strategy followed the philosophy of making the managers manage.

Main Components of the M&E System[2]

The Australian M&E system largely comprised a formal strategy for evaluations. It was based on a 1988 diagnostic review of evaluation practices in departments and of the overall level of evaluation activity in government. The strategy itself was progressively developed over several years (1987–1991). The strategy had three principal objectives: to encourage program managers to use evaluation to improve their programs' performance; to aid the cabinet's decision making and prioritization, particularly in the annual budget process, when a large number of competing proposals are advocated by individual ministers; and to strengthen accountability in a devolved environment by providing formal evidence of program managers' oversight and management of program resources.[3]

A centerpiece of the strategy was evaluation planning. This was done through formal portfolio evaluation plans (PEPs), which had to be submitted annually to the minister for finance (see box 8.1). These PEPs had a rolling, three-year coverage and indicated which programs or subprograms would

---

Box 8.1: Australia's Whole-of-Government M&E System

The main components of the M&E system were as follows:

Formal evaluation planning through PEPs, which listed the government programs the ministry intended to evaluate and the issues to be addressed in each evaluation. These PEPs were prepared annually, on a rolling three-year basis. They included major evaluations only, that is, evaluations of programs considered strategically important to the government: programs with large budgets; those of particular policy importance; problem programs; and pilot programs. The evaluations were conducted by the line ministry itself, usually with some sort of involvement by the finance ministry.

Requirement for every program to be evaluated at least once every three to five years. In practice, this meant that some aspects (such as particular subprograms) of each program were evaluated; most evaluations did not attempt to comprehensively address all aspects of a program's performance. In addition, there was also a requirement that all completed evaluations be published, with the exception of those with national security or industrial relations sensitivity.

Reviews of each ministry's program objectives and performance reporting. These reviews were conducted jointly by each ministry and the finance department, on a rolling basis over a three-year period.

---

be evaluated, which aspects evaluated, and when. There was a formal requirement that every program be evaluated every 3–5 years. These PEP evaluations were classified as major evaluations. Departments were also expected to initiate other, smaller evaluations, purely for internal management purposes. By the mid-1990s, about 160 PEP evaluations were under way at any one time.

The key issues for the PEPs were the choice of programs to be evaluated and the specific questions each evaluation would address; thus, the ToRs for each evaluation were crucial. These issues were decided through negotiations between the line departments and the DoF's budget sections. For the weaker departments, finance's priorities would largely prevail. For more powerful line departments, the balance of power was more even. Unresolved disputes concerning evaluation priorities would be escalated to the level of ministers or even to the cabinet if agreement could not be reached.

The line departments were responsible not only for evaluation planning, but also for the conduct of evaluations of their programs. Some of the larger departments such as the employment department—had an evaluation branch with some 20–25 staff responsible for planning evaluations,

providing advice on evaluation methodology, participating in evaluation steering committees, and conducting major evaluations.

Other departments had only small evaluation units, as part of a planning/coordination branch, and devolved the evaluation function to line program areas; they in turn would be responsible to the top management of the department for the quality and rigor of the evaluation (especially for smaller evaluations, which were often in the nature of rapid reviews). A number of evaluations were contracted out to individual consultants or consulting firms.

The DoF's budget sections also involved themselves in the conduct of individual evaluations wherever possible. This would often involve membership of interdepartmental steering committees for the major evaluations; these committees would usually include other relevant sector ministries and other powerful central departments such as the treasury and the department of the prime minister and the cabinet. This broad membership would allow the budget officials (1) to seek to influence the conduct of evaluations, to ensure that problems were fully investigated in an impartial manner, and (2) to comment on draft evaluation reports.

One feature of Australia's M&E system is that a broad definition of evaluation was used. Evaluation was defined as a form of disciplined inquiry: it included rapid evaluations, formal policy reviews, rigorous impact evaluations, and performance audits conducted by the national audit office. The cost of these evaluations varied widely: a sample of evaluations analyzed by the finance department ranged in cost (in 1993 prices) from about $43,000 to $430,000.[4]

The evaluation strategy was strengthened in 1991 in response to a performance audit that found that departments varied in their level of commitment to evaluation. The audit office report criticized some departments for poor choice of programs evaluated and for an insufficient focus on the effectiveness of government programs. In response, the DoF created a specialist evaluation unit responsible for providing advice, support, training, and encouragement to other departments, as well as to the budget areas of the DoF itself. This unit also monitored departments' evaluation planning and the number of evaluations conducted; the head of the finance department used this information to informally pressure line departments to improve their evaluation activities.

Australia's M&E system essentially stressed *evaluation*, which was viewed as providing the necessary in-depth, reliable information on the efficiency and effectiveness of government programs. Performance information was also understood to be important, but it was viewed as an issue for line departments to manage. By the mid-1990s, however, the finance department was concerned about the quality of this information and commissioned reviews of departments' annual reports and their budget documentation (which is tabled in the Parliament).

The deficiencies in these reports led the finance department in 1995 to mandate a rolling series of detailed reviews of each department's program objectives and performance information. These reviews were conducted jointly by the finance department and the line department, and recommendations for improvement were required to be implemented.

Performance Budgeting

While Australia's M&E system had three stated objectives, from the perspective of the finance department—which was the primary architect and the overseer of the M&E system—the objective to which it devoted most attention was to support the cabinet's decision making during the budget process. The DoF played a highly influential role in the budget process in Australia. It prepared policy analyses of all new spending proposals prepared by sector ministries, and these analyses accompanied the spending proposals sent to cabinet ministers for their collective consideration when making budget decisions. The DoF thus provided an independent policy analysis that typically constituted a view counter to that of the spending ministry. The work of DoF's budget sections also included the preparation of "savings options": policy proposals to cut or abolish existing government programs.[5]

The budget process entailed a "marketplace of ideas." In this inherently adversarial situation, having evaluation findings available about the performance of programs was an important means of ensuring a reliable evidentiary basis for budget decisions. Evaluations had the potential to provide a competitive advantage to those who relied on them. Thus it was important that the DoF's budget sections were fully involved in the evaluation planning of ministries and in the conduct of major evaluations. This ensured that the DoF budget officials were familiar with the quality and any limitations of the evaluations, were fully aware of the evaluation findings and recommendations, and were thus able to use them in their policy analysis work. Involvement of these officials in the evaluations would also increase their knowledge of the program's objectives and the realities of its operating environment—this understanding is important for their work.

It is worth noting here that finance ministries may not always be supporters of reforms designed to strengthen the amount of information available on government performance. Before the reforms, the Australian DoF was heavily involved in the detailed scrutiny of departments' spending activities. The danger is that this traditional focus on spending can mean that relatively little attention is paid to the results of that spending. And powerful finance ministries can even act as roadblocks to reform. Having the DoF responsible for evaluation oversight ensured that there was a direct influence on the divisional units within DoF that had oversight for line departments.

However, achieving the needed cultural change within the DoF was a slow process over a number of years and involved a substantial staff turnover. The DoF's greater focus on issues of value for money (rather than on spending issues) flowed through to the nature and quality of policy advice the DoF provided to the cabinet; that advice increasingly drew on available evaluation findings.

The most important feature of Australia's M&E system is the significant use made of evaluation findings to support the cabinet's budget decision making. The DoF conducted surveys of its budget staff each year to ascertain the influence of evaluations on each new policy proposal of line ministers and the savings options proposed by DoF (or by line ministers if they wished to fund new policies).[6] By 1994–95, about $1.75 billion (or 77 percent) of new policy proposals were judged to have been influenced by the findings of an evaluation, and in most cases the influence was judged to be direct. The corresponding figures for savings options were $380 million (65 percent of the total).

Evaluation findings influenced not only the policy options put forward for the cabinet's consideration, but also the cabinet's decisions. DoF budget officials were also surveyed regarding the extent to which evaluation had influenced the cabinet's decisions in the 1993–94 and 1994–95 budgets. The evidence is mixed, but it indicates that evaluation played a substantive role. In 1994–95, evaluation was judged to have influenced the cabinet's decision in 68 percent of the $2.846 billion of proposals considered (new policy proposals plus savings options).

Box 8.2: Influential Evaluations in Australia

In the 1996–97 budget the new government was determined to both reduce and reprioritize government spending. Particular focus was given to labor market and related programs, which accounted for $2.90 billion in spending annually. The minister for employment articulated the government's overall policy goal as being to provide assistance to the long-term unemployed and to those at risk of entering long-term unemployment. This focus was adopted both for equity and efficiency objectives, such as achieving a better match of labor supply and demand. At the same time, the minister wanted to achieve better value for money from labor market programs in the tight budgetary environment.

Australian and international evaluation findings were drawn on heavily to help guide the policy choices made. The minister highlighted the relative cost-effectiveness of different labor market programs. A key measure of this was estimated by calculating the net cost to government for each *additional* job placement from different programs—as measured by the *increased* probability of an assisted person being in a job some 6 months after he or she had participated in a labor market program. (The baseline was a matched comparison group of individuals who did not participate in a program.)

Evaluation findings showed that the JobStart program, which provided wage subsidies, had a net cost of $3,700 per additional job placement, whereas the JobSkills program, which was a direct job-creation program, had a corresponding net cost of $57,800. The minister noted, "The government will be ... concentrating its efforts on those programs which have proven most cost-effective in securing real job outcomes." As a result, the JobStart program was retained and the JobSkills program was substantially scaled back and more tightly targeted to job seekers who were particularly disadvantaged.

Total savings to the government from its reduction and reprioritization of labor market programs were about $1.14 billion over two years. The cabinet also commissioned a series of major evaluations of its new labor market programs and of the new arrangements for full competition between public and private employment service providers.

Source: Mackay 1998a.

Table 8.1: Strengths and Weaknesses of Australia's M&E System

Strengths	Weaknesses
• Evaluation findings heavily used for budget analysis, policy advice, and by the cabinet in its budget decision making • High utilization of evaluation findings by sector departments and agencies • Evaluation conducted as a collaborative endeavor between finance department, other central departments, and sector departments	• Uneven quality of evaluations • Insufficient availability of advanced evaluation training • Insufficient attention to regular performance information • A claimed administrative burden on departments

Source: Mackay 1998a, 2004.

The corresponding proportion for the 1993–94 budget, however, was only 19 percent of proposals. One important reason for this difference was the substantial revision of labor market, industry, regional, and aboriginal policies in the 1994–95 budget—the major policy review on which these decisions were based had been heavily influenced by a number of evaluations commissioned specifically to help guide the policy review.

Only a few programs were terminated as a result of an evaluation; given the emphasis in the budget process on portfolio (defined as a line department plus outrider agencies) budget envelopes—in effect, portfolio budgeting—any program termination would often result in spending reallocation within that portfolio. There were major instances where programs were significantly cut as part of a major reprioritization, for example, in the labor market and social security areas; these cuts reflected the desire to maximize value for money given the government's policy priorities (box 8.2).

Strengths and Weaknesses of Australia's M&E System

Strengths

Some commentators have observed that "program evaluation (in Australia) has been applied more extensively and systematically than in any other country" (Kim and others 2006). The outstanding feature of Australia's M&E system was the high utilization of evaluation findings in the budget process, as a key input for both high-quality policy advice (Uhr and Mackay 1996) and for the cabinet's budget decision making (table 8.1). As noted in the chapter 5 discussion on performance budgeting, the influence of evaluation findings on the government's decisions was typically indirect—ranging from a major influence in a number of cases to little or none in others. This is essentially the most that can be expected from a whole-of-government M&E system, in terms of potential utilization of the M&E information that the system produces.

The Australian auditor-general has commented, "In my view, the success of evaluation at the federal level of government . . . was largely due to its full integration into the budget processes. Where there was a resource commitment, some form of evaluation was necessary to provide justification for virtually all budget bids" (Barrett 2001).

Another strength of the M&E system was the high level of utilization of the information by line departments and agencies. A performance audit conducted by the Australian National Audit Office (ANAO) in 1997 concluded that line departments were making considerable use of their evaluation findings to help improve operational efficiency. To a lesser extent, they were also using these findings to help guide their own resource allocation decisions and in the design of service quality improvements (Australian National Audit Office 1997).

This high level of utilization by line departments reflected another strength of the Australian M&E system: evaluation was essentially a collaborative effort involving the DoF, other central departments, and the line departments. Although responsibility for evaluation was largely devolved to line departments, the involvement of the central departments in the planning and oversight of the major PEP evaluations helped achieve broad ownership of the evaluations themselves and of their findings.

This approach stands in contrast to that of Chile, for example, where the line ministries generally have little or no ownership of the evaluations the finance ministry commissions. The Australian approach also ensured that line departments' deep knowledge and understanding of their own programs were used intensively in evaluations; a danger with an evaluation system that relies on externally conducted, independent evaluations is that it can fail to draw on this program expertise.

Weaknesses

The downside of Australia's more collaborative approach, however, was an uneven quality of evaluations conducted by line departments. The ANAO performance audit analyzed a sample of evaluation reports and concluded that more than one-third suffered from methodological weaknesses of one kind or another.

One reason for this was that many of the program areas of line departments that had responsibility for conducting or commissioning evaluations lacked sufficient skills to ensure that high-quality evaluations were conducted. The DoF provided basic training in evaluation methods and issued handbooks on program evaluation and cost-benefit analysis. But the ANAO audit reported that 20 percent of line departments were concerned about the lack of available training in advanced evaluation techniques.

In retrospect, one option to address this issue of evaluation quality would have been for the DoF

to mandate creating sizeable central evaluation units in each department. Another option would have been to centralize the entire evaluation function in the DoF—this would have required the creation of a very large evaluation office and would have been contrary to the devolutionary nature of most of the public sector reforms.

Two other weaknesses of the Australian M&E system are worth noting. First is the relatively weak emphasis given to the regular collection and use of performance information. The DoF explicitly advised departments of the importance of developing sound program objectives and having sound performance information—not least to facilitate the conduct of evaluations. It was not until 1993, some six years after the evaluation strategy was initiated, that the DoF commissioned broad reviews of the quality of departments' annual reports and budget documentation.

Following these reviews, which were critical of the quality of program objectives and performance information, the DoF mandated a series of in-depth, rolling reviews of all departments' and agencies' program objectives and performance information. It required that action plans be implemented to address any problems identified. One lesson from this experience is that all M&E systems require ongoing review and adjustment; it is necessary to monitor and evaluate an M&E system, just as it is necessary to monitor and evaluate any other type of public sector reform.

A final weakness of the M&E system claimed by some departmental secretaries was that the formal requirements for evaluation planning and reporting were too burdensome. Some departments did create complex internal processes for evaluation planning and ended up preparing 120-page PEPs; yet the DoF guidelines did not mandate such complexity, and the guidelines recommended much smaller PEPs as good practice.

The Evaluation System—A Postscript[7]

The election of a conservative government in 1996 led to the considerable downsizing of the civil service; a substantial weakening of the policy advising process and the role of the DoF, especially in the budget cycle; and the dismantling of many of the remaining central controls and requirements. At the same time, a much higher level of autonomy was given to the heads of line departments—a return to the philosophy of letting managers manage.

Although line departments are still required to report their performance publicly to the Parliament, the DoF now applies no central controls or quality standards for M&E. As part of these changes, the decade-long formal evaluation strategy—and thus the government's M&E system—was dismantled. The Australian auditor-general has characterized these reforms as a deregulation of evaluation. While there remain some line departments that can be considered to be good practice "islands" of M&E,[8] in terms of their conduct, quality, and use of M&E, these appear to be the exception rather than the rule.[9] ANAO performance audits have highlighted the poor quality of performance information that most departments now provide to the Parliament.

Although the DoF still provides advice on departments' budgets, it lacks systematic, reliable monitoring information and evaluation findings on which to base this advice. As the OECD has concluded—

> *In Australia, the deregulation of the public service and the adoption of an arm's-length posture by the central agencies allowed management freedom but is currently considered to have deprived the Finance Ministry of the information necessary for it to adequately advise the Minister* (OECD 2002).

The Special Case of Africa

9

T he experience of African countries is relevant to poor countries in other Regions, especially those preparing poverty-reduction strategies. Africa also provides lessons on how to build M&E capacities incrementally, especially when there is the possibility of intensive donor assistance. These lessons are also relevant to middle-income countries, such as those that are not yet committed to comprehensive improvement of their M&E systems. In such countries, a more cautious focus on incremental changes can be appropriate if there is the potential to demonstrate that M&E is a cost-effective government activity.

It is widely accepted that the extreme poverty situation facing most African countries provides a clear priority for intensive development support. More than 30 African countries have prepared an interim or final PRSP, a document required for access to debt relief under the Heavily Indebted Poor Countries Initiative.[1] PRSPs set development targets and are intended to report on results achieved. In practice, this has meant a focus on the extent to which a country has achieved the MDGs.

This puts a premium on having adequate national statistics, which in turn is leading to intensive donor support for statistical capacity building, such as assistance for population censuses and household surveys. Particularly with their national statistical offices, countries appear keen to accept this support. PRSPs usually present their national monitoring (that is, statistical) systems as

synonymous with M&E, and the need to give priority to M&E has become a mantra that is widely accepted by governments and donors alike. In many cases, however, national monitoring systems are principally designed to meet donor data requirements (IEG 2004b).

Moreover, PRSPs end up focusing on the amount of budget and other resources spent on national priorities and national progress against the MDGs. These two issues are certainly important, but what is absent from this focus is what Booth and Lucas (2001a, 2001b) have termed the "missing middle": performance information on the intervening steps in the results chain, involving government activities, outputs and services provided, and their outcomes; and in-depth evaluative evidence linking government actions to actual results in the field.

Statistics on amounts spent and on poverty levels are both very important, but unfortunately neither is able to measure the government's performance in terms of the *results* of its spending—the outputs, outcomes, and impacts of the government itself. MDGs and other measures of poverty provide a bottom-line measure of *country* performance but fail to reveal the contributions of the government compared with donors, the private sector, and civil society groups such as NGOs.

Most African countries are simply too poor to be able to conduct evaluations and reviews; they rely instead on donors for such work. A difficulty is the heavy burden placed on countries to meet the M&E requirements of donors, in terms of inspection missions, provision of performance information, unharmonized donor evaluation criteria and methods, and so forth (IEG 2003a). Lack of donor harmonization has imposed a heavy burden of information supply on aid-dependent countries. However, donor cooperation and harmonization can be facilitated through sectorwide approaches. In Tanzania, for example, there is a health sector working group, made up of government and donors, that not only analyzes sector performance and policies but has also reviewed sector M&E systems and identified M&E capacity-building priorities. This sector working group also commissions evaluation or research into selected issues (Stout 2001).

The move toward greater use of programmatic lending to countries provides another way to mitigate the harmonization problem, because it reduces the scope for project-specific M&E and thus the scope for balkanized donor M&E. In Uganda, for example, the World Bank and other donors provide programmatic budget support to the government. Such programmatic support is becoming increasingly common in African and other debt-relief countries.

Lessons from Uganda[2]

Some African governments, such as Uganda and Tanzania, understand well the importance of having reliable and comprehensive performance information available. They use this information intensively in preparing their national plans and in determining budget priorities (see, for example, Government of Tanzania 2001; Ssentongo 2004; Government of Uganda 2004, 2006). A notable feature of both countries is that their national plans—in Uganda they are known as Poverty Eradication Action Plans (PEAPs)—predate the PRSP initiative. This experience made it easy for both countries to prepare PRSPs; indeed, they simply had to prepare summarized versions of their national plans to meet the PRSP requirement.

Uganda has had a number of M&E initiatives and systems. It was, for example, the first country in which PETS were undertaken (box 9.1). However, diagnoses of Uganda's M&E arrangements in 2001 (see table 9.1) and 2003 revealed a large number of uncoordinated and unharmonized monitoring systems at the sector and subsector levels—at least 16 separate systems (Hauge 2003). In addition, a detailed investigation of three sectors (health, education, and water and sanitation) revealed a considerable data-collection burden at the district and facility levels.

The management information systems for those three sectors collected data on nearly 1,000 performance indicators, involving almost 300,000 data entries per annum for each of the 110 districts in Uganda. These indicators largely focused on spending, activities, and the physical state of facilities such as schools and health clinics.

However, measures of client satisfaction and outcome measures, such as health status and learning outcomes, were largely missing. Unfortunately, the quality of the data was highly uncertain and often considered poor. As a result, the sector ministries and agencies relied heavily on inspection visits rather than on self-reported performance indicators. Hauge and others (2002) estimated that site inspections in the health sector alone were costing the equivalent of 1,400 staff years per annum, often consuming the time of qualified medical personnel.

The diagnostic findings concerning the multiplicity of M&E systems and performance indica-

Box 9.1: An Influential Evaluation in Uganda

In the early 1990s, Uganda, like many other developing countries, was concerned with the poor performance of public services such as education and health. A major cause was believed to be the "leakage" of funds that did not reach front-line agencies. With World Bank support, the PETS methodology was developed and applied in the primary education sector in 1996. Its purpose was to measure the proportion of funds provided by the central government that reached primary schools and the extent of the leakages and to recommend ways to reduce them.

The PETS analyzed the timing of budget flows through various tiers of government and compared budget allocations to actual spending on primary schools. As adequate public accounts were not available regarding actual spending, surveys were conducted in 250 government primary schools in 19 districts, and a panel dataset was created on spending and outputs for 1991–95. The study found that only 13 percent of earmarked (nonwage) funds actually reached schools in 1991–95. The remaining 87 percent disappeared or was used by district officials for other purposes. About 20 percent of funds allocated for teacher salaries went to "ghost workers" who did not exist or who were not working as teachers.

The study findings attracted considerable media attention, and the government decided that the information on the amount of funds allocated to, and received by, each school should be widely disseminated through local newspapers and radio stations and publicly displayed at each school. This helped ensure that parents became aware of the funding situation facing their child's school. This provided the information they needed to hold teachers and school principals accountable for lack of available teachers or for an inadequate supply of textbooks. These steps also demonstrated to local governments that the central government had resumed its oversight function.

Two follow-up PETS showed that the flow of nonwage funds reaching primary schools had improved from 13 percent in 1991–95 to between 80 and 90 percent in 1999–2000. This example demonstrates that quantitative data on public services are a powerful tool for mobilizing civil society's "voice." Although individual complaints can be brushed aside, public feedback backed by systematic comparative data is difficult to ignore and can provide a spark for public action.

The first PETS cost $60,000 and has been estimated to have helped increase the amount of funds reaching primary schools by more than $18.5 million per annum. This indicates that PETS are a highly cost-effective evaluation tool. The government of Uganda now routinely conducts PETS for each basic service sector.

Source: Bamberger, Mackay, and Ooi 2004, 2005.

tors—and the heavy burden imposed on frontline staff—caused considerable consternation within the government and led to the decision to create a National Integrated M&E System (NIMES) under the aegis of the Office of the Prime Minister. The objective of NIMES is to create an umbrella M&E system within which existing systems will be coordinated and harmonized and government capacities to conduct and use M&E strengthened (Government of Uganda 2004, 2006).

Various working groups have been created under NIMES addressing the following issues: M&E in local governments; policy research; evaluation; national statistical data; sector management information systems and spatial data; civil society organizations and M&E; and financial information. At least four donors provide funding support for NIMES, in the amount of some $7.4 million over a three-year period, in addition to the government's own funding.

NIMES is reducing the very large number of performance indicators, especially at the sector level, with a greater focus on outputs, outcomes, and impacts, as well as on the setting of targets. The World Bank and seven other donors now prepare a joint strategy for providing support to Uganda,[3] based on the national plan (PEAP) goals and objectives, and they rely heavily on the government's own monitoring information to assess their own performance. Donors still conduct their own separate evaluations, however.

In addition to the NIMES, the government has also embarked on a process to improve its performance and accountability. This includes the development of results-oriented management in public

Table 9.1: Uganda M&E—Summary Diagnosis of Strategic Issues, Challenges, and Possible Actions

Strategic M&E issues	Monitor and provide feedback on progress in poverty alleviation						
	1. Coordination and harmonization	**2. Development goals, targets, and performance indicators**	**3. Incentives to contribute to results**	**4. Devolution of managerial autonomy**	**5. Role of civil society in enforcing transparency and accountability**	**6. PEAP partnerships principles**	**7. M&E skills training**
Positive elements in Uganda	• Draft poverty monitoring strategy • Sector working groups as nexus of planning, budgeting, project progress reporting • Efforts to harmonize project progress reporting • Earmarking of five percent of poverty action funds for monitoring and accountability	• PEAP/PRSP as overall framework of poverty priorities • Training in results-oriented management being piloted • "Indicator retreat" as part of budget cycle	• Recognition of service delivery effectiveness as imperative of public management • NSDS 2000	• Decentralized responsibility for service delivery • Introduction of output-oriented budgeting • Comprehensive district plans • Local government development plan capacity development	• Consultative nature of PEAP process • Transparency of budget process • Practice of public notices • Significant capacity of NGOs • Government–civil society dialogue at central level	• Draft CDF partnership principles • Trend toward budget support • Consultative group meeting scheduled as part of budget cycle	• Awareness of M&E importance • Availability of local researchers and local academic and training traditions
Some challenges	• Separate planning and reporting formats for different funding sources • Sector/district policies, budgets, work plans approached as separate exercises • Alignment and coordination of different results management initiatives • One-third of official development assistance is technical assistance outside of government budget	• Inconsistent clarity of goals at sector level • PEAP goals correspond to ministerial activities rather than to poverty outcomes • Few goals are defined with measurable timeframe, baseline, or targets • Weak linkage between sector and district goals	• Performance assessed in terms of expenditure and bureaucratic activity • Weak linkage between resource allocation and performance • Rewards geared to good paperwork • Inconsistent enforcement of sanctions for poor performance • Corruption largely unpunished	• Generally weak management capacities at local levels • Prescribed spending ratios of conditional grant scheme gives little flexibility for managers to adapt to local needs • Number and level of posts directed from the center	• Need for improved stakeholder consultation in priority setting • One-third of official development assistance is technical assistance outside of government budgets and M&E practices • GoU/NGO dialogue at center is not mirrored at local levels	• One-third of official development assistance is technical assistance outside of government budget and M&E • Nearly 300 stand-alone projects remain • 20 separate annual program reviews • Local donors cannot depart from corporate M&E guidelines	• Weak management skills at local government levels • Likely increase in demand for management and conduct of M&E dealing with interrelationship between service delivery and poverty outcomes

Possible actions to address challenges						
• Identification of an M&E champion ministry or agency • Establishment of core M&E arrangements (such as through a formal M&E framework), harmonization of terminology, reporting formats, and periodicity • Improved coordination between inspection and audit agencies	• Cascading of PEAP goals and targets through planning, budgeting, and work planning at sector, district, and facility levels • Long-term expenditure framework focus on defining medium-term PEAP goals and targets	• Introduction of reach and outcomes as yardsticks of success and performance reward • Use of the NSDS as barometer of client satisfaction improvements • Introduce value for money concerns in finance act • Introduction of client service charters	• Allow greater local autonomy over recruitment, salaries, and non-wage expenditures • Ensure stronger local oversight as the quid pro quo • Introduce participatory M&E practices as key management function	• Extend transparency practice from allocation to execution • Client report cards as complement to the NSDS • Make NGOs eligible for poverty action fund monitoring and accountability funding • Introduce client service charters	• Leverage of donor support for the CDF and PEAP to increase synergy in planning, reporting, and review • Use poverty-reduction support operation policy matrix as joint planning and review mechanism	• Strengthen local capacity for evaluation skills training, for example, by training trainers at national institutions • Coordinate use of funding earmarked for M&E under poverty action fund, the local government development program, and Economic and Financial Management Programme II • Establish national evaluation association

Source: Hauge 2001.

Note: CDF = comprehensive development framework; GoU = government of Uganda; NGO = nongovernmental organization; NSDS = National Service Delivery Survey; PEAP = poverty eradication action plan; PRSP = Poverty Reduction Strategy Paper.

service organizations and its links with the budget process and with the staff performance appraisal process. The government's efforts include actions to strengthen both top-level political and civil service commitment and the demand for a greater performance orientation.[4]

Some Conclusions

Uganda and other African countries already possess M&E systems. They also receive donor support for statistical capacity building and have access to donor evaluations. The challenge these countries face is not developing new systems, but rationalizing and improving what already exists. There are problems with data quality and unharmonized donor requirements for M&E—a situation of *too much data, not enough information*. Compounding these problems on the supply side is the fact that in most other countries there is weak government demand for M&E information.

Although it would be unrealistic to expect most African countries to build comprehensive, reliable M&E systems, there are a number of important elements that they could feasibly undertake. What follows is a list from which African and other countries preparing a PRSP could draw, either with or without donor support. The advantages, costs, and limitations of some of these M&E tools are discussed in *Monitoring and Evaluation: Some Tools, Methods and Approaches* (IEG 2004b):

- Financial management information systems to support better financial tracking of government spending
- Public expenditure tracking surveys to identify "leakage" and to trace the effects of corruption
- Service delivery surveys of client satisfaction and perceptions of the quality of government services
- Rapid appraisals—for example, of "problem" projects or programs
- National and sector statistical collections—especially relating to national priorities such as the MDGs
- Sector ministries' administrative data.

The only caveat with this list is that, in some senses, less is more. One danger to avoid is the tendency to overengineer whatever M&E system is being created. It is therefore important to carefully monitor the extent to which each type of M&E information is being used. Where utilization is low, it is necessary to identify the reasons, such as low awareness of its existence, a low level of demand for it, poor quality data that are considered unreliable, or a lack of staff able to analyze and act on the information. This helps identify the steps necessary to improve supply or to increase the demand for M&E information.

PART III
LESSONS

Many developed and developing countries have accumulated substantial experience in building M&E systems. The consistency of these lessons across different countries and Regions is not surprising; they also reflect international experience with other types of public sector capacity building (chapter 10). The issue of utilization of M&E information is central to the performance and sustainability of an M&E system. Utilization depends on the nature and strength of the demand for M&E information—in other words, on the incentives to use M&E. Countries with little or no demand for M&E may be perceived as facing an insuperable barrier to efforts to build M&E systems, but this perspective is far too pessimistic. There are ways to increase demand by strengthening incentives, and these are discussed in chapter 11, which focuses on carrots, sticks, and sermons to ensure utilization of M&E information.

10

Building Country M&E Systems— Lessons from Experience

The growing literature on experience with strengthening government M&E systems suggests that there is broad agreement among experts on a number of key lessons (box 10.1) (see African Development Bank and World Bank 1998; Boyle 2005; Compton, Baizerman, and Stockdill 2002; DAC 2006; Development Bank of Southern Africa, African Development Bank, and World Bank 2000; Mackay 1998d, 2004; May and others 2006; OECD 1997a, 1997b, 1998a, 2004; Schiavo-Campo 2005; UNDP 2000).

The first and foremost lesson is that **substantive demand from the government is a prerequisite to successful institutionalization.** That is, an M&E system must produce monitoring information and evaluation findings that are judged valuable by key stakeholders, that are used to improve government performance, and that respond to a sufficient demand for the M&E function to ensure its funding and sustainability for the foreseeable future.

Efforts to build an M&E system will fail unless real demand exists or can be intentionally created, especially by ensuring that powerful incentives are in place to conduct and use M&E. It is not enough to issue an edict that M&E is important and should be done; this is likely to produce only lip service and is certainly unlikely to produce good quality monitoring information and evaluations. Such efforts at top-down compliance can, unless accompanied by a range of other actions, easily lead to ritual compliance or even active resistance.

Achieving substantive demand for M&E is not easy. And a barrier to demand is lack of knowledge about what M&E actually encompasses, particularly where the buy-in of key stakeholders such as government ministers or finance ministries is necessary before substantive effort will be put into creating and funding an M&E function. So there is frequently a chicken-and-egg problem: There is a lack of government demand for M&E because of the lack of understanding of M&E and what it can provide; there is a lack of understanding because of the lack of experience with it; and there is a lack of experience because of weak demand.

The way around this conundrum is to increase awareness of M&E—its range of tools, methods, and techniques—and its potential uses. Demand can be increased once key stakeholders in a government begin to understand it better, when they are exposed to examples of highly cost-effective monitoring systems and evaluation reports, and

Box 10.1: Elements of Successful Country M&E Systems

- Substantive government demand
- Strong role for incentives
- Diagnosis of existing M&E as first step
- Key role of a powerful "champion"
- Centrally driven by capable ministry
- No overengineering the system
- Reliable ministry data systems
- Utilization as the measure of success
- Training in M&E and in using M&E
- Limitations of relying on government laws, decrees, and regulations
- Structural arrangements ensure M&E objectivity and quality
- A long-term effort, requiring persistence
- Development in a nonlinear, less predictable manner
- Regular evaluation of M&E system itself.

when they are made aware of other governments that have set up M&E systems that they value highly. It can be persuasive to point to the growing evidence of very high returns on investment in M&E (Bamberger, Mackay, and Ooi 2004).

The supply side is also important—provision of M&E training, manuals, and procedures and identification of good M&E consultants, and so forth; M&E expertise is certainly necessary if reliable M&E information is to be produced. Those who view M&E in technocratic terms as a stand-alone technical activity tend to focus only on these issues.

But the supply side of producing M&E information is less important than demand. If demand for M&E is strong, then improving supply in response can be relatively straightforward, but the converse does not hold. Demand from governments is crucial for the utilization of M&E information and for the ongoing funding of M&E activities. Thus, it is necessary to secure the buy-in of the key stakeholders such as government ministers or finance ministries if substantive effort is to be put into creating, strengthening, or funding M&E func-

tions. Continuing reliance on donor funding and on donor M&E activities is not sustainable.

Incentives are an important part of the demand side. There need to be strong incentives for M&E to be done well, and in particular for monitoring information and evaluation findings to be actually used. In other words, strong incentives are necessary if the M&E function is to be successfully institutionalized (see box 10.2 on Ireland's experience, for example). This observation is also consistent with the extensive literature on achieving any type of institutional reform, particularly in the context of public sector management and sound governance (for extensive literature reviews see World Bank 1997a; OECD 2004, 2005).

Simply having M&E information available does not guarantee that it will actually be used, whether by program managers in their day-to-day work, by budget officials responsible for advising on spending options, or by a Congress or Parliament responsible for accountability oversight. This underscores both the dangers of a technocratic view, which sees M&E as a set of tools with inherent merit, and the fallacy that simply making M&E information available would ensure its utilization.

No governments build M&E systems because they have intrinsic merit. Governments build M&E systems because (1) those systems directly support core government activities, such as the budget process; national planning; development of policies and programs; and the management of ministries, agencies, programs, and activities, or (2) provide information in support of accountability relationships. Thus, M&E systems are often linked to public sector reforms such as performance-based budgeting (PBB), evidence-based policy making, results-based management, and the like; such initiatives share a number of common elements (see chapter 3).

In working to build or strengthen a government M&E system, it helps to **start with a diagnosis of what M&E functions currently exist** and their strengths and weaknesses—both on the demand

Box 10.2: Lessons from Ireland

Ireland developed its government evaluation system in response to the formal requirements for accession to the European Union. Since its accession, Ireland's system has been strengthened for internal reasons related to the government's wish to improve the value for money obtained from all areas of public expenditure. This has been reflected in the government's Expenditure Review Initiative.

For developing countries, Ireland provides a number of lessons about both success factors in and impediments to developing an M&E system. One lesson is that strong external pressures, linked to the availability of significant resources, can be a key catalyst in initiating an M&E system. (An analogy for poor countries is the requirement to prepare poverty-reduction strategies, with related M&E systems, in the context of debt relief under the Heavily Indebted Poor Country Initiative.) Once in existence, an M&E system can be used for additional, nationally driven purposes. Of course, country demand and incentives to utilize M&E information are very important for the institutionalization and sustainability of such a system. The case of Ireland again underlines the difficulty of ensuring a direct link between M&E information and budget decision making and other resource-allocation processes. Formal procedures and practices may be necessary to establish direct links.

Another lesson is the merit of periodically reviewing progress in developing such a system and reorienting the system—sometimes substantially—as a result. Ireland is continuing to pilot further improvements to its evaluation system.

Ireland has a small pool of evaluators, and this has been a constraint on the system, although it has enabled Ireland to develop rapidly its understanding of the requirements of the system. The small skills pool has underlined the importance of using this resource carefully; it has implications on both the demand and supply sides.

On the demand side, it suggests the importance of not trying to develop an overly complex or demanding system. Instead, it is better to focus on the most cost-effective M&E activities; these are determined by the likely utilization of the M&E information produced. On the supply side, there would be merit in working to expand the limited capacities in a planned manner—for example, through targeted training, curriculum development, on-the-job skills development, secondments, networking support, regular review of M&E quality, or period contracts with consulting companies. Where there is reliance on civil servants to undertake evaluations, it is particularly important to ensure that they are sufficiently trained and are provided with adequate guidelines and other support to enable them to function effectively.

Source: Boyle 2005.

and supply sides. The extent of actual (as distinct from the hoped-for) extent of utilization of M&E information must be clear, as well as the particular ways in which it is being used. Such diagnoses are themselves a form of evaluation, and they are useful not just for the information and insights they provide, but also because they can be a vehicle for raising the awareness of stakeholders in government, civil society, and the donor community about the importance of M&E and the need to build a new system or strengthen existing systems.

Another dimension to the demand side, and another success factor, is having a **powerful champion**—a powerful minister or senior official who is able to lead the push to institutionalize M&E, to persuade colleagues about its priority, and to

devote significant resources to creating a whole-of-government M&E system. A champion needs to have some understanding of M&E, in terms of tools and methods, and an appreciation of its potential usefulness for government—for one or more of the four main uses of M&E information (outlined in chapter 3).

Government champions have played important roles in the creation of some of the more successful government M&E systems, such as those of Chile, Colombia, and Australia (discussed for each country, respectively, in May and others 2006; IEG 2003b [chapter 11]; Mackay 2004). However, powerful champions constitute a success factor; they do not provide a guarantee of success. There are examples, such as Egypt, where the support of a group of key ministers for M&E has been substantially frustrated by skeptical mid-level officials (IEG 2004a; Schiavo-Campo 2005).

Creating a whole-of-government M&E system—whether focused solely on a system of performance indicators or encompassing various types of evaluation and review—requires a significant effort. It involves recruiting and training staff to conduct or manage M&E and use their findings; creating the bureaucratic infrastructure to decide which government programs should be evaluated and what issues should be addressed in each evaluation; and creating data systems and procedures for collecting, sharing, and reporting M&E information.

It also requires active oversight of the M&E system by senior—and usually very busy—officials. Like other systems, in areas such as financial management or procurement, it takes sustained effort over a period of years to make an M&E system operate efficiently. The OECD has concluded that—

> *It takes time to develop a performance measurement system and to integrate it into a management system. No OECD member country considers developing a performance measurement system as easy. On the contrary, it is perceived as an exhausting exercise which needs constant monitoring and controlling* (OECD 1997a, p. 19).

Thus, another feature of successful government M&E systems is the **stewardship of this process by a capable ministry** that can design, develop, and manage an M&E system. In many developed and upper middle-income countries (for example, Australia, Canada, Chile, and the United States) this has meant the finance ministry. It certainly helps to have the institutional lead of an M&E system close to the center of government (for example, a president's office) or the budget process (Bedi and others 2006). The need to have clarity concerning the roles and responsibilities of key stakeholders is also reflected in the Latin American experience (box 10.3)

In some countries, capable sector ministries have set up strong M&E systems. Perhaps the most

notable example is in Mexico, where the Secretariat for Social Development (SEDESOL), a capable and respected ministry, manages an M&E system that emphasizes both qualitative and impact evaluations. The ministry is also working to strengthen its system of performance indicators to better support the evaluations it conducts (Hernandez 2006).

The genesis for this sector ministry effort was a law passed by the Congress mandating the evaluation of social programs; Congress was concerned that the executive government might use its social programs to buy votes, and it wanted solid evidence of program performance before it would agree to fund programs. This law was influenced at least in part by the series of rigorous impact evaluations of the *Progresa* program.

Although these are among some of the most expensive impact evaluations ever done, costing millions of dollars, their quality has also been widely acknowledged, as has their enormous impact on the government. They were instrumental in persuading the government to retain the *Progresa* program and to expand significantly when it morphed into the *Oportunidades* program—by 2005, the government was spending about $6 billion on this program, which covers some 21 million beneficiaries, or about one-fifth of the Mexican population.

These evaluations, although expensive, can be viewed as having been very cost-effective. Governments in other countries find examples of highly influential evaluations to be quite persuasive in relation to the potential usefulness of evaluation and the merits of setting up a sound M&E system.

As noted in chapter 3, the success of M&E in SEDESOL has helped persuade the powerful finance ministry and the comptroller's office to join the national evaluation council to create a whole-of-government M&E system. This indicates the powerful demonstration effect a successful sector agency can have.

One point to note in passing: it is rarely if ever the case that a ministry that decides to create a strong

---

Box 10.3: Latin American Experience with M&E Systems

A World Bank–Inter-American Development Bank (IADB) Regional conference held in June 2005 focused on the experience of five leading or promising countries in Latin America: Brazil, Chile, Colombia, Mexico, and Peru. Several of these countries have achieved considerable success in creating M&E systems and institutionalizing them.

It was evident from the country experiences that there is no single "destination" for countries in terms of what a well-performing M&E system looks like. Some countries stress a system of performance indicators, and others focus on carrying out evaluations (program reviews or rigorous impact evaluations). And although most countries have created a whole-of-government approach driven by finance or planning ministries, some are more focused on sector M&E systems. One key characteristic of most of the systems in the Region is that they reflect country-led, rather than donor-driven, efforts to institutionalize M&E.

The shared experience of these countries has led to some collective wisdom about the development of solid M&E systems:

- There is a need to clearly define the roles and responsibilities of the main actors—the planning and finance ministries, the president's office, sector ministries, and Congress. It is also critical to create the right incentives to encourage these stakeholders to assume a greater role in M&E.
- Strengthening M&E systems is not only, even principally, a supply-side issue requiring a "technical fix." For an M&E system to be successful and sustainable, the information and findings of M&E have to be utilized intensively by all stakeholders, including sector ministries and, depending on how the system has been devised, civil society.
- Conservative ministries and staff may resist efforts to implement M&E systems and use M&E as a management and budget tool. It is essential to have a high level of commitment and ongoing support from powerful champions at the ministerial and senior official levels.
- There is an implicit debate on how to prioritize evaluations—to focus on problem programs, pilot projects, high-expenditure or high-visibility programs, or on systematic research to respond to questions of program effectiveness.

Source: May and others 2006.

M&E system has to start from scratch. Even in the poorest African countries there is usually a range of performance indicators available, and there will also be a number of evaluations conducted by donors. The problem is more the poor quality and partial coverage of performance information and its substantial underutilization.

A common mistake is to overengineer an M&E system. This is more readily evident with performance indicators—for example, Colombia's M&E system, SINERGIA, had accumulated 940 performance indicators by 2002; for Colombia, this number was unwieldy for its accountability uses of the information, and it has subsequently reduced the number to around 500 (Castro 2006a, 2006b; Mackay and others 2007; annex B of this volume). In contrast, Chile's M&E system includes 1,550 performance indicators. This is a very large number, but the highly capable finance ministry is able to use the information effectively. It would be best to regard Chile as the exception that proves the more general rule, that less is more.

The appropriate number of performance indicators also depends on the number of government programs and services and on the type of performance indicator. Indicators can focus on the various parts of the "results chain" for a program (defined in annex E): inputs, activities, outputs, outcomes, and impacts. Senior officials would tend to make use of high-level strategic indicators such as outputs and outcomes. Line managers and their staff, in contrast, would tend to focus on a larger number of operational indicators that target processes and services.

The regular production of this kind of detailed performance information is only a first step. Senior officials and managers would usually not have the time to scrutinize raw data. It can assist their work considerably if capable analysts review the data and provide summaries and analyses for senior officials.

Ministry data systems are often—and perhaps typically—uncoordinated, so a single ministry can possess several such systems, each with its own data definitions, data sources, periodicity of collection, and quality assurance mechanisms (if it has any). Mexico's SEDESOL, for example, had eight separate management information systems in 2004 (World Bank 2004c). In Uganda, one problem is the number of uncoordinated M&E systems—as many as 16 separate sector and subsector systems, which the government is now working to coordinate through a new national integrated M&E strategy (Hauge 2003; Government of Uganda 2006).

A problem in African countries, and perhaps in some other Regions, is that although sector ministries collect a range of performance information, the quality of data is often poor. This is partly because the burden of data collection falls on overworked officials at the facility level, who must provide the data for other officials in district offices and the capital but who rarely receive any feedback on how the data are actually being used, if at all.

This leads to another chicken-and-egg problem: Data are poor partly because they aren't being used; and they're not used partly because their quality is poor. In such countries there is too much data, not enough information. Thus, another lesson for the institutionalization of a government M&E system is the **need to build reliable ministry data systems**—to help provide the raw data on which M&E systems depend.[1] An audit of data systems and a diagnosis of data capacities can be helpful in this situation. It would provide the starting point for any necessary rationalization of data collections or improvements in their quality. It would give the data the credibility necessary to be used.

Data verification and credibility is partly a technical issue of accuracy, procedures, and quality control. Related to this issue of technical quality is the need for data to be potentially useful—for information to be available on a timely basis, easy to understand, consistent over time, and so forth. There is also an issue of honesty and objectivity; as performance information becomes important— particularly when it is used for accountability purposes—there will arise incentives to falsify the

data.[2] This is clearly of concern and requires specific measures to verify the data, such as through independent data audits. Verification could also involve accreditation of an agency's processes for data verification. Of course, efforts to falsify data can also be taken as a sign of success that the M&E system is starting to have an impact—that it is having real "bite."

Financial data on program spending comprise a fundamental type of information; quality and ready availability must be ensured. This information is supplied by financial management information systems. Sound performance budgeting, program management, and government accountability all require that information on the costs and results of government programs be linked. Ironically, many evaluations then fail to discuss the cost of the programs being evaluated; this makes it harder to gauge the cost-effectiveness of the program.

The objective of government M&E systems is never to produce large volumes of performance information or a large number of high-quality evaluations per se; this would reflect a supply-driven approach to an M&E system. Rather, the objective is to achieve intensive utilization of whatever M&E information exists to ensure that the M&E system is cost-effective—utilization in support of core government functions, as noted earlier. **Utilization is the yardstick of success of an M&E system;** conversely, it would be hard to convince a skeptical finance ministry that it should continue to fund an M&E system whose outputs are not being utilized. Such systems would deservedly be regarded as useless.

For an M&E system to perform well, it is necessary to have well-trained officials or consultants who are highly skilled in M&E. For this reason, most capacity-building plans place considerable emphasis on **provision of training in a range of M&E tools, methods, approaches, and concepts.** Those governments that contract out their evaluations need to ensure that their officials possess the skills and experience necessary to oversee and manage evaluations—this requires a broader set of competencies than the ability to simply conduct an evaluation. They also need to understand the strengths and limitations—the relative cost-effectiveness—of various types of M&E.

Introductory training in M&E can also raise awareness of and demand for M&E information. Training should also extend to the *use* of M&E information. Budget analysts and program managers need to be able to interpret monitoring data to understand trends, data definitions, breaks in data time series, and so forth. They also need to be discriminating consumers of evaluations; that is, they must be able to tell when an evaluation's methodology is flawed and is findings unreliable. Finally, parliamentarians and their staff need to be able to understand M&E information.

Another lesson is that there are **limitations when a country relies on a law, decree, cabinet decision,** or other high-level pronouncement to create an M&E system. In Latin American and francophone countries—those with the Napoleonic system of law—there is a tradition of relying on such legal instruments to create and legitimize M&E systems.[3] Thus, countries such as Colombia have a series of laws and decrees mandating evaluation; these were even enshrined in the Constitution in 1991. Yet in the intervening years, the fortunes of the government's evaluation system have waxed and waned, and it was only after a change in government in 2002 that the system started to perform strongly (Castro 2006a, 2006b; Mackay and others 2007).

The point here is not that a law or decree mandating M&E is irrelevant: on the contrary, these can be useful vehicles for legitimizing M&E, particularly in those countries where the presence of such a legal instrument is viewed as necessary for any government reform to be perceived as worthwhile and taken seriously.[4] But a law or decree on its own does not ensure that the considerable efforts required to build an M&E system will be undertaken.

The structural arrangements of an M&E system are important from a number of perspectives. One is the need to ensure the objectivity, credibility, and rigor of the M&E information the system produces. On the data side, some governments (for example, Chile) rely on external

audit committees to perform this function, some rely on the national audit office (for example, Canada) (Mayne and Wilkins 2005), and some rely principally on internal ministry audit units (for example, Australia). Some rely on the central ministry checking data provided by sector ministries (for example, Colombia), and others have no audit strategy (for example, Argentina) (Zaltsman 2006a).

On the evaluation side, issues of objectivity and credibility are particularly important. As noted in box 3.1, Chile (and most other Latin American countries) deals with this by contracting out evaluations to external bodies such as academic institutions and consulting firms; moreover, the evaluations are commissioned and managed by the finance ministry rather than by sector ministries, and the process of seeking bids and awarding contracts to conduct the evaluations is entirely transparent.[5]

The downside of this approach is a lack of ownership of these evaluation findings by the sector ministries, which do not make much use of the evaluations commissioned by the finance ministry. That may not be so great a problem in Chile, however, where the powerful finance ministry is able to use evaluation findings not only to support budget decision making, but also to impose management and program changes on the sector ministries (Rojas and others 2005). This centrally imposed system is unique.

Most OECD governments rely on sector ministries to conduct evaluations themselves (Curristine 2005), although this raises questions about the reliability of self-evaluations. In the United States, the OMB (the finance ministry) rates the performance of government programs and marks those programs with either no M&E information about their performance or with unreliable M&E information—see box 3.1.

Countries that have built a government M&E system have found that it is a **long-haul effort, requiring patience and persistence** (OECD 1997a; Mackay 1998b; Lahey 2005; May and others 2006). It takes time to create or strengthen data systems; to train or recruit qualified staff; to plan, manage, and conduct evaluations; to build systems for sharing M&E information among relevant ministries; and to train staff to use M&E information in their day-to-day work, whether that involves program operations or policy analysis and advice. Australia and Chile were able to create well-functioning evaluation systems (in terms of the quality and number and utilization of the evaluations) within four or five years; but in Colombia's case, it has taken more than a decade.

This is not to say that a slow and measured approach to building an M&E system is appropriate, however. Government champions will eventually depart, and the window of opportunity—indeed, the priority a government gives to any type of public sector reform—can close as quickly as it opened. This suggests that an approach of working in a focused, purposeful, and even intense manner to build various components of the M&E system is necessary, and that governments need to institutionalize them as quickly as possible.

It appears that **most countries with well-performing M&E systems have not developed them in a linear manner**—that is, starting with a clear understanding of what the system would look like once fully mature and then progressively achieving this vision. Instead, when one examines the experience of countries such as Australia (Mackay 2004), Canada (Lahey 2005), Chile (Zaltsman 2006a; see also chapter 7), Colombia (Mackay and others 2007), Ireland (Boyle 2005), and the United States (Joyce 2004; Lahey 2005), it is evident that these countries' M&E systems have been developed incrementally and even in a piecemeal manner, with some false starts and blind alleys along the way.

This would appear to be caused partly by the different amounts of time it takes to build particular M&E functions—a system of performance indicators relative to the conduct of program reviews or rigorous impact evaluations. It would also appear to be caused by a number of mid-course corrections made as the progress, or lack of progress, with particular M&E initiatives becomes evident. There is also the important influence of external factors, such as a change of government, which can not only alter the direc-

tion of an M&E system but can lead to it being significantly strengthened—such as in Colombia after 2002 and in the United States after 2000. A change in government can also result in an M&E system being substantially run down or even abandoned—such as in Australia after 1997 (chapter 8) and the United States after 1980 (GAO 1987).

There appears to be a rather worrying asymmetry with government M&E systems; they are slow to build up but can be run down quickly. For governments that have largely abandoned their M&E system, this would appear to reflect an ideological preference for "small government" rather than a considered decision about the cost-effectiveness of the M&E system; the negative effects on the M&E system thus appear simply to be collateral damage.

The frequency of mid-course corrections as M&E systems are being built indicates another lesson from experience: the **value of regularly evaluating an M&E system** itself, with the unsurprising objective of finding out what is working, what is not, and why. It is valuable to identify the nature of the roadblocks encountered and to indicate possible changes in direction. Such evaluations provide the opportunity to review both the demand and the supply sides of the equation and to clarify the extent of actual—as distinct from the hoped-for—extent of utilization of M&E information, as well as the particular ways in which it is being used.

The Chilean finance ministry's careful stewardship of that country's M&E system is exemplified by the review it commissioned the World Bank to conduct into the two principal evaluation components of the system (Rojas and others 2005). It commissioned this review partly to support the ongoing management and improvement of the M&E system and partly to apply the same standards of performance accountability to itself as it applies to sector ministries and the programs they manage—the finance ministry has, as a matter of course, reported the World Bank's evaluation findings to Chile's Congress. There are a number of diagnostic guides available to support such evaluations of government M&E systems (see chapter 12).[6]

Incentives for M&E— How to Create Demand

Efforts to strengthen government M&E systems are often viewed as technical fixes—involving better data systems, the conduct of good quality evaluations, and so forth. These supply-side issues are certainly important, but they are insufficient to strengthen the systems.

In chapter 10 we noted that, for the successful institutionalization of an M&E system—that is, the creation of a sustainable, well-functioning M&E function within a government, where good quality M&E information is used intensively—the demand side is particularly important. Demand focuses on the priority to *use* monitoring information and evaluation findings in support of core government activities. Uses include to assist resource-allocation decisions in the budget process; to help ministries in their policy formulation and analytical work; to aid ongoing management and delivery of government services; and to underpin accountability relationships.

Achieving strong demand within a country, however, is another matter. Having examples of other countries—such as Chile, Colombia, and a number of OECD countries—that have invested the effort necessary to build a well-functioning M&E system can be enormously influential in creating interest in M&E and building demand for it. And illustrating the cost-effectiveness of individual evaluations conducted in other countries can also persuade decision makers about the merits of M&E.

Some countries, such as Egypt, have developed a good understanding among key government ministers of the potential benefits of M&E. Yet efforts to institutionalize M&E in Egypt have been substantially frustrated by mid-level officials who did not buy into this vision of an M&E system.

The key issue this illustrates is the need to ensure there are sufficiently powerful incentives within a government to conduct M&E and to a good level of quality, and to use M&E information intensively. In other words, strong incentives are necessary if the M&E function is to be successfully institutionalized. This also highlights the importance of understanding the incentives facing ministries and individual civil servants to conduct—or not—M&E.

A public sector environment in which it is difficult for managers to perform to high standards and to perform consistently is hostile to M&E. Managers can do little more than focus on narrowly defined day-to-day management tasks. They are not willing to be held accountable for performance if they do not have some surety of the resources available to them or if they do not have substantial control over the outputs of their activities. In this environment, M&E is understandably seen by managers as irrelevant, as potentially (and probably) unfair to them, and as a threat rather than an aid.

The nature of incentives for M&E depends on how a country envisions using M&E information. If the main intended use of M&E is to assist line managers in all sector ministries and agencies—the learning function of M&E—then the broad civil service culture is important. But if M&E is conducted primarily for accountability purposes, then the key stakeholders, whose demand for M&E would be paramount, would be much narrower: the office of the president or prime minister, the Congress or Parliament, the finance and planning ministries, and the auditor-general.

If M&E is intended as a tool for performance budgeting, then the finance ministry and probably some other central ministries would be the key stakeholders. Sector ministries would also be stakeholders in a broad-based performance budgeting system (such as Australia's—see chapter 8) but would play a much less-important role in a more centralized budgeting system (such as Chile's—see chapter 6). Finally, if M&E is intended as a tool to support evidence-based policy formulation and analysis, then it is more likely to involve all ministries.

Clearly each of these intended uses of M&E involves somewhat different sets of stakeholders and thus incentives—to drive the system. As noted earlier, there is a tendency for government M&E systems to be conceived in an ambitious manner to include all possible uses of M&E information (see, for example, the case of Colombia—annex B). This approach would involve all stakeholders and thus a more complex set of incentives and may be unrealistic.

As we shall see in chapter 12, it is important that the issue of incentives is investigated when conducting a diagnosis of a country's or a ministry's M&E system; it is also a key issue when preparing an action plan to strengthen an M&E system. As already noted, the importance of understanding incentives is stressed in the extensive literature on achieving other types of governance reform (World Bank 1997b, chapter 9).

Three types of incentive are presented in table 11.1: carrots, sticks, and sermons.[1] Many of these incentives have been used to help institutionalize M&E in developed and developing country governments. Carrots provide positive encouragement and rewards for conducting M&E and utilizing the findings. They include, for example, public recognition or financial incentives to ministries that conduct M&E.

Sticks include prods or penalties for ministries or individual civil servants who fail to take performance and M&E seriously—such as financial penalties for ministries that fail to implement agreed-on evaluation recommendations. Finally, sermons include high-level statements of endorsement and advocacy concerning the importance of M&E. They also include efforts to raise awareness of M&E and to explain to government officials what's in it for them.

Table 11.1: Incentives for M&E—Carrots, Sticks, and Sermons

Carrots	Sticks	Sermons
• Awards or prizes—high-level recognition of good or best practice evaluation or of managing for results.	• Enact laws, decrees, or regulations mandating M&E.	• High-level statements of endorsement by president, ministers, heads of ministries, deputies, and so forth.
• Collegiate approach to M&E between key ministries—helps avoid the situation where a rival ministry controls M&E information.	• Have formal requirements for the planning, conduct, and reporting of M&E—create organizational momentum if ministries are forced to create committees and other formal structures for M&E.	• Government vision statements on public sector reform, good governance, or national plans, which highlight the merits of M&E.
• Budgetary incentives for high-performing programs—for example, Chile's bidding fund (Caveat: The desirable relationship between performance and funding is often unclear. For example, sometimes it is necessary to provide additional funding to an underperforming program to fix it—see Part VI, question 15.).	• Withhold part of funding from ministries/agencies that fail to conduct M&E.	• Frequent repetition of message of support at meetings of ministry senior executives, section heads, other staff.
• Provision of budget-related incentives to ministries/agencies to improve performance (thus putting premium on having M&E information to demonstrate performance)—for example, finance ministry provides greater funding certainty, forwards estimates through a medium-term expenditure framework, resource agreements, portfolio budgeting, program budgeting.	• Achieve greater transparency about government and managers' performance by regularly publishing information on all programs' objectives, outputs, and service quality. Performance comparisons across jurisdictions (states, provinces, districts, municipalities) are particularly effective in highlighting good/bad performance, emphasizing good performers, and embarrassing poor performers.	• Awareness-raising seminars/workshops to demystify M&E, provide comfort about its doability, explain what's in it for participants.
• Greater management autonomy provided to programs performing well.	• Highlight adverse M&E information in reports to Parliament/Congress and disseminate widely. This can be politically sensitive and overly embarrassing to government.	• Use of actual examples of influential M&E to demonstrate its utility and cost-effectiveness.
• Output- or outcome-based performance triggers in World Bank (and other donor) loans to governments—for example, Bank loan supporting Brazil's *Bolsa Família* program.	• Set challenging but realistic performance targets (for example, on a quarterly or annual basis) that each ministry, agency, and program manager is required to meet.	• Explain to service managers and staff how M&E can help them deliver better services to their clients.
• Rewards for compliance with M&E formal requirements (including for high-quality M&E).	• Include relevant performance indicators (outputs, outcomes) in the annual performance appraisals of managers.	• Pilot some rapid evaluations and impact evaluations to demonstrate their usefulness.
• Additional funding to ministries to conduct M&E.	• Require performance exception reporting where targets not met—requires that program areas explain poor performance (Colombia).	• Conferences/seminars on good practice M&E systems in particular ministries, in other countries, and so forth—demonstrates what M&E systems can produce.
• Careful knowledge management of evaluation findings—for example, providing easily understood executive summaries targeted to key audiences can reduce the cost of accessing and digesting the findings.	• Highlight poor quality evaluation planning, data systems, performance indicators, M&E techniques, M&E reporting—shames poor performance (a supreme audit institution, a central ministry such as finance or the president's office, and possibly internal audit, can play this role).	• A network of officials working on M&E—helps showcase good practice examples of M&E in ministries, demonstrates their feasibility, and helps encourage quality standards.
• Conduct regular "How Are We Doing?" team meetings (managers and staff) to clarify objectives, review team performance, and identify ways to improve it.	• Penalize noncompliance with agreed evaluation recommendations (Chile).	
	• Hold presidential town hall meetings with citizens to showcase good/bad government performance (Colombia).	

(Table continues on next page)

Table 11.1: Incentives for M&E—Carrots, Sticks, and Sermons (continued)

Carrots	Sticks	Sermons
• Performance contracts or performance pay for civil servants—that is, direct reward for performance. For example, new senior civil servants in Ceará (Brazil) receive up to 40 percent of their remuneration in the form of performance bonuses, which are based on achievement of performance indicator targets.	• Involve civil society in M&E of government performance results in pressures for better performance and accountability (Bangalore, Bogotá).	• Support for government M&E from multilateral and bilateral donors in their loans to governments—highlights and endorses M&E.
• Staff incentives—use M&E experience as one criterion for staff recruitment, promotion, and certification.	• Use accountability mechanisms such as citizen report cards—publicize poor performance of government agencies.	
• Assistance to program areas in conduct of M&E—via help desk advice, manuals and other resource materials, provision of free training, comments on ToRs, draft evaluation reports, and so forth. This makes it easier (reduces the cost) to do M&E and to use the findings.	• Provide ministerial feedback on quality of policy advice—provides criticism of poor quality of policy advice (for example, advice that does not have a sound evidentiary basis).	
• Ensuring that data providers—at the facility level, for example—understand how their data are used and the importance of providing accurate and timely data.	• Institute performance contracts or performance pay—direct penalties for poor performance.	
• Training for program managers and staff, budget analysts, to explain what M&E is and how to use it to improve ongoing work.		
• Identification and highlighting of good practice examples of evaluation planning, of M&E techniques, of evaluation reporting—provides models others can easily copy (a supreme audit institution, a central ministry such as finance or the president's office, and possibly internal audit, can play this role).		
• Systematic feedback from ministers to ministries on quality of policy advice for each policy brief sent to ministers. Provides praise for, and highlights, good quality advice—for example, Australia's department of employment.		
• A governmentwide network of officials working on M&E. This helps provide identity and support to evaluators (who often feel isolated within each ministry/entity)—for example, Australia, Canada, Niger.		
• Financial support and technical assistance for government M&E from multilateral and bilateral donors.		

PART IV

HOW TO STRENGTHEN A GOVERNMENT M&E SYSTEM

One of the lessons to heed in building an M&E system is the importance of conducting a country diagnosis (chapter 12). This provides a sound understanding of current M&E efforts, the civil service environment, and opportunities for strengthening M&E and using M&E information for core government functions. Perhaps equally important, a diagnosis helps focus key stakeholders within government and in the donor community on the strengths and weaknesses of current M&E arrangements in the government. Such a diagnosis can also ensure that these stakeholders share a common awareness of the issues. A diagnosis naturally leads to an action plan that identifies the main options for strengthening a government M&E system (chapter 13).

The Importance of Country Diagnosis

12

It should be apparent that there is a great diversity in country approaches to M&E. Countries such as Brazil stress a whole-of-government approach to setting program objectives and creating a system of performance indicators. Others, such as Colombia, combine this with an agenda of rigorous impact evaluations.

Yet others, such as Australia, the United States, and the United Kingdom, stress a broader suite of M&E tools and methods: performance indicators, rapid reviews, impact evaluations, and performance audits. Some countries have succeeded in building a whole-of-government M&E system. Others, such as Uganda, use a largely uncoordinated and disparate collection of about 16 separate sector monitoring systems. Most of the poorest countries—those required by multilateral donors to prepare poverty reduction strategies—stress the regular collection of performance indicators to measure progress toward the MDGs.

Why Conduct a Diagnosis?

This variety tells us that not only are the starting points faced by each country different, but so are the destinations to which they aspire. There is no single best approach to a national or sector M&E system.[1] Instead, which approach a country should use depends on the actual or intended uses of the information such a system will produce. As discussed in chapter 3, those uses range from assisting resource-allocation decisions in the budget process, to helping prepare national and sector planning, to aiding ongoing management and delivery of government services, to underpinning accountability relationships.

It is clearly important to tailor efforts to build or strengthen government M&E systems to the needs and priorities of each country. Conducting a diagnosis of M&E activities is desirable because it can guide the identification of opportunities for institutionalizing M&E. A formal diagnosis helps identify a country's current strengths and weaknesses in terms of the conduct, quality, and utilization of M&E. And a diagnosis is invaluable in providing the basis for preparing an action plan. The action plan should be designed according to the desired future uses of monitoring information and evaluation findings. An early diagnosis can help inform judgments about the likelihood of these intentions ever being achieved.

A diagnosis can be conducted—or commissioned—by government or donors, or it may be desirable jointly. The process of conducting a diagnosis provides an opportunity to get important stakeholders within government—particularly senior officials in the key ministries—to focus on the issue of institutionalizing an M&E system. For most if not all developing countries, there will already be a number of M&E activities and systems. But a common challenge is a lack of coordination or harmonization between them, which can result in significant duplication of effort. A diagnosis that reveals such problems can provide a stimulus to the government to address these problems, and by providing a shared understanding of the nature of the problems, it can also help foster a consensus on what is needed to overcome them.

Such consensus is particularly important for M&E, which is essentially a cross-cutting activity affecting all ministries and agencies. Any whole-of-government reform, such as the creation of a national M&E system, requires substantial effort and a high level of central coordination, as well as the active cooperation of sector ministries and agencies. Achieving real coordination among all these actors is typically not easy, so any process such as preparation of an M&E diagnosis provides one opportunity to get the key stakeholders to talk to each other about M&E and to attempt to reach some agreement on what to do about improving the government's approach.

This is illustrated by the experiences of Uganda, Mexico, and Australia. The finding that there were 16 M&E subsystems existing in Uganda produced a response of concern—even outrage—among senior officials. That response was instrumental in prompting a decision to create NIMES to address the problems of harmonization and excessive demands on the suppliers of monitoring information in sector ministries and agencies and at the facility level (see chapter 9). And the finding from a rapid diagnosis of M&E activities in Mexico's social development agency (SEDESOL), that there existed eight uncoordinated monitoring systems within that one agency, also prompted the senior management of the agency to take steps to harmonize these systems (World Bank 2004c).

The process of conducting a diagnosis in Australia in 1987 provided the basis for the government's evaluation strategy. Although this process did not lead to a consensus among sector min-

istries, which were largely opposed to the introduction of a mandatory set of requirements for conducting evaluations, it not only provided a sound factual basis for the evaluation strategy but also sensitized these stakeholders to the importance of the issue and fostered their somewhat grudging acceptance of the strategy itself.

A diagnosis also provides a baseline for measuring a country's progress over time; it is a long-haul effort to build and sustain both demand and supply for M&E. As noted in chapter 10, most countries have not developed their M&E systems in a linear, predictable manner; instead, they have developed them opportunistically, depending on emerging opportunities and roadblocks, and as they develop their understanding concerning which initiatives are or are not working well.

In this environment, it is important to regularly monitor and evaluate the M&E system itself—just as any area of public sector reform should be regularly assessed. Indeed, conducting regular M&E efforts to strengthen an M&E system is one way those in charge of such efforts can lead by example. Some aspects of an M&E system are amenable to regular monitoring, such as the number of evaluations completed or the extent to which their recommendations are implemented. Other aspects may require more in-depth evaluation from time to time, such as the extent of utilization of M&E information in budget decision making or the quality of monitoring data.

Thus a diagnosis is a type of evaluation and can identify the degree of progress achieved and any necessary mid-course corrections. It is also noteworthy that national audit offices have played an important role in reviewing the performance of M&E systems, through performance audits (see, for example, Australian National Audit Office 1997; Mackay 2004; Office of the Auditor-General of Canada 2003; GAO 2004) and in prompting their governments to make needed improvements—for example, in Australia, Canada, and the United States.

What Issues Should a Diagnosis Address?

In the simplest sense, a diagnosis would map out what is working and what is not—the strengths

Box 12.1: Key Issues for a Diagnosis of a Government's M&E System

1. Genesis of the existing M&E system—Role of M&E advocates or champions; key events that created the priority for M&E information (for example, election of reform-oriented government, fiscal crisis)

2. The ministry or agency responsible for managing the M&E system and planning evaluations—Roles and responsibilities of the main parties to the M&E system, for example, finance ministry, planning ministry, president's office, sector ministries, the Parliament or Congress; possible existence of several, uncoordinated M&E systems at the national and sector levels; importance of federal/state/local issues to the M&E system

3. The public sector environment and whether it makes it easy or difficult for managers to perform to high standards and to be held accountable for their performance—Incentives for the stakeholders to take M&E seriously, strength of demand for M&E information. Are public sector reforms under way that might benefit from a stronger emphasis on the measurement of government performance, such as a poverty-reduction strategy, performance budgeting, strengthening of policy analysis skills, creation of a performance culture in the civil service, improvements in service delivery such as customer service standards, government decentralization, greater participation by civil society, or an anticorruption strategy?

4. The main aspects of public sector management that the M&E system supports strongly—(i) Budget decision making, (ii) national or sector planning, (iii) program management, and (iv) accountability relationships (to the finance ministry, to the president's office, to Parliament, to sector ministries, to civil society)

   • Actual role of M&E information at the various stages of the budget process: such as policy advising and planning, budget decision making, performance review and reporting; possible disconnect between the M&E work of sector ministries and the use of such information in the budget process; ex-

istence of any disconnect between the budget process and national planning; opportunities to strengthen the role of M&E in the budget

   • Extent to which the M&E information commissioned by key stakeholders (for example, the finance ministry) is used by others, such as sector ministries; if not used, barriers to utilization; any solid evidence concerning the extent of utilization by different stakeholders (for example, a diagnostic review or a survey); examples of major evaluations that have been highly influential with the government

5. Types of M&E tools emphasized in the M&E system: regular performance indicators, rapid reviews or evaluations, performance audits, rigorous, in-depth impact evaluations; scale and cost of each of these types of M&E; manner in which evaluation priorities are set—focused on problem programs, pilot programs, high-expenditure or -visibility programs, or on a systematic research agenda to answer questions about program effectiveness

6. Who is responsible for collecting performance information and conducting evaluations (for example, ministries themselves or academia or consulting firms); any problems with data quality or reliability or with the quality of evaluations conducted; strengths and weaknesses of local supply of M&E; key capacity constraints and the government's capacity-building priorities

7. Extent of donor support for M&E in recent years; donor projects that support M&E at whole-of-government, sector, or agency levels—Provision of technical assistance, other capacity building and funding for the conduct of major evaluations, such as rigorous impact evaluations

8. Conclusions: Overall strengths and weaknesses of the M&E system; its sustainability, in terms of vulnerability to a change in government, for example, how dependent it is on donor funding or other support; current plans for future strengthening of the M&E system

and weaknesses of the M&E system—and the reasons why.

A diagnosis of M&E would be expected to map out a number of key issues (box 12.1). These key issues are relevant whether the focus of the diagnosis is at the national level or at the level of an individual sector ministry or agency, albeit with

somewhat differing emphases. The issues include the following:

• The genesis of the existing M&E system (assuming some sort of system or systems already exist)

• The system's management and the roles and responsibilities of the key stakeholders

- The public sector environment and whether there are incentives to take M&E seriously
- The current main uses of M&E information, especially the role of M&E information in the budget process and the use of M&E information by sector ministries and agencies
- The types of M&E most frequently used
- Responsibilities for collecting performance information and conducting evaluations
- The extent of donor support for M&E
- Overall strengths and weaknesses of the M&E system or systems.

The purpose of a diagnosis is more than a factual stocktaking. It requires careful judgment concerning the presence or absence of the success factors for building an M&E system, as discussed in chapter 10. Thus it is important to understand the strength of the government's demand for M&E information and whether there is an influential government champion for M&E.

Conversely, it is important to know if there are barriers to building an M&E system, such as lack of genuine demand and ownership; lack of a modern culture of evidence-based decision making and accountability (due, in some countries, to issues of ethics or corruption); lack of evaluation, accounting, or auditing skills; or poor quality and credibility of financial and other performance information. This understanding naturally leads to the preparation of an action plan to strengthen existing M&E systems or to develop a new system entirely (discussed in chapter 13).

Although the preceding issues are largely generic to all countries, it is necessary to adjust the focus according to the nature of the country. Thus middle-income or upper middle-income countries might well possess a strong evaluation community, centered in universities and research institutes. But the supply of evaluation expertise would be much weaker in many of the poorest countries—those that prepare poverty-reduction strategies, for example (see chapter 9). Also, poorer countries are likely to have a strong focus on poverty-monitoring systems in particular and are likely to experience much greater difficulties in coping with multiple, unharmonized donor requirements for M&E. Donor pressure is often the primary driver of government efforts to strengthen M&E systems, and the strength of country ownership of these efforts may not be strong. A deeper discussion of diagnostic issues is presented by Mackay (1998b).[2]

Depth of Diagnosis

A question that is often asked is how long it should take to conduct an M&E diagnosis. There is no simple answer to this question; it all depends on the purposes for which a diagnosis is intended, the range of issues under investigation, and the available time and budget. In some cases a week-long mission to a country has provided a sufficient starting point for a broad understanding of the key issues facing a government interested in strengthening its M&E functions. At the other end of the spectrum is a more formal, detailed, and in-depth evaluation of a government evaluation system, such as the one the Chilean government commissioned the World Bank to undertake (Rojas and others 2005). The Chile evaluation involved a team of seven people working for many months. It entailed several missions to Chile and involved interviewing large numbers of government officials in central and sector ministries, as well as detailed reviews of evaluation quality and evaluation utilization. Such in-depth diagnoses can cost as much as several hundred thousand dollars.

Other issues may need to be investigated in-depth, such as the quality and credibility of monitoring information and of the sector information systems that provide this information.[3] Another possible issue is the capacity of universities and other organizations that provide training in M&E; such training is a common element of action plans to help institutionalize M&E. A diagnostic guide for assessing training organizations is provided by Adrien (2003); an actual diagnosis for Ghana is also available using this guide (Adrien 2001).

In between the two extremes of a week-long mission and an in-depth evaluation are the Bank diagnoses conducted for Colombia and Uganda. Each involved several missions for discussions with senior officials and representatives of civil society, document review (such as government policy statements, documents relating to relevant donor projects, and any previous country diagnoses—of M&E, public sector reform, or public expenditure management issues, for example), and formal conference or seminar presentations on the government's M&E systems.

The Colombia diagnosis involved a number of Bank staff working closely with their government counterparts over the course of several missions to the country (Mackay and others 2007); this diagnosis is included in annex B. Illustrative ToRs for a possible future in-depth diagnosis of Colombia's M&E system are presented in annex C.

The Uganda diagnoses—in 2001, with a follow-up in 2003—were conducted by a Bank consultant over the course of several missions, with the close collaboration and support of government counterparts (Hauge 2001, 2003). The 2001 Uganda diagnosis is summarized in table 9.1.

The scope of a sector diagnosis would be narrower than one focused on the government as a whole, although many if not most of the key issues would be the same. A sector diagnosis would need to focus, among other things, on the role of sector M&E activities in contributing to any whole-of-government M&E systems. It would, of course, be possible to conduct a sector diagnosis as part of a national diagnosis; this could be useful in understanding the issues of institutionalizing M&E at the sector level, or if the government is considering piloting new M&E initiatives in selected sector ministries.

Depending on the issues to be addressed in a diagnosis, it might well be necessary to assemble a team of experts with a range of backgrounds. A team might therefore include individuals with expertise in some or all of the following: the management of a government M&E system; performance indicators and systems; statistical systems; evaluation; public sector management reform; and performance budgeting.

If a donor project to support the development of an M&E system is also envisaged, then it would be important to include in the diagnostic team some donor staff with relevant experience. Close involvement of senior government officials in the diagnosis is, of course, important—to tap into their knowledge and judgments about the current M&E system and the ways it could be strengthened and to ensure their acceptance of the diagnostic findings and recommendations.

Conclusions

A diagnosis of a country's systems for M&E can provide a solid understanding of their strengths and weaknesses. This is clearly important for developing an action plan that is appropriately tailored to some vision of the future M&E system, particularly in terms of the desired uses of monitoring information and evaluation findings, which are specific to each country. Such a diagnosis would also provide a baseline measure against which future progress can be evaluated, and further modifications can be made to the system as opportunities emerge and setbacks or barriers are encountered.

The process of conducting a diagnosis provides a vehicle for involving senior officials in the key central and sector ministries, together with donor staff, in considering the purposes, uses, and architecture of the government's M&E system(s). Diagnoses can provide surprising findings about a multiplicity of uncoordinated and duplicative systems. Such findings can help foster consensus on an action plan to strengthen the system.

Creating a consensus on roles and responsibilities under a whole-of-government M&E system may not be easy, however. Sector ministries and agencies might prefer not to be subject to centrally determined, formal requirements for M&E. And central ministries themselves might jostle for control of a new or rejuvenated M&E system.[4] A more collaborative, less adversarial approach can help reduce these differences.

A diagnosis should include a factual stocktaking and careful judgments concerning the presence or absence of the various success factors for building an M&E system, such as a committed, influential champion for M&E. A rapid diagnosis can provide an overview of a number of key issues but could not be expected to be either complete or balanced. A detailed, in-depth diagnosis would include drill-downs into specific issues considered important for the country, such as the quality of data systems or a detailed investigation of the current extent of utilization of M&E information.

Most diagnoses are neither very rapid nor very time consuming or in-depth; they fall between these two extremes. Nevertheless, a sound diagnosis does require considerable care; the expertise and quality of judgment of those who prepare the diagnosis is crucial.

13

Preparing Action Plans

A central theme of this volume is that there is no "best" model of what a government or sectoral M&E system should look like. Countries differ substantially in the emphasis they choose to give to the different purposes of an M&E system—such as to support budget decision making or ongoing management of activities, or for accountability purposes.

And each country is unique in terms of its M&E activities, functions, and systems and in terms of its public sector culture and environment. Thus, an action plan to create or strengthen an existing government system for M&E has to be tailored closely to country circumstances. This is why it is so important to conduct a diagnosis of a country's M&E strengths and weaknesses as a basis for developing an action plan (chapter 12).

Vision for the Future System

A diagnosis might ideally lead to a clear statement of what the M&E system would desirably look like at some time in the future. The dimensions of the system—its architecture—would include, in particular, the following elements:

1. Which of the four possible uses of M&E information will be the objectives of the system, recognizing the trade-offs between them: to support budget decision making or national planning; to help ministries in policy formulation, policy analysis, and program develop-

ment; to support ministries and agencies in managing their activities; or to strengthen accountability relationships (chapter 3).

2. The formal roles and responsibilities of the key stakeholders of the M&E system—those who would be expected to produce monitoring information and evaluations and to make use of them. It is important to locate responsibility for management or oversight in a powerful ministry, committee, or other entity.

3. Whether a whole-of-government system, including all central ministries, sector ministries, and agencies, is to be developed or if the system is to be more narrowly focused on individual sectors or agencies. Some governments develop an M&E system only for donor-funded operations in their country.[1]

4. The levels of government at which the M&E system will be developed: central, state/provincial, or local.

5. The range of M&E tools on which the system will focus: performance indicators, rapid evaluations, rigorous impact evaluations, and so forth. It is possible to create a reliable performance monitoring system without conducting any evaluations; however, conducting evaluations requires good performance information, either from a monitoring system or from special surveys, or both.

Implementation Issues

Once the vision of the fully functioning M&E system has been formulated, it is possible to develop an action plan to achieve it. This action plan should draw on the international lessons from building country M&E systems (chapter 10). Of course, it would not make sense to develop an action plan unless there is already some substantive demand for M&E within the government.

An action plan can also be designed to strengthen demand, for example, by ensuring that all key stakeholders play some substantive part in planning or managing the M&E system, such as through their involvement in an oversight or planning committee. Particular incentives might need to be created to further strengthen demand; these incentives could involve a mixture of carrots, sticks, and sermons (chapter 11). In other words, it would be a mistake to create an action plan that focused purely on technocratic, supply-side issues.

Strengthening an existing M&E system or building an entirely new one can be approached in many ways. Implementation issues that need to be addressed in an action plan include the following:

• The extent to which there will be a focus on strengthening what already exists: improving financial management information systems (to track budget appropriations and actual spending) or improving ministries' monitoring systems, especially administrative data on government activities, beneficiaries, and outputs (note that these data are typically collected at the facility level).
• Whether new approaches should be piloted, with a view to their subsequent mainstreaming if successful. These could include the implementation of new, formal requirements for

M&E in pilot ministries or agencies, for example, where there already exists a strong commitment to conducting and using M&E and where there is already some successful track record. Pilots could be developed at other levels, such as in individual states or municipalities. Pilots such as rapid evaluations or rigorous impact evaluations could also be envisaged for particular evaluation tools if there is little or no experience with them in the country.

• When and how quickly mainstreaming should occur. In Chile, for example, particular M&E tools were mainstreamed in a sequential manner: performance indicators in 1994, rapid reviews in 1996, rigorous impact evaluations in 2001, and comprehensive spending reviews in 2002 (chapter 6). Mexico is planning to mainstream its new, whole-of-government M&E system over a three-year period (2007–09) (Hernandez 2007).

The speed of implementation of an action plan is clearly very important. There is an issue here of "digestibility"—how much M&E change or reform ministries and agencies can absorb, and how quickly. We have learned from countries that have successfully created an M&E system that it is a long-haul effort requiring patience and persistence (chapter 10); M&E champions in government, in contrast, tend to be impatient when reforming their M&E systems. Another lesson is to institutionalize an M&E system as rapidly as possible before the champion(s) eventually depart.

As emphasized in chapter 10, it is helpful to regularly monitor and evaluate the M&E system itself, to identify how successfully its various components are being implemented. This provides a sound basis for any needed changes to the nature, scale, and timing of implementation of the action plan. And this is obviously important if a pilot approach has been adopted.

Action plans may focus on some or all of the following stakeholders: government ministries and officials, such as central and sectoral ministries and agencies; subnational governments at the state, province, or district levels; the Parliament or Congress, including elected representatives, committees, and their staff; and civil society groups, including universities, research institutes, and NGOs. Commonly adopted actions could include, for example, providing M&E training; promulgating any necessary laws, decrees, and regulations; preparing M&E guidelines and standards; strengthening and harmonizing monitoring systems; and conducting a range of types of evaluation, such as rapid reviews and rigorous impact evaluations.

Trade-Offs

There are many issues and trade-offs to consider when developing an action plan. One is that a whole-of-government M&E system that is managed by the finance ministry for purposes of performance budgeting would need to ensure broad coverage of all programs. One way to achieve breadth of coverage is to rely on performance indicators; their drawback, however, is that they usually provide little information on the reasons results have been achieved or not—in other words, the causes of good or bad performance.

Rapid reviews can provide some insights into causality, and as they are cheaper than some other evaluation methods, they can also provide relatively broader coverage of government programs. The most reliable evaluation findings can come from a rigorous impact evaluation, although these can be very expensive to conduct, so it is harder for a finance ministry to use them to evaluate a broad range of programs (chapter 2). There is often a trade-off between choice of M&E tools and the desired uses of M&E information.

Another trade-off is between who commissions evaluations and who is meant to use them. Chile's finance ministry commissions a range of types of evaluation and uses them effectively for its own purposes; but sector ministries and agencies are highly resistant to using these evaluations for their own, internal purposes—the entities do not "own" the evaluation findings (chapter 6). It can be difficult for a centrally imposed M&E system to be accepted by sector ministries.

Australia's finance department endeavored to address this by leaving to sector ministries the prime responsibility of planning and conducting evaluations—this ensured they had a high ownership of evaluation findings (chapter 8). However, this

ownership had a cost: up to one-third of the evaluations suffered from some kind of methodological weakness.[2] This is indicative of another trade-off: internally conducted evaluations may have high ownership, but external evaluations may be more likely to be rigorous and objective.

A simple results chain for building an M&E system is shown in figure 13.1. This provides a simplified representation of how an action plan would be expected to lead to various kinds of output, such as the number of officials trained in M&E, the number of evaluations conducted, and so on. These outputs in turn would be expected to lead to intermediate outcomes such as strengthened government demand for M&E, and to final outcomes, including the utilization of monitoring information and evaluation findings by government and others. It would be hoped that these outcomes would help lead to final impacts, including improved government performance, improved development effectiveness, improved service provision, and poverty reduction.

Menu of Actions to Improve M&E

Table 13.1 presents a menu of possible actions to achieve improvements in the demand for and supply of M&E. This menu is far from comprehensive. Rather, it illustrates the range and nature of actions that can be taken to build or to strengthen systems for monitoring and evaluation. One example of an action plan, which follows directly from a diagnosis of M&E in a country, is shown in box 9.2 for Uganda.

Another example is the World Bank project developed to help the government of Colombia strengthen its national M&E system, SINERGIA (chapter 7; annex B). This $14 million project has four components: (1) support better monitoring of government spending at the regional and local levels; (2) consolidate the institutionalization of SINERGIA within the government; (3) support the development of regional and local M&E systems, partly through a pilot approach; and (4) establish mechanisms to improve the quality, relevance, and cost-effectiveness of public information. This project is based on the Bank's diagnosis of SINERGIA (annex B). This project also includes a large

(Text continues on page 80)

Figure 13.1: A Results Chain for Building a Government M&E System

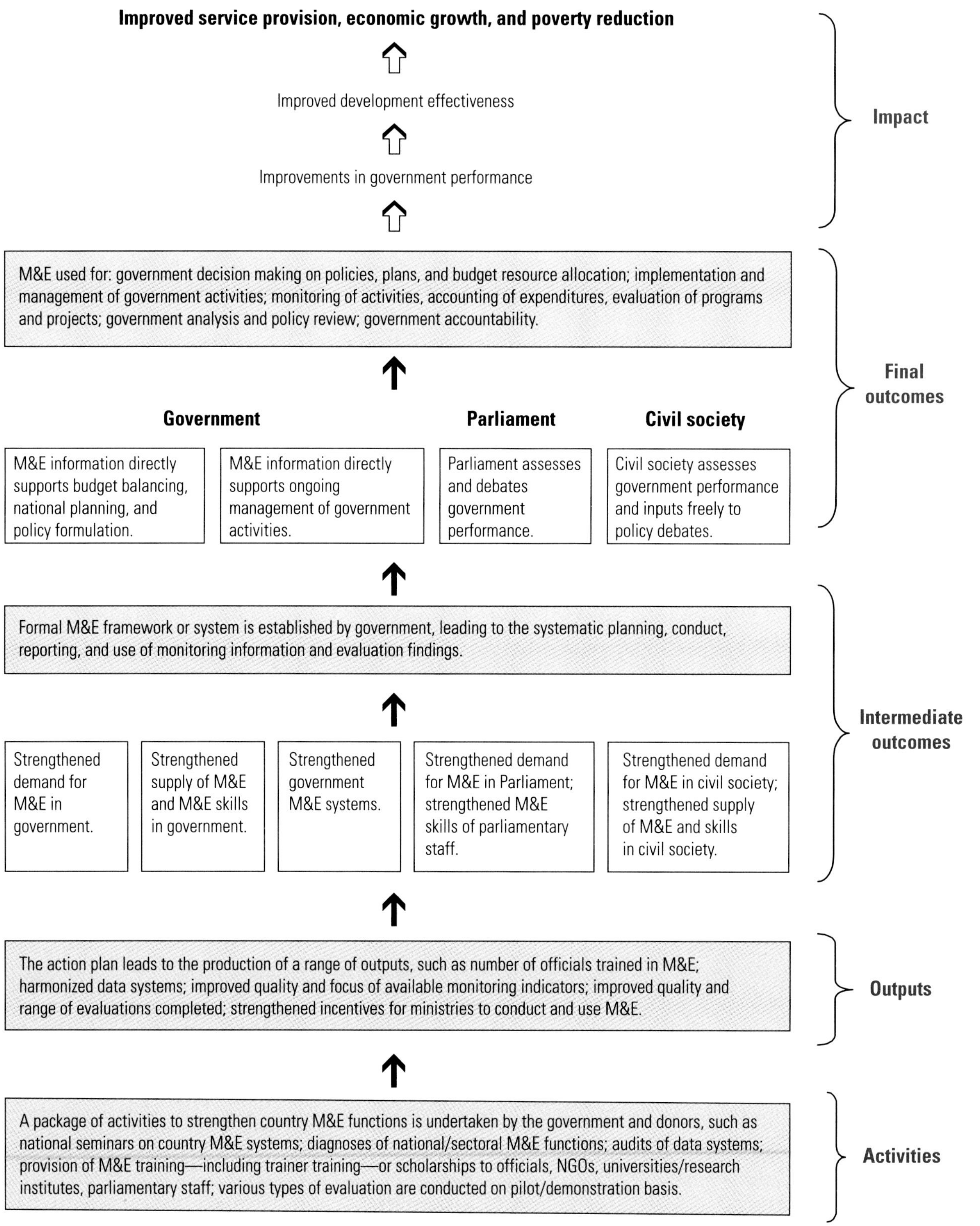

Improved service provision, economic growth, and poverty reduction

⇧

Improved development effectiveness

⇧

Improvements in government performance

⇧

Impact

M&E used for: government decision making on policies, plans, and budget resource allocation; implementation and management of government activities; monitoring of activities, accounting of expenditures, evaluation of programs and projects; government analysis and policy review; government accountability.

⬆

Final outcomes

Government　　　　　　　　　　**Parliament**　　**Civil society**

| M&E information directly supports budget balancing, national planning, and policy formulation. | M&E information directly supports ongoing management of government activities. | Parliament assesses and debates government performance. | Civil society assesses government performance and inputs freely to policy debates. |

⬆

Formal M&E framework or system is established by government, leading to the systematic planning, conduct, reporting, and use of monitoring information and evaluation findings.

⬆

Intermediate outcomes

| Strengthened demand for M&E in government. | Strengthened supply of M&E and M&E skills in government. | Strengthened government M&E systems. | Strengthened demand for M&E in Parliament; strengthened M&E skills of parliamentary staff. | Strengthened demand for M&E in civil society; strengthened supply of M&E and skills in civil society. |

⬆

The action plan leads to the production of a range of outputs, such as number of officials trained in M&E; harmonized data systems; improved quality and focus of available monitoring indicators; improved quality and range of evaluations completed; strengthened incentives for ministries to conduct and use M&E.

Outputs

⬆

A package of activities to strengthen country M&E functions is undertaken by the government and donors, such as national seminars on country M&E systems; diagnoses of national/sectoral M&E functions; audits of data systems; provision of M&E training—including trainer training—or scholarships to officials, NGOs, universities/research institutes, parliamentary staff; various types of evaluation are conducted on pilot/demonstration basis.

Activities

Table 13.1: Possible Actions to Strengthen M&E Systems at the Country/Sectoral Levels

Strengthen government demand for M&E	Strengthen supply and develop M&E skills within government	Strengthen M&E systems	Strengthen demand for M&E in civil society, Parliament	Strengthen supply and development M&E skills in civil society, Parliamentary staff
Provide carrots, sticks, and sermons to strengthen demand (see table 11.1).				
Donors advocate M&E and focus on *results*. Disseminate examples of influential evaluations.			Donors advocate M&E and focus on *results*. Disseminate examples of influential evaluations.	
Donors preserve and disseminate experience of other countries with M&E systems.		Donors preserve and disseminate experience of other countries with M&E systems.	Donors preserve and disseminate experience of other countries with M&E systems.	
Hold national brainstorming seminars on options for government M&E systems.		Coordinate/harmonize donor country M&E.	Hold national brainstorming seminars on options for government M&E systems.	
Hold seminars on donor evaluation findings (for example, World Bank's) relevant to the country—demonstrate the usefulness of evaluation.			Hold seminars on donor evaluation findings (for example, World Bank's) relevant to the country—demonstrate the usefulness of evaluation.	
Hold regional seminars on government M&E systems.	Foster regional networks of M&E managers and practitioners—a community of practice.	Encourage close coordination with work of other donors to strengthen the government's central and sectoral M&E systems.		
Conduct national/sectoral diagnosis of M&E functions—highlight problems and opportunities.	Conduct national/sectoral data audits. Conduct diagnosis of organizations that provide M&E training.	Conduct national/sectoral diagnosis of M&E functions—demand, supply, systems, options for action plans.	Conduct national/sectoral diagnosis of M&E functions—highlight problems and opportunities.	Conduct diagnosis of organizations that provide M&E training.
Embed M&E as component of donor/government public sector management and public expenditure management work.	Embed M&E as component of related public sector management/public expenditure management work, for example, on performance budgeting;	Donors give loans to support M&E systems. Link efforts to strengthen M&E systems with other performance-related government reforms.	Conduct service delivery surveys of client satisfaction and perceptions of the quality of government surveys and publicize the results widely (for example, CRCs).	

(Table continues on next page)

Table 13.1: Possible Actions to Strengthen M&E Systems at the Country/Sectoral Levels *(continued)*

Strengthen government demand for M&E	Strengthen supply and develop M&E skills within government	Strengthen M&E systems	Strengthen demand for M&E in civil society, Parliament	Strengthen supply and development M&E skills in civil society, Parliamentary staff
	results-based management and strategic planning; sectorwide approaches; sectoral reform programs; service delivery; financial management and accountability, including financial management information systems; statistical system capacity building (statistics offices, ministry management information systems, statistics production, including service delivery surveys); national audit office capacity building; government decentralization.			
Identify and support M&E champions. Promote collaboration among all key government stakeholders in the M&E system—especially in planning and oversight of the system.		Encourage stronger government internal coordination of M&E, including links between M&E, budget, planning and ministry, and management info systems.		
Seek to mandate M&E via government decisions, decrees, regulations, and laws.	Disseminate evaluation standards and methods.	Seek to mandate M&E through government decisions, decrees, regulations, laws. Develop M&E guidelines and manuals.	Seek to mandate M&E through government decisions, decrees, regulations, laws. Introduce freedom-of-information legislation.	Disseminate evaluation standards and methods. Support research institutes, universities, NGOs to evaluate and review government performance—for example, CRCs, budget analysis.
	Provide training in a range of M&E tools, methods, and techniques to officials—at national, state, municipal levels.		Encourage media to report on government performance.	Train parliamentarians and staff to analyze government performance. Provide a range of M&E training in a range of M&E tools, methods, and techniques to staff of universities, NGOs, and so forth.

	Provide M&E trainer training and support for civil service colleges, for example, via twinning arrangements with developed country counterparts.			Provide M&E trainer training and support for universities/research institutes, for example, via twinning arrangements.
	Review ministries' performance indicators. Strengthen ministries' management information systems. Support service delivery surveys.			
Create a fund for evaluation.	Create/staff M&E/statistics/policy analysis units.	Create evaluation fund—allow civil society access.		Create evaluation fund—allow civil society access.
Promote donor funding of major impact evaluations/reviews—to demonstrate feasibility and utility.	Donors fund major evaluations/reviews—on "public good" grounds.	Support community involvement in participatory poverty assessments, and so on.		Donors subcontract evaluations/reviews to universities/research institutes.
	Allow greater donor reliance on national M&E expertise when conducting evaluations.	Encourage civil society and parliamentary scrutiny of government evaluation reports.	Allow greater donor reliance on government to undertake M&E of donor-funded projects and programs.	
Support development of government evaluation networks and national evaluation associations.	Support development of government evaluation networks and national evaluation associations.			Support development of national evaluation associations.
Seek donor support for joint evaluations with governments and for country-led evaluations.	Donors support joint evaluations with governments and country-led evaluations.			

Note: If actions in these five columns are similar or related, this can be seen by looking along each row. CRC = citizen report card; NGO = nongovernmental organization.

number of planned diagnoses of more detailed, specific issues:

- A review of existing institutional arrangements, particularly the extent to which M&E information from SINERGIA has been used to support national planning and budget decision making. This review will recommend increasing the government's level of utilization of M&E information.
- A review of M&E structures, institutional arrangements, and capabilities in two line ministries. This will help establish M&E quality standards, which will be required of all ministries and agencies.
- An assessment of the M&E capabilities of the unit in the DNP that manages SINERGIA and provides technical assistance to other ministries and agencies.
- A review of existing laws, decrees, and regulations relating to M&E.
- A review of the cost, quality, and cost-effectiveness of the various evaluation tools and techniques currently used in the SINERGIA system.
- A diagnosis of the capacities needed to establish PBB.
- A diagnosis of the quality and utilization of performance information and of information systems in two pilot municipalities.
- An assessment of mechanisms for local accountability in some good practice municipalities.
- An assessment of the methodology currently used by the DNP to assess the performance of all 1,100 municipalities in Colombia.
- A review of data quality and the extent of data harmonization among the main monitoring systems in Colombia's central government.
- An assessment of the quality, relevance, and use of the DNP's main system for monitoring government performance.

Conclusions

A useful strategy for building a government system for M&E is to start with a diagnosis of current M&E activities within the government. At the same time, a vision of what a well-functioning system would look like should be developed. These basic building blocks naturally lead to the development of an action plan, including a phased approach to its implementation.

By now it should be abundantly clear that it would not make sense to attempt to apply a standardized, "cookie-cutter" approach to developing a government M&E system. The action plan for building a government M&E system needs to be tailored closely to each country's individual circumstances and to the government's particular vision of the future system. This vision would encompass the specific uses to which it intends to put monitoring information and evaluation findings, whether that is to be a whole-of-government system or an individual ministry or agency, the levels of government to which it will apply, the particular range of M&E tools to be adopted, and so on.

There are many possible dimensions to an M&E system, and there are many trade-offs to be considered carefully. An action plan for building an M&E system does not have to be enormously complex, although there is always the danger that the desired system will be overdesigned and thus much harder to achieve; it is very much the case that less is more. A similar danger is that the speed with which a system can be built will be overestimated.

A concrete action plan provides a focus for key stakeholders in the government and for donors. It also provides a yardstick against which actual progress toward the vision of the future M&E system can be gauged—by regular M&E of both the system and the action plan. This will not only facilitate identification of emerging opportunities; it will also enable any implementation difficulties to be identified early and addressed. The emergence of roadblocks and opportunities explains the experience of many countries: because of these challenges, government M&E systems are usually not developed in a linear, predictable manner (chapter 10).

The international community is still accumulating experience on how best to strengthen government M&E systems—which approaches and systems are most effective and in which types of country, such as in middle-income countries or in poor countries with very weak capacities. This underlines the importance of further building the body of evidence concerning how best to institutionalize an M&E system. These and other frontier issues are considered in Part V.

PART V
REMAINING ISSUES

Part V maps out some remaining issues. There are other issues about which international experience is either not well understood or not well documented. These are frontier, cutting-edge issues—topics that are important for the institutionalization of M&E but where current knowledge appears to be insufficient (chapter 14). They include, among other things, the cost-effectiveness of alternative approaches to strengthening government M&E systems; how much evaluation is enough; good practice models of M&E at the sector and subnational levels; and ways to foster the involvement of civil society in monitoring and evaluating government performance. Many if not all of these topics would merit more detailed research.

Frontier Issues

Knowledge about building government systems for monitoring and evaluation is a work in progress. Considerable experience has been accumulated and analyzed in OECD countries (chapter 3), and the literature on the experience of developing countries has started to grow over the last 10 years in particular.

But there are many issues that are either not well understood or not well documented (box 14.1). Nine frontier issues are suggested here. Most if not all of these issues deserve additional, in-depth investigation through a long-term research program.

Cost-Effective Approaches

As flagged in chapter 13, one important issue is **which approaches to strengthening government M&E systems are most effective, and in which types of country.** A long list of different types of actions has been presented in this volume, but the relative cost-effectiveness of each is unknown. One yardstick is provided by the evaluation criteria that can be applied to any type of capacity-building effort, such as its efficiency, effectiveness, sustainability, and so forth.[1]

Donors are becoming increasingly active in helping governments strengthen their M&E systems, and we can expect a number of donor evaluations of those capacity-building projects in coming years. Until now, most donor support that has been provided through lending projects has been as part of a larger reform effort, and thus when the projects are evaluated, relatively little attention is devoted to issues such as the cost-effectiveness of individual actions—such as those listed in table 13.1.

The IEG, which has had an M&E capacity-building program for more than 20 years, conducted a self-evaluation of its work (IEG 2004a); this evaluation is discussed in annex D. More evaluations of donor and government efforts to build M&E systems are needed to deepen our understanding of what works best in different situations. The World Bank is currently preparing its first project devoted solely to strengthening a government M&E system, for Colombia. The future monitoring and evaluation of this loan should provide invaluable lessons.

The growing literature on government M&E systems focuses on good practice or promising practice countries (chapter 5). This is understandable for at least two reasons. First, donors working in this topic and governments interested in strengthening their M&E systems want to replicate success; thus, they want to understand the key capacity-building actions and underlying success factors. Second, donors that advocate government M&E systems as a desirable means for improving sound governance need to be able to identify credible examples of well-functioning M&E systems.

What is missing from this approach are **examples of countries that have tried but failed to strengthen their M&E systems.** We know as evaluators that we often learn as much from failure as from success. But there are few documented examples.[2] Once more donor evaluations of capacity-building work in this area have been conducted, it will be important to focus specifically on these "failures."

Another question of interest is **which types of M&E system**—each with its own specific purposes, such as for performance budgeting or for better program management—**are most cost-effective.** A yardstick here is provided by the extent of utilization of M&E information in different ways and the value of that utilization—a consistent argument in this volume is that utilization is the bottom-line measure of success of an M&E system. An example here is Chile; its M&E system costs the government about $0.75 million per year, and the M&E information it produces is used intensively by the finance ministry for its budget decision making and for imposing man-

agement improvements on sector ministries and agencies (chapter 6).

The value of M&E information is an interesting question, but it may be not be possible to provide a clear answer; much depends on the circumstances and level of demand (or commitment) of each individual government. It is likely that some types of M&E systems—for example, those relying on an agenda of rigorous impact evaluations—might be too demanding and costly for the poorest governments. In such a situation, it might, however, be possible to rely on donors to fund and manage such evaluations.

Related to this issue is the question of **how much evaluation is enough.** How much should governments be prepared to spend annually on their M&E system, once it has been created? The evaluation literature occasionally makes passing reference to this issue, and there has been some suggestion that it would be appropriate to allocate around one percent of an organization's total spending on evaluation. But this number has no logical or empirical basis. The issue remains important, however. Chile's annual government budget is about $20 billion, and the finance ministry spends only $0.75 million annually on the M&E system. Is this enough, or is it too much?

Chile's finance ministry funds fewer than 20 evaluations per annum. Compare this to Australia, where, in the mid-1990s, some 160 major evaluations were under way at any one time (chapter 8). As in Chile, Australia's evaluations were used intensively in the budget process. Which country produced the optimum number of evaluations? This is not an easy question to answer. The parsimonious approach of Chile's finance ministry would seem to imply that it would never finance a series of expensive impact evaluations on the scale of Mexico's *Progresa* evaluations (discussed in chapter 6). Yet the Chilean government utilizes the M&E information intensively and considers its system highly cost-effective; the returns it has derived from its investment in M&E are highly positive. Thus, it should spend more—and arguably much more—on its M&E system.

If we accept that utilization of M&E information is the basic yardstick of success of a system, this suggests a simple decision rule as to how much to spend on M&E: Continue to spend on the M&E system if the benefits from using the M&E information are judged to be high; and if the potential benefits from a proposed increase in spending on M&E are also judged to be high, then spend that additional amount—using either the government's budget funds or donor loans. This puts the onus on those who manage the M&E system to demonstrate credibly that M&E information is indeed being heavily used and that the system is cost-effective.

This again underlines the value of undertaking regular M&E of the system itself. In those situations where M&E information is not being used intensively, clearly an analysis of the reasons needs to be conducted. If there are perceived problems with the reliability of the M&E information, then more money might have to be spent to improve it. And if there are problems of weak government demand, even for reliable information, then steps would need to be taken to strengthen demand. If those steps do not work and it is not possible to increase demand, then one can argue that the M&E system might need to be scaled back, or perhaps even abolished.

Most of the discussion in this volume is focused on national, whole-of-government M&E systems. This is typically the domain of finance or planning ministries or the president's office. On the donor side, the staff who work on such issues are often public sector management or public expenditure management experts whose work is largely concerned with systemic issues of sound governance; these staff also tend to have a focus on the central ministries of a government.

Sector Systems

Another frontier issue is **sector systems for M&E,** such as often occur in health and education ministries. Donor staff who work at this level are often sectoral specialists. National and sectoral systems are clearly related; indeed, a national system usually has to rely on sectoral systems for much of the monitoring information it requires. That information may come from administrative records, or possibly from special surveys and censuses conducted either by sector entities or by the national statistical office.

Sector systems for M&E are clearly important in their own right and also because of the role they play in a national system. Yet the literature on government M&E systems, and the literature on government statistical systems,[3] appears to concentrate largely on national systems. This gap needs to be filled. There are some sector ministries and agencies in developing countries that appear to have well-performing M&E systems, especially in the health, education, and social welfare sectors. But we don't know enough about these possible islands of good practice, the factors that led to their existence, or their sustainability.

There are at least some documented examples of high-quality work on sectoral M&E systems, and these in themselves merit greater attention. One example is the Health Metrics Network (HMN), a global partnership supported by the World Health Organization, which promotes the development of health sector information systems.[4] The Network has prepared a detailed diagnostic tool for assessing the performance of health information systems, identifying critical weaknesses, and monitoring the performance of efforts to address those weaknesses. This tool can be used to assign ratings to a large number of dimensions of a health information system, and these ratings are assigned to five categories of performance, ranging from "highly adequate" to "not functioning."[5]

This volume takes the approach that the lessons from institutionalizing national M&E systems—those discussed in chapter 10—also apply to sectoral M&E systems. There is some evidence to support this belief, such as the analytical work conducted in relation to Mexico's social development agency, SEDESOL (World Bank 2004c; Hernandez 2006). But more research is warranted into this proposition that sectoral M&E issues are essentially a microcosm of the issues facing a national M&E system. At the very least, there are likely to be some important differences in emphasis. Collectively, we need to understand what these are.

Subnational M&E Systems

A comparable issue to sector M&E systems is **subnational M&E systems,** especially where there is not a unitary system of government. Many governments have a federal system with several layers, with varying degrees of devolution and decentralization of functions.

The relationships between these layers of government can be complex, including accountability relationships and formal requirements for provision of information. Few case studies have been prepared on M&E at the subnational level. Yet it is clearly important because of the complexity of the relationships.

Another reason this is relevant is the reality that typically most monitoring information is collected at the facility level—thus, the nature of the relationship between individual facilities and sector ministries/agencies on the one hand, and subnational levels on the other, may help determine the quality of the information provided, as well as the extent of use of that information by the facilities themselves. As noted in the case of Uganda (chapter 9), the information workload at the facility and district levels can be onerous, with highly negative implications for the quality of data.

Donor Harmonization

A perennial issue in the donor evaluation community is **donor harmonization,** or the lack of it. This has multiplied the workload imposed on donor countries because of their need to comply with the different donor requirements for M&E. In the 2005 Paris Declaration, donors pledged to endeavor to harmonize these requirements and to align themselves as much as possible with country systems and approaches to "results frameworks and monitoring"—that is, **country alignment** (High Level Forum on Harmonisation, Alignment, Results 2005).

Donors and countries have also committed to working jointly to strengthen country capacities

and demand for results-based management. It will be interesting to learn to what extent, if any, these objectives have been met; a series of evaluations of the results of the Paris Declaration are under way, and they will be reported over the 2008–10 period.[6]

One bright spot is the evidence of a growing number of donor/government impact evaluations. The World Bank, for example, is currently planning or conducting around 30 rigorous impact evaluations jointly with governments in Latin America, typically as part of Bank projects with governments; it appears that these are being conducted in a highly collaborative manner. It is likely that there are some lessons here for the conduct of other types of evaluation and for joint donor/government evaluations in other Regions.

Examples of **civil society involvement in monitoring and evaluating government performance** are presented in chapter 3—the Citizen Report Card Initiative, which was first conducted in Bangalore, and the comparable *Bogotá Cómo Vamos* approach. These initiatives have successfully pressured municipal governments to improve their performance. The CRC has been replicated in a number of other cities in India and other countries.

The challenge for the donor community is how to encourage the replication of this kind of civil society engagement in other countries. This will depend in part on each country's circumstances and the space that civil society has in the country.

The World Bank and some other donors face an additional difficulty because their primary interaction is with governments. Nevertheless, it is possible for the Bank to use its convening power to help ensure that the voice of civil society is heard. The Bank can and has showcased to civil society groups in various countries a range of examples of civil society engagement in monitoring and evaluating government performance. The hope is that this will stimulate civil society's interest and demand for involving itself in this issue (see, for example, Mackay and Gariba 2000). It is important that the donor community, and civil society itself, identify additional ways of fostering this type of engagement.

Formal Standards

One final frontier issue is suggested here: whether there is a need to establish **formal standards for good practice M&E systems.** Similar standards are applied by the international community—especially by donors—for national and some sector statistical systems and for government financial management systems.[7] It would be possible to develop standards for government M&E systems based on the checklist criteria developed as part of the various existing diagnostic guides (chapter 12; Mackay 1998b).

One argument in favor of such formal standards is that this would provide clearer guidance to governments as to what standards they could, and perhaps should, aspire to. A second argument is that it would facilitate periodic monitoring and evaluation of the M&E systems themselves; as argued in chapters 12 and 13, it is important that efforts to strengthen a government M&E system are monitored and evaluated, and the assessment of an M&E system against explicit criteria would facilitate this. One argument against a standardized list of criteria, however, is that there is no single good practice model—or even handful of models—for M&E systems governments should aspire to. Rather, there is a very wide array of possible models.

Concluding Remarks

15

The focus of this volume is on government systems for monitoring and evaluation and how they can help achieve better government. Most OECD countries and a small but growing number of developing countries place considerable emphasis on ensuring that monitoring information and evaluation findings are available.

These governments use M&E information in four possible ways: to support policy making, especially budget decision making; to help government ministries in their policy development and analysis work; to support ministries and agencies in managing their activities; and to strengthen accountability relationships.

It is argued here that these four uses of M&E place it at the center of sound governance—as a necessary condition for the effective management of public expenditures for economic development and poverty reduction. Examples are given of highly influential evaluations that have been conducted in developing countries; these indicate the potentially high returns that governments can derive from investment in M&E.

The purpose of this volume is to help governments in their efforts to build, strengthen, and fully institutionalize their M&E systems, not as an end in itself but to achieve improved government performance. Case studies of well-performing country systems for M&E are presented, together with a large number of lessons from these and other

countries about how to build such systems, as well as lessons about mistakes to avoid.

A consistent theme of this volume is that the bottom-line measure of "success" of an M&E system is utilization of the information it produces; it is not enough to create a system that produces technically sound performance indicators and evaluations. Utilization depends on the nature and strength of demand for M&E information, and this in turn depends on the incentives to make use of M&E. Some governments in developing countries have a high level of demand for M&E; in others the demand is weak or lukewarm. For these latter countries, there are ways to increase demand by strengthening incentives.

One of the key lessons to incorporate into building an M&E system is the importance of conducting a country diagnosis of M&E. It can provide a sound understanding of M&E activities in the government and the public sector environment and opportunities for using M&E information to support core government functions. Such a diagnosis is an important building block for preparing an action plan. A diagnosis can also be a vehicle for ensuring that key government and donor stakeholders have a shared understanding of the issues and of the importance of strengthening M&E.

There is a considerable and growing body of knowledge about country experience in building M&E systems, and the key lessons are presented in this volume. In addition, answers are provided to frequently asked questions from officials and others working to strengthen government M&E systems. But there are also a number of issues about which less is known, such as good practice models of M&E at the subnational and sectoral levels, or ways to foster the involvement of civil society in M&E. These are frontier, cutting-edge issues, and this volume argues for a long-term program of research to investigate them.

PART VI
Q&A—Commonly Asked Questions

Answers are provided in Part VI to a number of questions that commonly arise at national and international conferences on the topic of government M&E. The frequency with which similar questions are raised helps identify key issues that must be addressed when seeking to institutionalize an M&E system.

Q&A—Commonly Asked Questions

Officials, academics, consultants, donors, and others interested in strengthening government M&E systems often raise similar issues about how to do this and how to overcome the perceived challenges. Answers to 21 of the most frequently asked questions are provided here. These issues help highlight the many related dimensions of a government system for M&E and clarify the nature of the trade-offs that may need to be made.

1. How can a governmentwide system for monitoring and evaluation be introduced progressively? It is too big a step for my country to introduce a system all at once.

A good first step is to conduct a diagnosis of existing government M&E functions and systems (chapter 12). This should provide a sound understanding of the strengths and weaknesses of what currently exists. It should also help clarify who needs what M&E information, for what purposes, and when. This in turn should help identify a menu of possible actions to strengthen existing M&E systems or create a new system entirely (chapter 13). Clearly a threshold issue is to clarify the main intended uses of M&E information in the future.

One possible approach is to implement a range of M&E tools and methods in a progressive, whole-of-government manner. Chile did this by implementing a performance information system in

1994, followed by comprehensive management reports in 1996, rapid reviews in 1996, rigorous impact evaluations in 2001, and comprehensive spending reviews in 2002 (chapter 6). Most governments, however, might not have the patience to pursue such a protracted approach.

There are some M&E actions that, while important, can take a long time to achieve—such as extensive improvements to performance monitoring systems or a rigorous impact evaluation—if good data are not already available. Champions for the M&E system may or may not be willing to wait for these actions to be taken; even if they are patient, champions will eventually depart, perhaps unexpectedly.

This is an argument for trying to include some quick wins in the M&E action plan. These might include a range of pilot activities, such as conducting some rapid evaluations to feed into the budget process (by revealing the performance of individual programs); conducting a public expenditure tracking survey to reveal the extent of "leakage" of government funds; or conducting a rigorous impact evaluation where good data already exist or can be readily collected (see chapter 2).

Such demonstration activities can highlight the value of M&E information and thus help raise awareness of and demand for it. Although it is always a good idea to have a well-prepared action plan, including a number of stages for development of the M&E system, one important lesson from experience is the importance of being able to respond flexibly when new opportunities for M&E arise (chapter 10).

2. Demand within my government for monitoring information and evaluation findings is weak. What should I do about this disinterest if I want to build a government M&E system?

Weak demand is a serious obstacle to building a government M&E system, but there are a number of steps that can be taken to strengthen demand (see chapters 10 and 11). First, it can be helpful to raise awareness of M&E among senior officials: explain what M&E is and the many ways it can be valuable to a government—such as to achieve more informed decision making in the national budget or to improve ongoing management of all government activities. Senior officials can often be persuaded by examples of influential evaluations and well-performing M&E systems in other countries (chapter 3). Finding powerful champions and allies is also important, and they in turn can help advocate and support M&E more widely.

Every government is already conducting *some* M&E work, even if it only comprises ministries' systems of administrative records, the sector data of national statistics agencies, and the information governments provide to donors. It can be eye opening to conduct a rapid diagnosis of current M&E activities and to discover the extent of duplication and inefficiencies in existing monitoring systems. This can provide the impetus to streamline existing systems and ensure they provide in-

formation that is more useful to the government, as happened in Uganda (chapter 12).

3. How can a performance culture be created in my government's civil service?

This is difficult to achieve, particularly for civil servants who have spent the whole of their careers conforming to rigid rules and procedures. It is easy for civil servants and their managers to focus only on activities or processes, such as the number of health clinics constructed or the number of checks paid to welfare recipients. But ideally they would focus on the goals and objectives of these activities and specifically on their *results*—the outputs, outcomes, and impacts of their efforts.

There is no simple answer to this issue, but there are a number of steps that can help change the mindset of civil servants. One is the introduction of committed, reform-oriented champions who occupy powerful positions in the government. Another is the use of powerful incentives to encourage a greater focus on results and a greater client orientation—a service culture (see chapter 11, for example). Conducting regular "How Are We Doing?" team meetings for managers and their staff can help clarify objectives, current team performance, and ways to improve it.

Provision of greater autonomy and flexibility to managers who achieve high levels of performance—that is, *results*—can provide powerful incentives, and these can flow down to their staff (World Bank 1998). Such autonomy can include greater access to funding and more power to hire and fire staff on the basis of their performance. Achieving such broad-based reforms throughout an entire civil service is difficult, but it may be feasible to pilot such reforms for selected agencies.

4. My government is already under a lot of workload pressures and stress. Why should we now devote effort to building an M&E system?

See the answer to Question 2. Your government is already devoting a lot of effort to M&E, especially the monitoring efforts of your ministries and the achievement of donor evaluation requirements. For example, a diagnosis in Uganda discovered 16 monitoring subsystems; another diagnosis in the social development agency in Mexico discovered eight uncoordinated monitoring systems in one agency.

There will almost certainly be potential to reduce inefficiencies and duplication in your existing systems and to produce only the core information you need and can use. There are a growing number of countries around the world that are already devoting significant effort to M&E—they include most OECD countries, some notable middle-income countries (such as Chile and Colombia), and even some of the poorest countries, including Uganda and Tanzania. They are doing this because they understand that an investment in M&E can produce high returns.

5. My government is keenly interested in strengthening our M&E work, but our institutions are weak. How can we proceed?

The short answer is to build incrementally on what you already have. Simplify and rationalize your monitoring systems. Seek donor support and expertise, both for your M&E systems and to access donor funding for some evaluations for demonstration purposes. Prioritize those evaluations in areas (such as health or education) where important government decisions will have to be made in the future. It is best to start modestly, seeking to showcase the benefits from M&E, and to build incrementally on these efforts. It is best to avoid the common mistake of overengineering an M&E system (chapter 10).

6. How much should my government spend on evaluations? How much is enough?

There is a myth that one percent of a program's spending should be devoted to evaluation. Although there is no logical or empirical basis for this number, it is indicative of the scale of effort and resources that should be devoted to evaluating any activity. If a program is evaluated every three to five years, then even a cost of one percent is equivalent to only one-third to one-fifth of

one percent on an annualized basis. Thus, the evaluation would need to result in only a very modest improvement in the effectiveness or efficiency of the program for the evaluation to be cost-effective. Some of the evaluations highlighted in this volume have been much more cost-effective than this (see also IEG 2004b, 2006).

The cost of an evaluation will be substantially lower if there already exist good monitoring data, especially on program beneficiaries and program outcomes. This is an argument for establishing sound administrative data systems and for investing in national statistical systems.

Of course, evaluations should never be conducted for their own sake; the bottom-line measure of success for any evaluation is that it is used intensively. Annex A provides lessons on how to ensure that evaluations are influential.

7. How can we prioritize our evaluations? Our funds are limited, and we cannot evaluate everything we'd like to.

Prioritizing evaluations is a common issue for the managers of an established M&E system. Standard criteria used to help select programs for evaluation include the following: large spending programs; programs of particular policy importance; programs that have suspected major problems with their performance; and pilot programs the government is considering scaling up. Additional criteria to prioritize evaluations include the feasibility of conducting the evaluation, whether the evaluation will provide timely information (such as whether the evaluation findings will be available in time to influence the government's decisions), and whether there are enough resources (funds, staff, and so on) to conduct the evaluation.

As always, when deciding which programs to evaluate, it is a good idea to consider questions such as who needs what evaluative information, for what purposes, and when.

For M&E systems that are not yet established, the challenge is to make every evaluation count— to ensure that they will have high visibility to senior decision makers and will also be highly influential. It is helpful in this context to try to anticipate important decision points, such as a planned major review of social spending, an incoming government, or preparation of a new national plan. If these decision points can be anticipated sufficiently far in advance, it should be possible to ensure that the evaluation's findings will be available in time to feed into the government's decisionmaking.

The time required for the evaluation will depend on the type of evaluation, the existence of suitable data, and so forth. For such "demonstration" evaluations, it would be prudent to seek to minimize the risk that the evaluation's findings will be judged irrelevant because of poor quality, poor timing, or political sensitivity.[1]

8. Who should pay for evaluations? They are expensive, and it is not reasonable to expect poor countries to pay for them.

It is true that very few evaluations are commissioned and paid for by African countries, for example. Although evaluations do not have to be expensive—as outlined in chapter 2, rapid reviews and similar types of evaluation can be conducted quite cheaply, costing even just a few thousand dollars—many evaluations are much more expensive than that. There does appear to be a public good argument to have evaluations in poor countries funded by international donors, partly because of the poverty of the countries and partly because the findings from evaluations may well be of benefit to other countries in the Region.[2]

In addition to funding, donors can also bring their technical expertise in evaluation. The downside, however, may well be a much lower level of government ownership of the evaluation findings if senior officials have played no role in the choice of program to evaluate, the management of the evaluation, or its funding. This provides a strong argument for a collegiate approach to evaluation, involving a government-donor partnership.

9. Aren't rigorous impact evaluations, particularly those involving randomized control trials, the gold standard for evaluation? Isn't any other type of evaluation relatively weak and perhaps even not worth doing?

This is a highly controversial issue.[3] Some proponents of rigorous impact evaluations do appear to argue this. It is certainly the case that a randomized control trial, if performed well, can provide strong evidence of the impacts of a program; this is the standard experimental method for measuring the effects of new medicines, for example. A serious limitation of such rigorous impact evaluation methods, however, is that it is often not possible to apply them to sectorwide or nationwide interventions. These evaluation methods are also typically very expensive, which makes it harder for governments to fund them. Chile, for example, conducts a limited number of impact evaluations each year, while it also conducts a greater number of inexpensive desk reviews (chapter 6).

10. Shouldn't evaluations always be conducted externally to the entity whose work is being evaluated?

In Latin American countries it is usual for evaluations to be commissioned by government departments but conducted externally. The advantage of this approach is that it avoids a potential conflict of interest. It helps to ensure that the evaluations are more objective and "independent" than if they had been conducted within the government. This increases their perceived credibility and reliability.

Chile's M&E system has experienced the downside this approach can have—the ministries whose programs are being evaluated generally have little "ownership" of the evaluation findings and thus do not make much use of them. Colombia has combined the advantages of external evaluations with the advantages of sector ministry ownership; they are full partners in commissioning and managing the external evaluations (chapter 7).

In OECD countries, it is more usual for evaluations to be conducted internally; this helps ensure that the evaluations draw on the program expertise of the agency's staff. It also encourages agencies to use the evaluations (Curristine 2005). In Australia, sector ministries evaluated their own programs, but the central ministries would usually play some role in overseeing the evaluations and reviewing the evaluation reports (chapter 8).

11. How many performance indicators should my government/ministry/agency/ program collect?

There is no simple answer to this question. It depends on who in government needs performance indicators for their work, how many indicators they can make use of, and their cost. Chile's finance ministry collects 1,550 performance indicators, which is a large number by international standards; the finance ministry would like to have even more information but realizes that this number is at the limit of what budget analysts can meaningfully use. In contrast, Colombia's system for monitoring the 320 presidential goals comprises some 600 indicators; this information is publicly available on a Web site (annex B).

It is perhaps more meaningful to view a system of performance indicators as being like a pyramid—with a small number of high-level, strategic indicators focusing on outputs and outcomes at the top, for use by senior officials. For mid-level officials it would be appropriate to provide a greater number of operational indicators, focusing on inputs, processes, and outputs. And at the bottom of the pyramid it would be appropriate to provide a much larger number of operational indicators focusing on processes and services, for use by line managers and their staff at the agency and facility levels. Any individual line manager would only be interested in a small subset of these latter indicators, that is, those directly relevant to that work unit.

A common mistake with performance monitoring systems is collecting too many indicators—which leads to a situation of too much data and not enough information (chapter 10). Unused data can provide a disincentive to data providers to ensure the data are of high quality, and this can lead to a vicious circle of low data utilization and low data quality.

12. Would it be best for a governmentwide M&E system to be designed and managed by the finance ministry?

Not necessarily. It is true that a number of countries have anchored their whole-of-government M&E systems in the finance ministry—such as Australia, Canada, Chile, and the United States. But there are advantages and disadvantages to this approach. Finance ministries typically have a great deal of power, particularly on matters concerning budget funding. These ministries may well be able to create incentives for sector ministries to actively support the M&E system. In some countries they also play an important role as an architect or overseer of public sector reforms. Their powerful position allows them to initiate actions to strengthen M&E in the government, particularly in pursuit of PBB.

On the other hand, finance ministries can be bastions of conservatism and resistance to change, both at senior levels and at the level of the budget sections that oversee each sector ministry and agency. In Australia the leadership of the finance ministry was committed to reforms, including the development of a governmentwide M&E system. This leadership wanted to reorient the work of the budget sections to focus less on spending details of line items and much more on big-picture issues of policy relevance and the efficiency and effectiveness of government spending. The ministry leadership therefore embarked on a process of cultural change within the ministry, seeking to influence division heads, section heads, and their staff. This involved some focused recruitment, promotion, on-the-job training, proactive turnover of staff, and recognition of good practice use of M&E information in the ministry's policy advice (chapter 8; Mackay 1998a).

In some countries, finance ministries have acted as roadblocks to reforms like strengthening national M&E systems. For this reason, it is important to have the cooperation of the finance ministry in these efforts, or at the very least to avoid any active opposition on their part. The support of other central ministries, such as the president's office and the civil service ministry, can also be expected to be a success factor—particularly if the central ministries act in a collegiate manner to support a national M&E system. A diagnosis can identify the extent of support or opposition of each of the powerful central ministries to the strengthening of the M&E system; this can also act as a vehicle to achieve shared understanding of the benefits of M&E and help foster a consensus on an action plan to strengthen the system.

13. Don't sector ministries resent having formal requirements for M&E—designed by one of the central ministries—imposed on them?

No one likes being told what to do, particularly if he or she has no say in the decision to create the formal requirements and if there is no obvious benefit from the M&E information produced. This has been the case in Chile, where the powerful finance ministry has in effect imposed a set of M&E requirements on sector ministries and agencies; the sector entities make little use of the evaluation findings the system produces.

It can be difficult to achieve consensus on the merits of M&E reforms, but it is well worth making the effort. Lack of agreement might cause sector ministries and agencies to not comply with centrally imposed M&E requirements, or at least to provide only lip service. It is these entities that usually have the main responsibility of providing the monitoring data the M&E system requires. If these entities consider they have no incentives to ensure good quality information, then the whole system will suffer (including the quality of evaluations, to

the extent that these rely on data supplied by the ministries). This is one of the key lessons to emerge from the diagnostic work conducted for Uganda (chapter 9).

Another lesson is to avoid the dangers of multiple, uncoordinated monitoring systems at the central and sectoral levels. These place a considerable burden on data suppliers, particularly at the ministry, agency, and facility levels.

Negative incentives—"sticks" imposed by central ministries—are not likely to be appreciated by sector ministries, although they may still be necessary. Positive incentives—carrots such as the certainty of greater funding for those ministries able to demonstrate their performance—are more likely to win hearts and minds (chapter 11).

14. Is there any way to ensure that monitoring information and evaluation findings will be used in the budget process?

There is no way to guarantee use of M&E information in the budget process, but there are ways to increase the probability of this happening. Clearly it is important that the key stakeholders in the budget process and in budget decision making—including the president or prime minister, the finance minister, other key ministers, and the finance ministry, among others—have demanded M&E information so they can better develop policy options and make better decisions. If that demand is weak or absent, then steps can be taken to improve awareness of M&E, in terms of what it encompasses and what it can offer.

And there may be options for key stakeholders to provide incentives—carrots, sticks, or sermons—to encourage use of M&E information in the budget (chapter 11). These incentives could include, for example, strong statements of support for M&E from influential champions within government; regular feedback from ministers to policy analysts concerning the quality of policy advice provided (including the extent to which that advice makes good use of available M&E information); inclusion of ratings of program performance in published budget documents; and provision of support to the finance ministry to pilot some rapid evaluations in order to demonstrate their usefulness.

15. Doesn't PBB imply that less money should be spent on poorly performing programs?

Not necessarily. The overriding consideration will be whether the program is a priority for the government. Some programs—such as primary education—are simply too important to be abolished or even to have their funding cut. In these cases, the challenge will be to fix the performance problems that monitoring information and evaluation findings have identified, for example, inefficient service delivery or poor targeting to the intended beneficiaries. Thus it might well be necessary to spend more money on the program, at least in the short term, to fix these problems.

Finance ministries in countries such as Australia have used resource agreements with agencies in such situations; these provide short-term increased funding for a priority program, in exchange for a medium- to long-term overall reduction in funding. They require that specific actions be taken to improve performance (OECD 1997a).

For low-priority programs, however, evidence of poor performance is more likely to lead to a government decision to cut the program or even abolish it entirely. Chile is one country that may abolish a program if there is evidence of poor performance, but it is an exception; the finance ministries of most OECD countries rarely abolish programs when M&E information reveals poor performance (Curristine 2005).

16. Is it possible to introduce PBB on a pilot basis, or does it have to be introduced all at once for the entire budget?

PBB can be introduced on a pilot basis. There are three types of PBB (box 3.1, p. 10). The first involves a direct relationship between budget funding for a program and its performance. This approach is used in only a few rather narrowly de-

fined cases such as formula-based funding for hospitals or university education. Thus, it is possible to introduce such direct performance budgeting on a pilot basis for specific programs.

The second type of PBB is indirect performance budgeting, where M&E information provides an input into budget funding decisions. It might seem odd to consider using M&E information as one input to budget allocation decisions for only a handful of pilot programs. Governments may have reasonably good performance information available for all programs, but few governments have good evaluation findings available for all programs in all sectors. Thus, it is necessary to use whatever information is available, however piecemeal or imperfect that information might be. In other words, budget decisions have to be made irrespective of whether there exists good M&E information available on the performance of a program, or little information at all.

So, yes, it is also possible to pilot the use of M&E information to assist in budget allocation for only some programs. Whether PBB is introduced on a pilot basis or for the entire budget, it is inevitable that there will be disparities in the amount of M&E information available for different programs. And this in turn places a priority on sound evaluation planning, to ensure that evaluation findings will be available to help budget decision making for key government programs. One strategy when piloting this type of PBB is to commission strategic evaluations of "hot" policy issues to try to ensure utilization of the evaluation findings in the budget—to achieve a demonstration effect.

The last type of PBB is presentational performance budgeting, whereby the government reports publicly its past or expected performance for each program. Again, the level of M&E information available for different programs is likely to vary widely,[4] so again it is possible to pilot this type of PBB. In Colombia, for example, this type of PBB has been piloted for the investment budget but not for the recurrent budget (annex B). The government of Guatemala is currently piloting performance-based budget allocations for the education and health ministries.

17. Does program budgeting help in creating an M&E system?

Yes. Program budgeting typically groups all activities with the same objective—such as achieving a specific improvement in infant nutrition—into a single program.[5] This makes it much easier to estimate the total amount the government is spending to achieve the objective. It also facilitates both the measurement of the total volume of outputs of these related activities (that is, baseline measures) and the setting of performance targets.

This clarity contrasts strongly with the more traditional, line-item budgeting, which identifies the total amount spent by an agency on all activities, with information only on the types of expenditure, such as salaries, office rents, telephones, travel, and so forth. Knowledge of how much is being spent to try to achieve each government objective is very useful for senior officials and budget analysts, as it helps them assess whether the amount of that spending is commensurate with the level of importance of the objective; this is essentially a results-based management perspective. It also helps them assess whether the results of that spending are likely to justify the expense, as well as to compare alternative spending options for achieving the same objective.

But before these assessments can be made there needs to be M&E information available concerning the effectiveness of the spending (that is, the outputs, outcomes, and impacts achieved by that spending). A final advantage of program budgeting is that it encourages a longer-term focus on goals and objectives, and on the intermediate steps needed to achieve them.[6]

The alignment of program budgeting with M&E requires alignment of information systems. Thus, a financial management information system and a performance monitoring system would need to be harmonized. This would require a significant effort.

Chile has been able to construct a robust M&E system without having program budgeting in place (although it is now working to build a pro-grammatic structure). But the disadvantage of the lack of structure has been that the evaluators of Chile's programs have to try to decide which government activities should be considered as part of the program being evaluated. This is a time-consuming and ad hoc approach. Most OECD countries have implemented program budgeting.

18. What role should the national audit office and the Congress or Parliament have in M&E?

In principle, both the national audit office and the legislative arm of government—the Congress or Parliament—should play leading roles in M&E. National audit offices are the fiduciary watchdogs of the legislature. They traditionally conduct compliance audits of the financial management practices of ministries and agencies. An increasing number of national audit offices also conduct performance audits, a type of evaluation that focuses on the efficiency and effectiveness of government spending. And in some countries they have reviewed the performance of the government's M&E system and have thus prompted the government to make needed improvements to the system (chapter 12).

The legislative arms of government are also, in principle, concerned with the performance of the executive arm. It is the legislature that usually has the legal power to approve—or not—the government's funding requests; it often has the power to modify these requests as it sees fit. In considering funding requests it also has the opportunity to review the past performance of the government—its stewardship of public monies. That said, however, it appears that legislatures are generally not well equipped for the task of reviewing government performance; they usually do not have the skills, the resources, or the time to perform this function.

19. Isn't M&E for PRSPs just another type of donor conditionality?

In many ways, yes. One important reason that PRSPs emphasize M&E is to ensure that governments as well as donors focus on country results, as well as on the amounts spent to achieve these results. This has become even more important since the World Bank initiated the debt relief initiative for heavily indebted poor countries (chapter 4). A common defect of most PRSPs is that they focus on *country* performance but give little attention to the specific contribution of the government—or individual sectors of the government or subnational governments—or donors (or the private sector) to those results (chapter 9). Reasons for this deficiency include the weakness of government M&E systems and the weakness of donor support for these systems. But in some countries, such as Uganda and Tanzania, the government's concern with M&E predates the PRSPs; in other words, these governments realized the value of investing the time and effort to build a government M&E system to support better national planning and better budget resource allocation.

20. Don't donors make M&E harder—not easier—for developing countries?

It is certainly the case that donors have failed to harmonize the M&E requirements that they expect countries to meet. This situation has created a significant burden on some countries. One conundrum is that the weaker government capacities and systems are, the more donors apply their own systems and conditionalities, which can undermine governments' efforts to strengthen their own systems. However, donors are able to offer a number of different types of capacity-building support to governments to strengthen existing M&E systems. In addition, donor evaluation offices have undertaken a large number of evaluations over many years, and these collectively offer a goldmine of information—a library of evaluation findings—that governments could use to good effect.

21. What are the main dangers and pitfalls to avoid when trying to strengthen M&E in a country?

There are many. Six main challenges are discussed in this volume:

- **The belief that M&E has intrinsic merit**—an "M&E mantra." This argument is particularly unconvincing to skeptical, overworked government officials. Rather, the way to persuade is to be able to point to particular evaluations that have been highly influential and to other, similar governments that have devoted considerable effort to building an M&E system and become strong proponents of M&E. This perspective stresses that M&E is worthwhile only to the extent that it is actually used to improve government performance (chapter 3 and Part II).

- **A technocratic approach to capacity building** that focuses solely on creating monitoring systems, conducting evaluations, and providing M&E training. These supply-side activities are necessary but are far from sufficient for successful M&E systems. Demand-side issues are crucial, particularly the nature and strength of incentives to conduct and to use M&E information (chapters 10 and 11). Training that raises awareness of the uses and value of M&E—its strengths and limitations—can help strengthen demand for M&E.

- **Rigid adherence to a predetermined action plan** for building an M&E system. It is always worthwhile to start with a good vision for the M&E system, how it will operate, and the uses that will be made of the information the system will produce once it has been fully built. Yet experience reminds us that most successful M&E systems have developed in an opportunistic, nonlinear manner, as roadblocks are encountered and new opportunities emerge (chapter 10). These unforeseen developments may reflect, for example, the departure of key champions, changes in government, or fiscal crises that increase the premium placed on having M&E information available. Thus, developing an M&E system can best be viewed as an evolutionary process, and one that needs to be adjusted and managed carefully. Regular M&E of progress in developing a system will provide the understanding necessary to make these necessary adjustments (chapter 12).

- **The limitation of relying on laws, decrees, and regulations** as the main means to institutionalize M&E within government. A strong legal basis can provide partial aid to the institutionalization of an M&E system, but much more is needed (chapters 10 and 11).

- **The danger of overengineering an M&E system**, particularly through multiple monitoring systems with an excessive number of performance indicators (chapters 9 and 10).

- **The search for the ideal government M&E system** among other countries. Some officials seek exemplary systems, such as Chile's, with a view to replicating it in their own countries. This is a mistake: not only are the starting points faced by each country unique, but so are the destinations—depending on the actual or intended uses of the information their M&E system will produce (chapter 12).

ANNEXES

ANNEX A: LESSONS ON HOW TO ENSURE EVALUATIONS ARE INFLUENTIAL

A consistent theme in this volume is that utilization of monitoring and evaluation (M&E) information is necessary for the system to be considered a "success." This is partly an issue of a government obtaining the maximum benefit from its M&E efforts—reflecting the cost-effectiveness of the M&E system.

However, low utilization is not only a missed opportunity; it can also pose a threat to the sustainability of the system. Government officials usually do not view evaluations as having inherent merit, so there would likely be little enthusiasm for continuing to invest large amounts of money in evaluations that were being ignored.

Utilization is particularly important in the early years of an M&E system, before it has been fully established and accepted as part of the normal business of government. In this initial period it is important for evaluations to have a powerful demonstration effect—through demonstrating their usefulness—by persuading unconvinced or skeptical senior officials that M&E is worthwhile and has real value to the government (see chapter 3 for a discussion of the different ways in which evaluations can be used by governments). In other words, during the start-up phase of an M&E system it is important to make every evaluation count. This puts an onus on the managers of an M&E system to plan their evaluations carefully.

The same definition of success of an M&E system can be applied to an individual evaluation. And this naturally leads to the question, "What does it take for an evaluation to be used intensively—to be influential?" The following discussion draws on an in-depth analysis of eight evaluations that have been found to be highly influential; this study lists a number of detailed lessons on how to design an influential evaluation (Bamberger, Mackay, and Ooi 2004, 2005). These lessons are also consistent with the academic literature on evaluation utilization (for example, Patton 1997), and with the findings of the Bank's own Independent Evaluation Group (IEG) concerning the utilization of its own evaluations (IEG 2006). Five main lessons are summarized here:

1. The importance of a conducive policy or management environment. An evaluation's findings and recommendations are much more likely to be used if they address important policy issues that the government is currently addressing. For example, a newly elected government might have decided to considerably expand the level of support to the unemployed but might be uncertain of the most cost-effective means of doing so. Evaluations of alternative types of government intervention, such as job creation, wage subsidies, or training programs for the unemployed, would be very helpful to the government's decisions (see box 8.2 for an example from Australia).

A conducive environment would also include the commitment of the management of an agency to implementing an evaluation's findings—perhaps because the agency has a strong service orientation and managers and staff are keen to provide the best possible quality of service to their clients. In this situation it could be said that the agency possesses a strong service or performance culture.

2. The timing of the evaluation. The likelihood that an evaluation's findings and recommendations will be used is greatly enhanced when they become available in time to have input for policy or management decisions. Thus, Chile's finance ministry plans its evaluations carefully, with the budget deadlines firmly in mind, to ensure that evaluations will be completed in time for their results to be used by policy analysts and decision makers in the current budget cycle (chapter 6).

This puts a particular priority on planning and managing the timing of each evaluation. But it can be difficult to anticipate opportunities to influence the government's policy agenda, which could be influenced by unforeseen circumstances, such as a change in government or a macroeconomic crisis.

An example of an evaluation completed too late to influence a government's policy decision is provided in annex B, box B.2. An incoming government in Colombia decided to terminate a job-creation program before the evaluation's findings became available.

As it turned out, these findings were critical of the program's performance relative to the program objectives. A rigorous impact evaluation was conducted. These can provide the most in-depth and reliable evaluation findings, but they can usually only be conducted after the program has been operating long enough that its outcomes and impacts have revealed themselves. And this type of evaluation can also take a long time to conduct, especially if a considerable amount of data needs to be collected.

This example from Colombia highlights the trade-offs the managers of an M&E system have to consider when deciding which programs to evaluate, which type of evaluation methodology to use, and when there might be a good opportunity to influence the government's policy debate.

3. Understanding the potential role of evaluation. Evaluators need to avoid the misconception that their findings and recommendations will be—and should be—the main influence on government policy makers or managers. Rather, an evaluation is usually only one of many sources of information and influence on government,

only one piece of the puzzle. Ideally, an evaluation will provide new knowledge and understanding.

Sometimes governments use evaluation findings to justify decisions they would have made in any case, particularly if those decisions might have been unpopular. Or an evaluation might provide the final "nail in the coffin" for an underperforming program. Evaluation recommendations that focus on detailed implementation issues would typically be less controversial than recommendations relating to the overall worth of the program or whether the program should continue or be abolished. A particularly useful role for an evaluator is to bring a fresh, external perspective.

4. Who should conduct the evaluation. For an evaluation to be influential requires that the evaluator be perceived as credible, objective, and competent. In many situations this will also require that the evaluator is viewed as independent from the program—and sometimes also the agency—being evaluated. In Latin American countries, it is usual for evaluations to be conducted externally; this stands in contrast with Organisation for Economic Co-operation and Development (OECD) countries, where it is more usual for evaluations to be conducted internally (see part VI). Thus, there can be a trade-off between the objectivity, independence, and credibility of evaluations and the evaluator's understanding of the program and the ownership of the evaluation findings by the program manager and staff.

The expertise of internal or external evaluators is another issue to consider here. One way to combine the benefits of both approaches—internal and external evaluations—is to ensure that both internal and external stakeholders play an oversight role in the evaluation, regardless of whether the evaluation is conducted internally or externally.

5. Building a relationship with the client and communicating and marketing evaluation findings and recommendations. Another fallacy, and one apparently held by many evaluators and managers of evaluation offices, is that the evaluator's job is simply to produce competent evaluation reports. Similarly, dissemination of an evaluation's findings and recommendations might (naively) be viewed as mailing out the evaluation report to a long list of names and addresses.

When conducting an evaluation it is important for the evaluator to maintain a good relationship with key stakeholders, including in particular the principal client that commissioned the evaluation. The client should be kept fully informed about the progress of the evaluation, and key stakeholders should be informed before the evaluation is completed about the likely findings, especially if these would be controversial. In other words, there should be no surprises.

Communication and knowledge management are particularly important for evaluation offices. Thus, another important function for both evaluators and evaluation offices is to extract the key findings that are likely to be most relevant and useful to key stakeholders. Stakeholders include policy makers and program managers. Senior officials usually do not have the time to read lengthy evaluation reports, so it is helpful to provide short, easy-to-read executive summaries and to prepare précis documents that identify the most relevant, notable findings and recommendations.

More sophisticated approaches to knowledge management include, for example: the use of evaluation Web sites (both for individual evaluations and for the evaluation office's library of evaluation findings); formal launches of evaluation reports, including seminars and conferences; and maintenance of a dissemination list of key stakeholders who have expressed an interest in receiving evaluation summaries. IEG, which has been in existence since 1973, now uses its extensive library of evaluation findings to address immediate needs for evaluative findings and lessons of experience (IEG 2006, chapter 3).

It is doing this through a new type of "quick-turnaround" products, including notes and presentations and briefing papers for Bank senior managers, line managers, and staff. One example of this is the materials prepared at short notice concerning lessons for dealing with natural disasters; these were prepared in the wake of the major earthquake in Pakistan in 2005.

The Importance of Measuring Utilization

Related to all this is the importance of an evaluation office knowing the extent to which its evaluations are actually being used, and for what specific purposes. This is particularly important for a newly established evaluation office, whose sustainability might not be assured. Where utilization is not high, it will be necessary to take specific steps to increase it.

IEG is actually one good practice model. It prepares an annual review of the evaluation activities of the World Bank's operational areas. This review also includes a self-evaluation of IEG's own evaluation activities, including the perceptions of key stakeholders concerning the value of IEG's evaluation work. These stakeholders include the Bank's Board and staff, including country directors, sector managers, and task team leaders (who manage the Bank's lending projects). Focus groups and structured interviews are conducted with samples of individuals in each of these groups. The main issues these focus groups and interviews address are the use and usefulness of IEG's evaluation findings, products, and information and the challenges, incentives, and disincentives to using M&E information in their work.

As part of the same self-evaluations, IEG also conducts internal surveys of large numbers of World Bank staff, Board members, and their advisors. It also conducts external surveys of external clients including governments, donor organizations, nongovernmental organizations, academia, and the general public. These surveys focus on specific IEG evaluation reports. They ask questions about—

- Readership and awareness of these reports
- Perceptions of their quality (relevance, ease of understanding, conciseness of presentation, timeliness, usefulness of recommendations, unbiased and objective analysis, transparency and clarity of the methodology, strength of the link between conclusions and evidence, depth of analysis, and whether all available information was incorporated)

- Extent of influence of the evaluation, such as on respondents' understanding of the subject area
- Use of the evaluation (for Bank staff, various possible categories of use in their work are investigated, such as in their provision of advice, their work to design new strategies, and in modifying existing Bank projects and strategies)
- How to improve the quality of the recommendations in IEG's evaluations.

The findings from such focus groups, interviews, and surveys can be quite eye opening for an evaluation office and for individual evaluators too. Such approaches apply the same rigor to an evaluation office as the office would apply to the programs it evaluates. This, in turn, can help to enhance the credibility and influence of the evaluation office.

ANNEX B: A COUNTRY DIAGNOSIS—THE EXAMPLE OF COLOMBIA[1]

This diagnosis was also published separately (Mackay and others 2007). Preparation of this rapid diagnosis was a collegiate endeavor involving a number of staff from the Bank's Latin America and the Caribbean Region, as well as IEG's coordinator for evaluation capacity development.

1. Introduction

The World Bank is preparing a programmatic loan to support the government of Colombia in its continuing efforts to strengthen its national system of monitoring and evaluation (M&E)—SINERGIA (Sistema Nacional de Evaluatión de Resultados de la Gestión Pública, or National System for Evaluation of Public Sector Performance). The purpose of this rapid diagnosis is to assist the Bank team and the government in their joint understanding of key aspects of this M&E system, including:

- Its genesis
- Legal framework
- Objectives, and the roles and responsibilities of key stakeholders
- Principal M&E components of SINERGIA: SIGOB and impact evaluations
- Extent of utilization of the M&E information which SINERGIA produces
- SINERGIA: strengths, challenges, and future directions
- Conclusions.

The information base on which this rapid diagnosis relies consists of a number of government reports and policy statements, documentation on a broad range of lending and donor projects funded by the World Bank which have either supported SINERGIA or have supported specific activities under the broad aegis of SINERGIA, formal con-ference presentations by senior government officials, information collected by Bank staff who have participated in numerous project preparation and supervision missions, and feedback on this diagnosis from government officials in the Department of National Planning (DNP, or Departamento Nacional de Planeación). Bank missions have included meetings with officials from central and sector ministries, the general comptroller's office, municipal governments, and civil society groups, concerning M&E issues including the strengths and weaknesses of SINERGIA. These meetings have been a valuable source of information, although a more structured approach to capturing the views of relevant officials would be necessary to present a more considered, in-depth picture.

This paper seeks to document what we know, and what we do not know, about SINERGIA. It should be viewed very much as a work in progress—as a vehicle to seek further information, comments and judgments about the many detailed facets of SINERGIA and its possible future directions. One challenge facing outside observers is to be clear about which of the various components of SINERGIA and other budget/planning systems are working reasonably well and which exist largely on paper. A more in-depth diagnosis will be necessary to resolve a number of important, outstanding issues on which current evidence appears weak or inconclusive. Draft terms of reference for such a diagnosis are attached in an annex; this diagnosis would constitute, in effect, a formal evaluation of SINERGIA.

2. Genesis and Broad Development of SINERGIA

The genesis of Colombia's M&E system was the decision of the finance minister to replicate in

Table B.1: Funding Support for SINERGIA: 2002–06 ($'000)

Source of funds	2002	2003	2004	2005	2006	Total 2002–2006
World Bank PFMP II	350	300	305	288	300	1,543
World Bank Social Sector loans	1,500	—	450	—	—	1,950
IADB	2,666	—	2,509	—	—	5,175
USAID	—	—	50	200	200	450
UNDP	—	—	400	—	—	400
Government	250	250	256.7	270	270	1,297
Total	4,766	550	3,970.7	758	770	10,814

Source: Department of National Planning.

Colombia the World Bank's own approach to evaluation. With technical assistance from the Bank, the government mapped out the basic architecture for an M&E system. This first stage of the system's evolution ran from 1990 to 1996 and included a formal requirement for evaluations in the revised 1991 constitution. SINERGIA—the national system for evaluation of management and results—was formally created in 1994. The Bank provided ongoing support to SINERGIA through this period, mainly via the Public Financial Management Project I (1994–2001). The second stage in SINERGIA's evolution, from 1996 to 2002, marked a period when the standing of SINERGIA within the government reportedly declined, partly due to a perception of difficulties with the management of the system. The option of abolishing it was raised during this period because of doubts as to its relevance to the public sector reform agenda. However, the constitutional requirement for evaluation precluded this option. Toward the end of this period, in 2001, the Bank intensified its support for SINERGIA not only via a new Public Financial Management Project (PFMP II), but also by cosponsoring with the Inter-American Development Bank (IADB) a series of impact evaluations of two major government programs, *Empleo en Acción* (a job-creation program) and *Familias en Acción* (a conditional cash transfer program).[2]

The third stage, from 2002 to the present, was initiated with the election of a reformist president, Álvaro Uribe. The new government was dismayed to note that the large increases in government spending in areas such as schools and health care had not been matched by corresponding increases in government performance (outputs and outcomes) in these areas (see CONPES 2004; Castro 2006a). At the same time, President Uribe stated his strong desire for a new culture of public administration, based closely on social accountability—"social control." Thus he introduced a system for monitoring and reporting progress vis-à-vis presidential goals and the country's development goals (Sistema de Programación y Gestión por Objetivos y Resultados, or System of Programming and Management by Objectives and Results SIGOB); he has actively sought to implement the constitutional mandate for evaluation and has issued a presidential directive[3] and policy statement on results-based management (CONPES 2004). He integrated SIGOB into SINERGIA and has re-energized SINERGIA. This led to the appointment of a new head of the evaluation unit which manages SINERGIA, located in the department of national planning, and to the recruitment of staff and consultants to this unit.

During this third stage, the Bank substantially increased the range and level of support it provided to government M&E, via two structural adjustment loans and a related technical assistance loan, a social safety net loan, sectoral work and a second public financial management project. Other donors have also been active in supporting SINERGIA during this period of rejuvenation, as shown in table B.1. Since 2002, $10.8 million has been spent on SINERGIA, with almost half of this total funded by the IADB, 32 percent by the World Bank, and 8 percent by USAID and the United Nations Development Programme (UNDP). During this period, when there were severe macroeconomic fiscal constraints, the government itself funded only 12 percent of SINERGIA's costs; clearly, this low level of government financial support is not sustainable in the long term.

3. Legal Framework

The following discussion is based on a rapid stock-taking and analysis of legal instruments in Colombia. The Bank is currently preparing a more detailed analysis to help identify overlaps and gaps, and what types of legal instrument will be needed to fill these gaps—decree, law, or policy statement.

A detailed legal framework has been built to support SINERGIA in the years since the creation of the Constitutional mandate in 1991. This stipulated the focus of the evaluation system as being "to assess the public sector's management and results." Laws in 1993 regulated the fiscal control function (exercised by the Contraloria) to include "results control systems," and also regulated the internal control function within public sector agencies to include management evaluation and control systems. A law of 1994 gave DNP responsibility for creating SINERGIA and for reporting annually to the National Council for Economic and Social Policy (CONPES), the high-level policy committee which is headed by the president, on the results of the evaluation system. SINERGIA itself was created through a DNP resolution in 1994, which operationalized the constitutional and legal mandate and also assigned responsibility for self-evaluation to all agencies in the executive branch of government. In addition, DNP assigned to itself the responsibility for developing methodologies to guide the system's evaluation activities. More recently, a 2003 law stipulated that the national budget include details on the objectives, intended results and management indicators for all government activities.[4] Other laws during this period have added to the complexity of the legal framework. That said, it is commonly accepted in Colombia that a detailed legal and regulatory basis is required to provide direction and legitimacy for any area of government reform, such as

M&E. Of course, while such a framework is considered necessary, it is not sufficient to ensure that the function performs well. Other factors discussed below, such as the strength of leadership for the reform, the resources provided to support it, the establishment of routine rules and procedures, and incentives for the utilization of M&E information, are also key to a system's success.

The government itself has recognized that the multiplicity of laws and decrees has led to a profusion of M&E concepts, methodologies and instruments, and that greater clarity is needed now that SINERGIA is entering a more mature stage of development. This led to the policy document issued by the CONPES (#3294) in 2004: "Renovation of Public Administration: Management by Results and the Reform of the National System of Evaluation."

4. Objectives, Roles, and Responsibilities

4.1 Objectives

The government's latest policy statement on SINERGIA—CONPES 3294—articulates the objectives of the M&E system as follows:

1. To improve the effectiveness and impact of government policies, programs, and public institutions
2. To help improve the efficiency and transparency of the planning and allocation of public resources
3. To stimulate transparency in public management, in particular by stimulating oversight by citizens—that is, social control.

These broad-ranging objectives can be disaggregated into six different types of desired utilization of the M&E information produced by SINERGIA: (1) to support resource allocation and decision making in the national budget by providing information on the actual and likely performance of alternative spending priorities; (2) to support national planning decision making, both when the four-year national plans are developed and when annual priorities are identified under the national plan; (3) to ensure the cohesion of government action around those development priorities; (4) to assist sector ministries in their policy

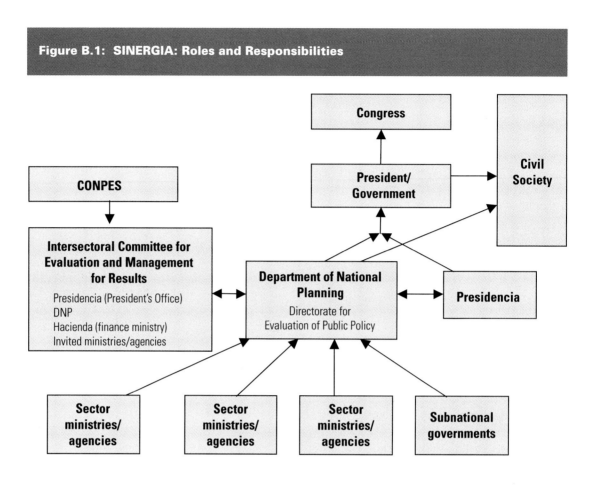

Figure B.1: SINERGIA: Roles and Responsibilities

development and planning work; (5) to support the ongoing management of government activities by ministries and agencies; and (6) to ensure the transparency of government performance by making M&E information available to the Congress and to civil society—that is, fostering accountability through "social control."

Of these objectives, as we shall see below, the one which Colombia's SINERGIA has most successfully emphasized, particularly since 2002 at least, has been social control.

4.2 Roles and Responsibilities of Key Stakeholders

The Directorate for Evaluation of Public Policy (Dirección de Evaluación de Políticas Públicas, DEPP) in DNP is the lynchpin of SINERGIA. This unit coordinates the system, provides advice on methodologies and types of evaluation, and manages some evaluations; it also provides technical advice and financial support for some of the sophisticated impact evaluations and other types of

evaluation conducted by sector ministries and agencies. It advises subnational governments piloting M&E systems, and also entities such as the Ministry of Social Protection (Ministerio de Protección Social, MPS), which is establishing a monitoring and evaluation system. DEPP manages the information system which tracks progress against the president's goals, SIGOB, and it is jointly responsible with the Presidencia for preparing annual and end-of-administration reports on the government's performance vis-à-vis commitments under the national development plan; these reports form a key input to the President's own annual reports to the Congress (figure B.1). DEPP has a staff of 31, of whom about 70 percent are currently employed as consultants.[5]

DEPP coordinates the reports of sector ministries and agencies, and subnational governments, which provide the monitoring information needed for the SIGOB (discussed below). These entities and subnational governments are formally responsible for *managing for results*. DEPP also acts as the secretariat to the Intersectoral Committee for Evaluation and Management for Results (Comité Intersectorial de Evaluación y Gestión por Resultados). This committee, which was created by a decree of December 2002, has a formal responsibility for coordinating M&E actions among government units deciding the four-year evaluation agenda—corresponding to the president's term of office—and the corresponding annual agenda of evaluations to be conducted. This committee also decides technical standards and agrees the evaluation methodology for individual evaluations; it acts, in effect, as a steering committee for individual evaluations. Other members of this committee include other directorates of DNP, the Presidencia (the president's office), Hacienda (finance ministry), and sector ministries and agencies invited to participate when their programs are being evaluated. The committee has met six times since its creation in early 2004, and it, in turn, reports to CONPES. In 2004 the CONPES issued a policy statement on *managing for results* and on needed reforms of SINERGIA.

5. Principal M&E Components of SINERGIA

Government monitoring and evaluation usually encompass a broad range of tools, methods and approaches. These can appear confusing to the layman, but it is important to understand their range, and particularly their uses, advantages and limitations, and the costs, skills and time required for each. It is important to understand that these various types of M&E are complementary; each has strengths and limitations, and the challenge is to decide how best to combine them in a national M&E system.

SINERGIA's two main components are SIGOB, a system of performance indicators which tracks progress against the president's goals, and its agenda of impact evaluations.

5.1 SIGOB

There are about 500 performance indicators that relate to the 320 presidential goals,[6] and for each indicator SIGOB records the objective, baseline performance, annual targets, actual performance against these targets, and the imputed amounts spent by the government; thus SIGOB includes a large number of indicators on government performance that include input, process, output and outcome measures. The information is disaggregated by region, including for the major cities. In addition, where a target has not been met, there is a requirement that the goal manager prepares an explanation for the reasons for the shortfall. These "exception reports" are included in the SIGOB database, the core of which is publicly available on a real-time basis.[7] The Web site also encourages accountability by identifying the goal manager, their ministry and formal position, and their e-mail address.

An initial, basic version of SIGOB was developed in 2002 with UNDP support, and was initially located in the Presidencia. Responsibility was subsequently transferred to DNP in 2005, under the aegis of SINERGIA, where a new software package with increased functionality was developed. DNP negotiates the annual targets with each ministry and agency. DEPP is also supporting pilot work to replicate SIGOB in the municipality of Pasto.

The data which comprise SIGOB are supplied by ministries and agencies. In addition to whatever data controls are applied by the entities which supply these SIGOB data, DEPP itself endeavors to identify any data problems or inconsistencies, and has a team responsible for monitoring the quality of the SIGOB data and for following up on suspected data problems with the entities which supplied them. However, in the absence of a system of regular, detailed data audits, the reliability of the data is unknown and has certainly not been demonstrated. One partial exception is the Ministry of Education (MEN), which, with Bank support, is reportedly undertaking some limited audits of the data provided by departments and municipalities;[8] as funding allocations to the states are based on school enrollment data, there exist incentives for states to over-estimate enrollments.

The government's policy statement on SINERGIA (CONPES 3294), which was drafted by DEPP/DNP, has flagged the need to address the problems with the reliability of SIGOB data, including their quality, consistency (where problems have arisen from multiple, uncoordinated data sources), regularity, and verification. This policy statement also raises explicit concerns about ministries "gaming" the data which they provide for SIGOB.

5.2 Evaluations [9]

These constitute the second principal M&E component of SINERGIA. About 16 evaluations are currently underway or have been completed, with another 17 to be conducted over the next five years or so (table B.2). Most of these are impact evaluations and entail a sophisticated statistical analysis of program beneficiaries with control or comparison groups. They also usually include a focus on operational efficiency and other management issues. A small number of other types of evaluation are conducted, and these focus narrowly on management and institutional issues.

Since 2002, at least two-thirds of the total amount spent on SINERGIA from all sources—mainly the IADB, the World Bank, and the government—has been spent on evaluations. Their cost has ranged from $15,000 up to $2 million for the rigorous impact evaluation of the rural component of Familias en Acción. For the evaluations which have received funding support from the Bank, the main vehicle for this support has been sector-specific loans, particularly in the social sectors. The level of additional financial support from sector ministries and agencies for these evaluations is not known. CONPES has endorsed impact evaluation as an instrument of social policy (CONPES 3188).

Table B.2 also shows that the cost of many of these evaluations is high. This arises from the need to conduct detailed data collection for many of the evaluations, due to the absence of adequate administrative, household, and other data. This issue, and the potentially high cost-effectiveness of this type of evaluation, is discussed in greater detail below.

DEPP has used a competitive bidding process to contract out these evaluations to academia or to domestic or international consulting firms. These evaluations are contracted out to help ensure the objectivity, reliability, and credibility of the evaluations, and also because of a scarcity of impact evaluation expertise within government. Another objective is to help build local capacities for evaluation. DEPP and the sector ministries

typically work closely in managing these impact evaluations.

Thus for DEPP, the priority is to be able to manage or oversight these evaluations, rather than to conduct them itself. The skills base which exists in DEPP to support this work is limited; and DEPP's reliance on contract staff—who account for 22 of DEPP's 31 staff—may have acted as a barrier to the development of professional skills, for example, through their ineligibility for training scholarships. A priority for DEPP will be to strengthen its capacity to manage these evaluations.

The government has stated that decisions as to which activities should be subject to sophisticated impact evaluation are based on five criteria: (1) amount of resources they consume; (2) the characteristics of the population they service (for example, the poor, or the displaced); (3) importance of the activity, in terms of whether it is a priority for the national development plan; (4) innovativeness of the activity (for example, a pilot); (5) potential for replication. SIGOB's performance information does not appear to have been used to flag "problem" government programs for which an evaluation would be warranted, but it would be worthwhile for DEPP to adopt such an approach. In Chile, for example, indications of poor program performance are used as one trigger to warrant a more in-depth investigation of the causes of poor performance through a formal evaluation—either a rapid evaluation or a sophisticated impact evaluation.

As noted earlier, the Intersectoral Evaluation Committee has formal responsibility for deciding both the four-year and the annual evaluation agendas. So far, however, the agenda of evaluations has been decided in a bottom-up manner rather than in a planned, top-down manner. Thus the evaluation agenda is currently determined on the basis of evaluations funded by international donors as part of their loans to the government, together with some additional evaluations which are largely funded by individual sector ministries and agencies, and with some financial and technical support from DEPP. This approach can be expected to have helped achieve a high level of acceptance of the findings of these evaluations, on the

Table B.2: Agenda of Impact and Other Evaluations
(US$ cost of each evaluation in parentheses)

Evaluations completed	Evaluations under way	Evaluations planned (2006–10)
Empleo en Acción ($1.5m)	Familias en Acción—Rural ($2m)	Cursos de Formación Complementaria—SENA ($200,000)
Adulto Mayor ($50,000)	Familias en Acción—Grandes Ciudades ($180,000)	SENA—Institucional ($60,000)
Corpomixtas ($15,000)	Jóvenes en Acción ($670,000)	ICBF—Institucional ($30,000)
Programa de Apoyo Directo al Empleo—PADE ($66,000)	Vivienda de Interés Social—VIS ($226,800)	SENA—Otros Programas ($95,000)
	Programa de Renovación de la Administración Pública—PRAP ($311,000)	Reinsertados ($119,000)
	Hogares Comunitarios ($1.36m)	Familia Guardabosques ($119,000)
	Fondo Colombiano para la Modernización y Desarrollo de las Micro, Pequeñas y Medianas Empresas—Fomipyme ($88,000)	Programas del Sector Agrícola ($119,378)
	Sistema General de Participaciones—SGP (Parte 1) ($419,000)	Familias en Acción Desplazadas ($119,378)
	Red de Seguridad Alimentaria—RESA ($125,000)	Banco de Pobres ($198,000)
	Programa de Paz y Desarrollo y Laboratorios de Paz (etapa 1) ($206,000)	Red de Apoyo Contra la Pobreza Extrema—PEP ($198,000)
	Desayunos Infantiles	Evaluación Programas Sector Justicia ($119,000)
	Estratificación Socio económica ($200,000)	DANE—Institucional ($60,000)
		MinInterior—Institucional ($25,000)
		Rapid evaluation pilots ($98,000)
		Evaluación Plan Decenal de Cultura ($150,000)
		Mujer Cabeza de Familia Microempresaria ($150,000)
		Programas de alimentación escolar en Colombia ($600,000)
Total: $1.631m	**Total: $5.786m**	**Total: $2.460m**

Source: Department of National Planning.

part of the ministries and agencies whose programs have been evaluated, and on the part of DNP and other central ministries. However, it also means that the evaluation agenda has been heavily dependent on donor support and evaluation priorities. It would be worthwhile for the Intersectoral Evaluation Committee to play a substantive role in overseeing SINERGIA's performance and in developing its future directions.

5.3 Other M&E Activities

DNP/DEPP has been active in a number of other aspects of M&E, such as efforts to strengthen public accountability in government performance, provision of technical assistance to some ministries/agencies which are trying to develop their internal M&E systems, M&E capacity build-

ing in the public sector and in academia, advancing the piloting of performance-based budgeting at the municipal level, the preparation of a performance-based investment budget report, and the development of policy guidelines on M&E. Aspects of these initiatives are considered below.

6. Extent of Utilization of M&E Information Produced by SINERGIA

6.1 Accountability—Political and Social Control

A unique feature of Colombia is President Uribe's strong commitment to the use of M&E information to enhance political control of the executive government and to support social control. The SIGOB database is loaded in his personal computer, and he uses this information in his monthly "management control" meetings with each minister and DNP. During these meetings, the progress being made against each presidential goal is reviewed, and ministers are required to provide reasons for any shortfalls in performance. Performance indicators and actions to meet these targets are also agreed. The president has met with ministers to ensure they are all skilled in the use of SIGOB. The president also uses this SIGOB information in his weekly town hall meetings in different municipalities around the country, and also in the annual television presentation to citizens, in which the president and his ministers discuss the government's performance and answer citizen questions on these issues.

This strong presidential commitment to using M&E information to monitor and report on his government's performance appears to be unique in Latin America and perhaps in the world. It sends powerful signals to individual ministers and civil servants in their ministries and agencies, and can be expected to have fostered a performance culture; the actual extent to which such a culture has developed is not known, however— this is one issue which an in-depth diagnosis would be able to investigate. There does not appear to have been a widespread adoption of M&E practices by all ministries and subnational governments, however. That said, there are several ministries, agencies, and municipal governments, discussed below, which are currently working to strengthen their M&E systems, some of them with the active support of DEPP.

Another unknown issue is the credibility of the information which government reports to civil society.[10] Some prominent representatives of civil society have cast doubt on the credibility of the SIGOB data—the main argument being that these data are produced by government and that they are thus inherently unreliable. SINERGIA's reliance on the government reporting on its own performance is thus viewed by some as a structural weakness of the accountability arrangements (see below). The SIGOB Web site allows readers to give their judgments about government performance

vis-à-vis its promises (as reflected in the national development plan), and about the accessibility, quality, and usefulness of the publicly available SIGOB information on government performance.[11] In addition, DEPP surveyed over 3,000 households in 13 capital cities in July 2006, to ask them directly an expanded set of similar issues, including also the transparency, responsiveness, and accountability of the government and of different types of government entity, availability of information about government performance, the importance of citizen participation in public management, and the quality of a range of public services.[12]

Another aspect of SIGOB is that it is essentially a monitoring tool. Explanations of over-performance or under-performance need to be informed by program and policy evaluations that, in turn, need to be based on rigorous policy and program formulation linked to presidential goals and the country's development goals.

DEPP has developed an ambitious set of initiatives to further promote social control, and it appears that the first of these has made some progress. These include:

- Colombia Lider—an independent, civil society partnership of media, banking, foundations, and other organizations to promote good governance and social control. This consortium, which has been encouraged and supported by DEPP, will highlight good performance of municipal mayors, and will monitor government plans and spending, and analyze their impact on poverty.
- Partnerships with civil society organizations to disseminate M&E information.
- Use of TV and radio stations to produce programs on government performance.[13]
- Contracting of sectoral experts to analyze and report on government performance. This would also provide some complementary quality assurance of the government's M&E information, such as the SIGOB data.

Although progress on the last three initiatives appears modest, these efforts to engage directly with civil society could have a significant pay-off if eventually successful, and would also be very difficult to reverse in future years. A strong example of such a civil society initiative, which was developed independently of the national government, is *Bogotá Cómo Vamos*. This initiative was created by a consortium of a private foundation (the Corona Foundation), the main daily newspaper in Bogotá (*El Tiempo*), and the Chamber of Commerce (Cámara de Comercio de Bogotá), and it appears to be fully institutionalized.[14] *Bogotá Cómo Vamos* involves widespread publication of data on municipal government performance together with data from public opinion surveys. The three partners in this venture are supporting the replication of the approach in Barranquilla, Cali, Cartagena, and Medellín. This initiative is an excellent example of the type of mechanism that can be supported to promote social control of government performance.

The president also reports formally to the Congress each year, on the extent to which the national plan's goals and objectives have been attained. The extent to which Congress is able to use this information is unclear, however. Congress plays only a weak role in the budget process (World Bank 2005b, 2005c). Congressmen have little technical support to enable them to easily digest performance information and evaluation findings, and Congress' discussion of the annual budget in any case tends to focus on narrower political issues. This experience is perhaps similar to many other countries; the potential for Congress to play any significant role in SINERGIA therefore appears to be weak—unless Congress takes the initiative in demanding government M&E information and institutionalizing its usage.

6.2 Support for Budget Decision Making and National Planning

Budget Rigidities. DNP is responsible for preparing the four-year national development plan and also has responsibility for the annual investment budget. The latter includes infrastructure and other investments, as well as investments in human capital (such as education and training);

the investment budget comprises about 15 percent of the total national budget. Hacienda is responsible for the remainder—the recurrent budget—which also includes ongoing funding for civil servants and their administrative activities, government debt servicing, pension payments, and transfers to subnational governments.

The extent to which there is potential for M&E information to influence budget decision making and national planning in Colombia is not clear. There exist considerable budget rigidities in Colombia for several reasons, including the constitutionally-mandated transfers to subnational governments and a range of permanent entitlements and revenue earmarks. As a result, as much as 95 percent of the budget is earmarked and is thus inflexible in the short-run.[15] But while performance information and evaluation findings may be able to exert only limited influence on national budget allocations in the short-run, there might well be considerable potential in the medium to long run, especially if there exists clear evidence about government performance in attaining presidential goals and other government priorities (see box B.1). And even in the short-run, there is potential for subnational governments to themselves use M&E information; these governments account for over one-third of the federal budget spending and have greater flexibility in budget allocations.

For this reason the pilot approaches to performance budgeting in Medellín and Pasto are potentially significant. For example, the municipal government of Medellín conducts surveys of around 23,000 households to obtain detailed indicators on human development. These are then mapped to identify the poorest districts. Government spending has been heavily reoriented to favor these districts, and performance baselines and targets are set to assist in monitoring government performance. The lack of evaluations is a constraint on understanding the results of this spending, but the government employs local academics to analyze the likely results chains of alternative options for government spending— this helps the government to decide the types of

Box B.1: An Influential Evaluation in Colombia

Familias en Acción is a government conditional cash transfer program which provides income support to poor families which commit to ensuring that their children receive preventive health care, enroll in school and attend classes. The program was created in 1999 in response to the economic crisis.

A rigorous impact evaluation of the program, whose final stage is to be completed in 2006, was contracted out to external consultants, under the supervision of DNP. The evaluation found that the program had achieved impressive nutrition, education and health impacts. These findings persuaded the government of President Uribe to not only retain the previous government's program but to commit to a doubling of its coverage, from 500,000 to 1 million poor families. In late 2006, the government decided to further increase the program's coverage, to 1.5 million families.

The Familias en Acción evaluation has cost $1.5 million so far. While this is a large amount, it is relatively small when compared with total government spending on that program (around $100 million at the time of the evaluation). Due to its major influence on the government, it can be judged to have been highly cost-effective.

erated commitments by the local government to improve various aspects of service delivery. These municipal models provide lessons for the introduction of performance budgeting at the federal, department, and municipal levels throughout the country.

An example of the government's ability to respond nimbly to emerging priorities is the creation of the *Empleo en Acción* program during the economic crisis of the late 1990s. The government also agreed to undertake a major impact evaluation of this program; however, the government decided to terminate the program before the evaluation findings were available. Many valuable lessons for evaluation planning can be drawn from this case study (box B.2).

One interesting performance-based budget initiative is the management contracts which have been piloted between DNP/Hacienda and two social sector agencies, the Colombian Institute for Family Welfare (Instituto Colombiano de Bienestar Familiar, or ICBF) and the Vocational Training Institute (Servicio Nacional de Aprendizje, or SENA), with World Bank support. These contracts involved the setting of performance indicators and targets for service delivery and administrative implementation.[16] When the targets are met, the budget allocations of the two agencies are increased by allowing them to retain a greater share of the non-tax revenues they collect. It is unclear whether or not these pilots will be retained or scaled up.

Performance-Based Budgeting and Planning.
DEPP has prepared "performance-based budget" reports, for both 2005 and 2006, for Colombia's investment budget. These reports are presented as an annex to the regular budget documents, which continue to be presented on a line-item basis. The performance-based reports use a programmatic classification to group government activities according to common objectives, which in turn were based on the Presidential Goals and the national development plan. The reports showed the stated objective for each "program," the corresponding performance targets (using SIGOB data), and also the corresponding investment

activity on which it should spend. With support from DEPP, the municipal governments of Pasto and Medellin have prepared performance-based budget reports for fiscal year 2007, and are preparing organic budget laws to formalize this approach. Their performance budgeting work is supported by monitoring systems and tools similar to SIGOB. On the demand side, mechanisms for social and political control have been promoted in both cities, drawing lessons from the *Bogotá Cómo Vamos* experience. In Pasto, the local alliance for accountability has undertaken a survey of 1300 households on themes analogous to the national survey conducted by DEPP, but placing greater emphasis on issues of citizen participation and local governance. An independent study on subsidized health services was commissioned and publicly discussed with the city mayor, and this process gen-

Box B.2: The *Empleo en Acción* Program: Lessons for Evaluation Planning

The government requested Bank support for a new direct job-creation program, based on public works, in response to the economic crisis of the late 1990s. A Bank loan became effective in early 2001, and the loan included funding for a sophisticated impact evaluation; this evaluation was a condition of the Bank's lending. Some delays were experienced in implementing the project and at the same time economic conditions started to improve. By early 2004 the new government had decided to terminate the *Empleo en Acción* program; by then, some $183 million had been spent on it.

The findings of the impact evaluation, which cost about $1.5 million, became available later that year. The evaluation found that the program had succeeded in transferring income to the poorest households, and it had increased the employability of program participants. It had also produced public works that benefited local communities. However, the program failed to meet the targets for the number of individuals who would benefit from the program, and it also failed to meet the target for the level of net annual earnings which the program provided to beneficiaries. An implementation completion report on the Bank project has recently concluded that the program was, overall, not cost-effective compared with similar direct job creation programs in other countries and compared with other types of support for the unemployed.

Although the impact evaluation was not influential, it does provide several lessons for evaluation planning, and these are highly relevant to the management of SINERGIA. One is the need for a high level of care in planning an evaluation, particularly one which is complex and expensive, and will take quite some time before its results are available. Unforeseen events external to the evaluation are always a possibility; the challenge is therefore one of risk management. It is also important to plan evaluations so that findings will be available to feed into likely decision points, such as the election of a new government (when a new national plan will be prepared), and the annual budget cycle. Another issue for evaluation planning is prioritizing evaluations—deciding which government activities should be evaluated, when the findings are likely to be needed, and to what depth of analysis (and cost) should the evaluation be conducted. Prima facie, for a major government program such as *Empleo en Acción*, it is highly appropriate to conduct an in-depth impact evaluation. Even if such an evaluation provides only a marginal improvement in the program's performance—that is, its efficiency and effectiveness—spending $1.5 million on the evaluation of a program which spent $183 million (and potentially might have spent a lot more) would be highly cost-effective. Where evaluation funds are constrained, or where there are tight timing constraints, then other, more rapid types of evaluation are more likely to be appropriate. A final lesson for SINERGIA is the value in conducting regular in-depth reviews of its own M&E activities, to find out which have been effective, which have not, and the reasons why.

Note that the impact evaluation of *Empleo en Acción* has added to the "library" of evaluation findings available to the government. These findings should prove valuable to the government in the current debate on the desirability of creating a new public works program.

budget for that year. However, programs have not been rigorously constructed (following logframe or similar methodologies) and budget allocations are frequently estimates of the financial support given to such a program under different budget lines. Publication of these ex ante reports—that is, before budget execution—is a form of performance budgeting, albeit the weakest type since the reports are unlikely to have any influence on budget decision making in the absence of an explicit mechanism to achieve this; thus they might best be viewed as accountability documents. Note that the other types of performance budgeting which a country could adopt are performance-informed budgeting, where M&E information provides one input to budget decision making (as is the case in Chile and in most OECD countries), and direct performance budgeting, where budget allocations are based on an explicit formula or grading (examples here include higher education funding based on number of students and the type and topic of their degree, and health funding based on the "casemix" method).[17]

There does not appear to be any relationship between the level on which SINERGIA focuses—the presidential goals—and the much more micro, project focus of the work of DNP in preparing he annual investment budget. At the start of each new, four-year administration, the DNP, with the imprimatur of the president, submits to Congress the national development plan. This indicates proposed investments over the period. The investments included in this plan constitute the "Programs and Projects Bank" from which specific investments (and only those) can be selected for inclusion in subsequent annual budgets. DNP's Directorate for Investment and Public Finance (Dirección de Inversiones y Finanzas Públicas, DIFP) sets the standards that projects must meet. Entities prepare projects—either by themselves or through outsourcing—and send them to DIFP. Then DIFP checks whether projects meet the prescribed standards and ranks them according to government priorities.

In making the annual selection, DIFP conducts an ex ante evaluation of individual investments, although in practice this comprises more of a technical "assessment" than a formal evaluation; a review of DIFP's evaluation methodology has recently been completed. Ministries and agencies are meant to conduct ex post self-evaluations, but the reliability, credibility, and rigor of the self-evaluations which are conducted are open to question, and have been questioned by DIFP itself. It is unclear to what extent DIFP has been able to make substantive use of SIGOB information or the findings of the small number of SINERGIA evaluations which have been completed so far. The newly created sectoral spending committees, which include DIFP, DEPP, and Hacienda, provide a potentially important forum for utilization of SINERGIA's M&E information in the future, particularly as the volume of evaluation findings expands rapidly in coming years as a result of the ambitious evaluation agenda which is under way.

An important test of the relevance of the M&E information which SINERGIA has produced to date will be the extent to which it was used in the new four-year national development plan which DNP prepared and which was submitted to the Congress in November 2006. DEPP believes that DNP and sector ministries have made good use of information from SINERGIA to define the goals embodied in the national plan, as well as to report the government's (and ministry) performance in terms of the extent to which the goals have been achieved.

The M&E work of SINERGIA appears to be largely separate from the M&E activities of another directorate within DNP, the Directorate for Sustainable Territorial Development (Dirección de Desarrollo Territorial Sostenible, DDTS). The DDTS is responsible for monitoring and evaluation[18] of the work of subnational governments— the 1,100 municipalities and the 32 departments which oversight them—funded by transfers from the central government. The quality of the information provided to DDTS by the municipalities is reportedly poor, with many data gaps. Note that the municipalities separately provide the information on which sector ministries and agencies rely, and which they in turn input to SIGOB. The municipal-level work of DDTS and that of DEPP— on performance budgeting in several municipalities, for example—have not been coordinated.[19]

The split investment/recurrent budget also has implications for the use of M&E information from SINERGIA in the preparation of the recurrent budget; it raises issues of information exchange between DNP and Hacienda, coordination, and decisions on evaluation priorities. The option of unifying the investment and recurrent sides of the budget was recently considered within the government, but no consensus was reached. At present, the structure of the national budget in Colombia constrains the scope for use of M&E information.

Four other issues will also influence the ability of the government to undertake performance budgeting. The first is the December 2005 decision to implement a medium-term expenditure framework. One advantage of such a framework is that it provides greater surety in outyear funding for government ministries and activities. It can also provide an environment in which greater flexibility and responsibility is given to ministries and agencies, and these can be used to promote a greater performance orientation within government, as adopted by a number of OECD countries.

A second issue is the lack of a programmatic structure to the budget. DEPP's "performance budgets" for the past two years have reported planned budget spending on a program basis, and it constructed this programmatic classification of activities on an ad hoc basis. The investment and recurrent budgets continue to rely on conventional line-item budgeting, however; DEPP's performance budget reports are attached as an annex to the conventional budget reports.

There are many potential benefits from a program budgeting approach.[20] It links cost items (that is, activities) which have common objectives, and it assists program and spending prioritization; it also makes it easier to expand, reduce, or even terminate programs and the activities which they comprise. It facilitates evaluation by grouping linked activities, and also facilitates the setting of baseline measure of performance and performance targets. It helps clarify who is responsible for performance. However, while a program budgeting approach facilitates the use of M&E information during the budget process, it is not a prerequisite to a well-functioning M&E system which is intensively utilized by government, as the case of Chile amply demonstrates: Chile possesses the best-functioning M&E system in Latin America, in terms of a mature system of M&E which is fully utilized in the budget process, yet Chile continues to rely on line-item budgeting.

A third, related issue for Colombia is the apparently weak links between the integrated financial management information system (Sistema Integral de Información Financiera, SIIF) on which the budget is based and SIGOB. This makes it harder to link government spending on particular activities to the outputs, outcomes, and impacts produced by those activities. Thus DEPP's performance budget reports have involved the manual matching of SIGOB performance information with the cost data produced by SIIF. Chile has to conduct similar manual matching—which is time consuming—when it estimates the budget spending on the programs which it evaluates.

Related to this is a fourth issue: the limited information which DIFP possesses concerning actual government spending at the subnational level. While information on budget allocations is available, data on budget execution by individual departments and municipalities are simply not. This makes it impossible to compare government outputs of goods and services with the amounts spent on them, and it is an impediment to better budgeting and planning, and to performance-based budgeting.

This preliminary analysis of the work of DIFP and DDTS suggests that the M&E initiatives of DEPP have generally not been closely integrated into the work of the rest of DNP. Considerably closer coordination of DNP's M&E work can be viewed as a prerequisite for the achievement of performance-based budgeting and performance-based planning. Similarly, the apparent lack of M&E coordination with the budgeting work of Hacienda would appear to be an obstacle to a greater emphasis on performance budgeting by that key ministry.

Rapid Evaluation Pilots. One significant, recent development is the work of DEPP, in consultation with DIFP, to conduct two pilot rapid evaluations. These are intended to provide a rapid, low-cost method of evaluation which would better complement the more sophisticated and usually expensive impact evaluations on which SINERGIA has hitherto largely focused. These rapid evaluations will clarify the objectives of the two programs being evaluated, the logic of the program design, and will attempt to assess their activities, management, cost and performance. The innovative methodology which DEPP has developed is based on a combination of the rapid evaluation methodologies used by the Chilean and United States governments. The new methodology is called the *Evaluación Ejecutiva* (E^2). It is intended that such evaluations will be able to be completed within 3 months at a cost of $15,000–20,000 each.

Hacienda has no direct involvement in either SIGOB or the evaluations, and makes no direct use of them. However, another significant development is Hacienda's recent agreement to pilot two additional rapid evaluations—these will essentially comprise desk reviews, using Chile's "evaluations of government programs" methodology. Hacienda is also investigating the possibility of pursuing performance budgeting on a systematic basis.

Mix of M&E Tools. The piloting of rapid evaluations will provide an important addition to the range of M&E information available for budget decision making and national planning. For budgeting and planning to be done well requires the analysis and provision of advice on the performance of a very broad range of government activities—on those already under way and on possible new activities being considered. SIGOB already provides performance information for all government spending, and it focuses at the level of the presidential goals. Such information is relatively inexpensive to produce, and it achieves breadth of coverage. But its limitation is that it provides little or no understanding of the reasons why government goals have, or have not, been achieved. In contrast, SINERGIA's impact evaluations have the advantages of depth and rigor—they can identify causal relationships and prove definitively whether individual government actions are, or are not, producing the intended results. But sophisticated impact evaluations are typically rather expensive and time-consuming to conduct.[21] This is why rapid evaluations are a useful addition to the M&E toolkit: they are relatively quick and inexpensive, and can be used to evaluate a much broader spectrum of government activities than the large, one-off impact evaluations. Their disadvantage is that their findings are considerably less reliable than sophisticated impact evaluations.

The various M&E tools discussed here are complementary. Each has strengths and limitations, and each has a role to play as part of Colombia's M&E toolkit. The challenge for the government is to choose the mix which provides the most cost-effective use of the funds available for M&E.

Note that Chile has successfully employed a range of M&E tools in its budget cycle: the Hacienda uses performance indicators (some 1,560), rapid reviews (14 are completed each budget), sophisticated impact evaluations (4 are completed per budget), and comprehensive spending reviews of an entire sector (one per budget). Chile funds its M&E system using its own budget funds, without any donor funding support.

6.3 Support for Results-Based Management by Ministries and Agencies

There appear to be several entities which have devoted considerable effort to building their own M&E systems for their own, internal purposes. DEPP provides a range of support to these ministries, depending on circumstances. For some, it involves advising or even initiating sophisticated impact evaluations (such as for some components of the *Familias en Acción* program); for others it entails assistance in creation of ministry monitoring systems (such as for the MPS).

It would be useful to investigate the genesis and motivation underlying the creation and institutionalization of these entities' M&E systems, to identify lessons which might have broader applicability across government. These entities include the MEN. It has a management information system which includes program goals, objectives, performance indicators, targets, baselines, and exception reports. This database is comparable to SIGOB, but it reportedly includes many more performance indicators. One difficulty faced by MEN has been the generation of data for SIGOB. Despite MEN's detailed database, the information it provides cannot interface directly with SIGOB; instead, the MEN data have to be extracted manually and adjusted to meet the SIGOB definitions. It is possible that this disconnect partly arises from the different levels of focus of the two systems: SIGOB is very clearly focused on the level of the presidential goals, whereas MEN's system is focused on serving the much more specific and detailed requirements of ministry planning and activity management. It would seem reasonable to assume that most if not all other ministries and agencies face greater difficulties in providing data for SIGOB. It is not clear if there is scope to achieve greater harmonization of performance indicators—in terms of data definitions, periodicity, geographical coverage, and so forth—between the whole-of-government SIGOB system and ministry/agency systems.

Another entity to note is the Colombian Institute of Family Welfare (ICBF), which has created its own evaluation office to assist ICBF's own management and planning. The evaluation office has prepared evaluation guidelines, and it oversights the sophisticated impact evaluations which it contracts out to academia and consultants. (ICBF also undertakes some other types of evaluation.) It cofinances the impact evaluations with the World Bank (through social sector loans), the IADB and DEPP; ICBF also receives technical assistance from these entities. Some of the evaluations of ICBF programs have been led by the multilateral donors. ICBF has an overall budget of some $500 million, and its evaluation budget is expected to be about $2 million in 2006 (compared to $3 million in 2005, when it financed a large survey of nutrition). All of ICBF's impact evaluations are counted by DNP as coming under the aegis of SINERGIA.

Ministry/agency M&E systems can be expected to make it easier for entities to satisfy the information needs of SINERGIA, but they should be viewed as quite distinct from SINERGIA, whose objectives are very much focused at the whole-of-government level. And entities with good practice M&E systems appear to be very much the exception, however. As already noted, there has not occurred any widespread adoption of M&E practices in ministries and agencies across the government. An in-depth diagnosis would be necessary to determine if sector ministries and agencies collectively make much use of the two main information components of SINERGIA: SIGOB and the impact and other evaluations. In other words, are most entities simply suppliers of data, produced on an ad hoc basis, to SINERGIA?

7. SINERGIA: Strengths, Challenges, and Future Directions

7.1 Strengths and Challenges

The government of Colombia has achieved a considerable success in the creation and strengthening of SINERGIA. It is one of the strongest whole-of-government M&E systems in Latin America, in terms of the types of M&E it undertakes, its overall credibility, and its utilization; much of this progress has been achieved since 2002. Creation of the SIGOB system for monitoring the progress against the presidential goals has been notable, as is the intensive use made of this system by the president, the presidencia, and the DNP. Indeed, the president's role as the key champion for, and user of, such a monitoring system is unprecedented within the region. The ambitious agenda of impact evaluations is also impressive.

The CONPES policy document on SINERGIA (#3294) lists four challenges facing this M&E system: (1) lack of a single, clear conceptual framework, (2) a need to clarify the roles and responsibilities of the organizations which support SINERGIA, (3) absence of clear links between planning, budgeting, and evaluation, and (4) problems with the availability and frequency of data, as well as problems with data quality controls.

This rapid diagnosis concurs that these substantive issues clearly need to be addressed. The main challenge facing any government M&E system is its full institutionalization. This entails not only the creation of a system which provides good quality information, but one where that information is used intensively in supporting sound governance, and where the system is fully sustainable—in other words, a system which is likely to survive changes in government and to continue to be relied upon by future administrations. This definition of a "successful" M&E system provides the yardstick against which SINERGIA can be compared. It also provides the destination toward which options for the future development of the system, and for World Bank support, should be framed.

Utilization of SINERGIA information has been substantive for accountability purposes: the accountability of the president to civil society and to the Congress, and the accountability of ministers (and their ministries) to the president. Prima facie, this unique emphasis on accountability seems unlikely to continue to such a high degree when the current president leaves office in 2010. Nevertheless, if in the meantime the processes and popular support for presidential accountability have become established, there will be continuing demand for the type of information provided by SIGOB. DEPP has recently drafted a CONPES document intended to establish policy guidelines for government accountability and social control.

DEPP believes that SINERGIA information has also been used by the planning area of DNP and by sector ministries to assist their work in preparing the 2006–2010 national development plan. This issue has not been subject to detailed investigation, however.

There is little evidence that the four other potential uses of the M&E information produced by SINERGIA have been realized to any significant degree so far: (1) to support resource allocation and decision making in the national budget; (2) to ensure the cohesion of government action around those development priorities; (3) to assist sector ministries in their policy development and planning work; and (4) to support the ongoing management of government activities by ministries and agencies. An in-depth review of the use of M&E information by sector ministries and agencies might well reveal that the President's use of SIGOB information prompts some of them to take this information seriously in their planning and policy development work. And it is possible that as a growing number of sophisticated impact evaluations and rapid evaluations are completed in coming years, they will increasingly be used for budget and national planning purposes—although it would be a misconception to assume that the supply of evaluation findings automatically leads to their utilization.[22]

A recurring issue is the quality, availability and cost of the data used by SINERGIA and by ministries and agencies for their own work. One difficulty is lack of harmonization of data definitions. Another is the substantial absence of formal data audits. And the cost of impact evaluations has been driven up by the need for more detailed information than is available from either the regular household surveys conducted by the national statistical office (Departamento Administrativo Nacional de Estadística, DANE),[23] or from the administrative data produced by entities. Prima facie, there is an important role which both DANE and the high-level data coordination committee (Comisión Intersectorial de Políticas y Gestión

de Información para la Administración Pública, COINFO, or Intersectoral Committee for Information Policy and Management), which was created in 2003, could play here. The government is aware of these difficulties and it has decided to give a high priority to strengthening administrative and other data by, for example: promoting greater harmonization of data; the regular collection of core socioeconomic, health and nutrition data; and the development of minimum data standards. It has also signaled the need to improve data coordination through support to both DANE and COINFO.

The evaluation agenda is also costly. The cost of the impact evaluations underway or recently completed is $7.42 million, with an additional $2.46 million to be spent on new evaluations planned for the next five years. While this evaluation agenda might appear, prima facie, to be expensive, its cost represents only a very minor percentage of total government spending on the evaluated programs—thus the evaluations would need to result in only a relatively minor improvement in the effectiveness of government spending to make them highly cost-effective.

That said, there are ways in which the cost of evaluations could be reduced considerably, although some of these options would take several years to achieve (Bamberger 2006). A number of the large evaluations have to collect data by means of large, one-off, expensive surveys. The need for such ad hoc surveys could be reduced through an expansion of national statistical collections, such as longitudinal databases which track samples of the population over time; readier availability of data would also reduce the length of time needed to conduct an impact evaluation. The expansion of national statistical collections would itself be costly, and would take a number of years to complete, but would help to further increase the cost-effectiveness of SINERGIA. Another option is to rely much more on local Colombian evaluation consultants, rather than expensive international consultants. DEPP is using the rapidly increasing number of evaluations being conducted as an opportunity to increase the domestic supply of capable evaluators.

The government is pursuing an ambitious and broad-ranging strategy for strengthening SINERGIA. The initiatives include, among others:

- SIGOB
- Support for replication of improved SIGOB-type databases in municipal pilots (Medellín and Pasto)
- The agenda of impact and other evaluations, conducted jointly with DNP/DEPP, social sector ministries/agencies, and donors
- Development of a rapid evaluation methodology, and the pilots being planned by DEPP/DIFP and in Hacienda
- Efforts to engage directly with civil society, to encourage utilization of M&E information
- Preparation of government performance reports for the president, Congress, and civil society
- Preparation of performance budget reports, linking national development plan activities with their imputed costs, on a pilot, programmatic basis
- Support for performance budgeting efforts at the municipal level (Medellín and Pasto), with a view to mainstreaming these pilots
- Efforts to coordinate the generation of information feeding the M&E system, and to ensure the quality of the information—with a particular emphasis on the data registry for subsidy programs
- The Constitutional provision for evaluation, and laws, regulations, decrees; and the CONPES policy statement on M&E
- Support for the Intersectoral Committee for Evaluation and Management for Results
- Support for COINFO.

This broad-ranging strategy has been opportunistic, and this is wholly appropriate for two reasons. First, it is important to trial a number of initiatives to see which ones are more successful in the Colombian context: building a whole-of-government M&E system is an art, not a science, and it is often difficult to judge which initiatives are likely to be successful. None of those governments which have successfully built a whole-of-government M&E system did so in a linear, predictable model where the whole system was clearly envisaged from the start and progress was made incrementally, step by step, to achieve this vision. Rather, successful countries such as Chile, Australia, and Canada have started with some view of what a "successful" system would look like, but have also worked to create a whole-of-government system in an opportunistic manner, adjusting their plans as new opportunities emerge and as particular roadblocks have been encountered. These opportunities and roadblocks are not only country-specific, but are also government-specific, according to the strengths and weaknesses of individual ministries and other bodies (such as the national audit office), and according to the depth of commitment to a results focus of the key stakeholders in government. The arrival, or departure, of an M&E champion such as President Uribe is enormously influential, but it is also fortuitous. Similarly, the Hacienda's consideration of the possibility of pursuing performance budgeting provides a discrete window of opportunity to pursue this potentially significant use of SINERGIA information.

The downside of this opportunistic approach is the apparent absence of strong linkages between many of the various initiatives. From this perspective, it might be argued that SINERGIA is not so much an integrated M&E system, but rather a collection of performance-related activities with two main (and largely unrelated) components: SIGOB and the impact evaluation agenda. In parallel with these multiple initiatives, donor support appears, prima facie, to have been highly balkanized. Given the priority for SINERGIA to now enter a period of consolidation (discussed below), emphasis should be placed on achieving much better coordination among donors.

A good practice feature of DEPP's management of SINERGIA has been its willingness to present the approaches, methods and results of SINERGIA to public debate via the international conferences which DEPP sponsors—in 2004, 2006, and annually in the future.[24] These also provide a forum in which plans for the future strengthening of the national M&E system can be debated. Continual review and adjustment of the strategies underlying a national M&E system are highly desirable.

Table B.3: Stages of Maturation in SINERGIA Activities

	Demonstration	Expansion	Consolidation
More successful	• SIGOB pilots in municipalities		• SIGOB • Impact evaluations
Uncertain	• Rapid evaluation pilots • Performance budgeting pilots in municipalities • "Institutional incentives" involving public recognition of high-performing organizations and civil servants	• Performance budget reports • Easy-to-read reports on M&E information (for civil society and Congress) • Institutional framework for accountability (draft CONPES document)	• Regulatory framework, including Intersectoral Evaluation Committee
Less successful	• Direct engagement with civil society		

A second argument for a broad-ranging strategy is that the institutionalization of SINERGIA can be expected to be stronger, the greater the performance orientation of numerous stakeholders inside and outside of government—such as sector ministries/agencies, subnational governments, the Contraloria, the Congress, and civil society. Demand from these stakeholders for M&E information is likely to be cumulative and mutually reinforcing. It is also likely to lead to efforts to strengthen the supply side of M&E—such as improvements in the quality of data which feed into SIGOB, and in the availability of data needed for evaluations. Thus the greater are the synergies amongst all the performance-oriented M&E initiatives, the greater will be the probability that SINERGIA will thrive. The downside of this complexity, however, is a growing burden on DEPP in terms of management and coordination challenges. A careful balance between breadth and depth therefore needs to be achieved.

There are many performance-related activities which do not fall directly under the aegis of SINERGIA—such as the project evaluation work of DIFP and entities, the assessment of municipal performance by DDTS, and the M&E systems created by social sector entities for their own internal uses. To the extent these other performance-related activities are strengthened, this could provide useful demonstrations of the value of M&E, which in turn could strengthen the lessons for other ministries and agencies, and would also help to further legitimize M&E (and SINERGIA) within the government. DNP will need to consider carefully the extent to which DEPP becomes involved in these efforts, many of which are not directly related to the development of SINERGIA. The clearest relationship between SINERGIA and these other M&E activities arises from the need to achieve some harmonization of data requirements, standards, and procedures; the degree of actual (or potential) overlap between SINERGIA and other M&E systems and activities is not clear, however. This is another issue which would benefit from in-depth review.

DEPP's efforts to institutionalize SINERGIA can be classified into three categories, in a sequential chain: demonstration; expansion; and consolidation (table B.3). These can be further categorized into those which appear to have had some success, those whose level of success is uncertain, and those which have encountered real challenges. The extent of success can not be judged clearly, however, and an in-depth diagnosis would ideally be undertaken to assess this more definitively. Indeed, one observation is that progress in institutionalizing SINERGIA should be subject to continuous monitoring, through agreed performance indicators and targets, and regular evaluation; thus the government should apply high expectations to SINERGIA in terms of regular and credible monitoring and evaluation of it. This is an important, potential role for the Intersectoral Evaluation Committee.

Clearly, demonstration activities should only be expanded once they have achieved some substantive measure of success. And activities which are at the expansion stage, such as the performance (investment) budget reports, could usefully be broadened to include the recurrent budget. Activities in the final stage of maturity, such as the work of the Intersectoral Evaluation Committee—whose role, responsibilities and membership still have to be fully defined—should be helped to rapidly improve and consolidate.

7.2 Options for Consolidation of SINERGIA

Within this framework, and given the unique window of opportunity over the next three and a half years during the second administration of President Uribe, what steps might offer the greatest potential for achieving a high level of institutionalization of SINERGIA, and of maximizing its prospects for sustainability? The priorities for consolidating SINERGIA would appear to include the following:

- Ensure a much more focused, strategic approach to evaluation planning, under the leadership of the Intersectoral Evaluation Committee, to ensure that the range and depth of SINERGIA's evaluations best support the government's budget decision making and national planning.
- Foster much greater ownership of SINERGIA's M&E information by sector ministries and agencies through their broader involvement in the Intersectoral Evaluation Committee, and through clearer roles, responsibilities and functions for the Committee.
- Give the Intersectoral Evaluation Committee the responsibility to consider and agree on the recommendations from the large number of evaluations which will be completed in com-

ing years, and to ensure the implementation of these recommendations through their close monitoring.

- Achieve a demonstration effect, encourage a broader range of sector ministries and agencies to undertake evaluations through creation of a central pool of some evaluation funding to support rapid and impact evaluations. Such funding, which would ideally be overseen by the Intersectoral Evaluation Committee, would also help ensure the continuity of the government's evaluation agenda. It could also attract a range of donor funding.
- Support the rapid evaluation pilots to be trialed by the Hacienda and DNP, with a view to their rapid expansion and consolidation if the pilots are judged to be successful. Seek close collaboration between the two ministries in these efforts.
- Identify good practice M&E approaches adopted by social sector entities (such as, possibly, MEN and ICBF), and use these as a basis on which the Intersectoral Evaluation Committee would mandate specific M&E functions which all ministries and agencies are required to undertake.
- Strengthen the municipal pilots which are pursuing performance budgeting, and expand the pool of pilots to include some much weaker municipalities, with a view to the eventual consolidation of the approach at the subnational level—involving centrally determined standards and requirements—if the pilots are found to be fully successful and replicable.
- Ensure much greater quality assurance of the data which ministries, agencies and subnational governments provide for SIGOB—independent data audits will be required if a high level of credibility of SIGOB data is to be achieved.
- Review the various data systems which central ministries maintain, with a view to seeking greater harmonization, simplification and coordination to prepare a set of basic standards of administrative data.
- Ensure that both DANE and COINFO play an important role to guarantee the quality of data used by SINERGIA—in SIGOB and in evaluations—and to reduce its cost.

- Explore ways to further reduce the cost of the impact evaluations conducted under SINERGIA—such as via the expansion of national statistical collections, and greater reliance on local Colombian evaluation consultants.
- Establish the necessary linkages between the country's development goals, policies (properly structured), programs, and projects; only when these linkages are established can there be proper evaluation of Presidential Goals. Such policy evaluations should be piloted.

8. Conclusions

SINERGIA is a well-performing, whole-of-government M&E system. The main challenge it now faces is its full institutionalization, so that it will continue to thrive and to support good governance after a change in administration. For SINERGIA to be fully sustainable in this sense will require the strengthening of both the demand and supply sides of M&E; these are closely related. The supply side can be strengthened by improving the quality and credibility of monitoring information, reducing the costs of data supply, and increasing the volume and breadth of types of evaluations which are conducted. The demand side can be strengthened by promoting greater awareness of, and confidence in, the monitoring information and evaluation findings which the system produces—awareness among ministers, civil servants, and in civil society. Greater utilization of M&E information will require that key ministers and their ministries—especially the Presidencia, DNP and Hacienda—play a leading and even forceful role in championing the usefulness of the M&E information produced by SINERGIA. This support will need to go well beyond simple advocacy, and will need to include steps to ensure the utilization of the M&E information to support budget and national planning decision making and social accountability.

Sector ministers and their ministries also have a role to play in ensuring utilization of M&E information, in sector ministry policy development and planning, and in the ongoing management of government activities by ministries and entities. Their use of M&E information would be expected to encompass both the information produced by SINERGIA, and M&E information which their own ministries are meant to collect.

Thus on both the demand and supply sides, there is a need for greater clarity and focus of M&E roles, responsibilities, and accountabilities. It is argued here that the CONPES and the Intersectoral Committee for Evaluation and Management for Results should play a significant role in the oversight of SINERGIA and in ensuring its full institutionalization to further strengthen sound governance.

ANNEX C: TERMS OF REFERENCE FOR AN IN-DEPTH DIAGNOSIS OF COLOMBIA'S M&E SYSTEM

Introduction

The government of Colombia has been working since 1990 to create a robust and sustainable M&E system. The World Bank and other donors have provided a range of support for this purpose, including loans and technical assistance.

The objective of the current assignment is to prepare a diagnosis of the strengths and challenges facing the institutionalization of M&E in Colombia. Particular, but not exclusive, attention will be paid to the government's M&E system, SINERGIA. The World Bank has published a guide that provides an overview of concepts and issues and that will assist in this diagnosis.

Tasks

These terms of reference (ToRs) specify the tasks to be undertaken in the assignment.

1. Prepare a diagnosis, of about 60–80 pages in length, providing an overview of the Colombian government's approach to M&E, with a particular focus on SINERGIA. The types of issues the paper will be expected to address will include the following (an expanded listing of these issues is provided in the attachment to these ToRs):

   - The genesis of the government's approach
   - Legal and institutional framework
   - Use of M&E for political and social control
   - Role of M&E in the budget
   - Role of M&E in preparation of national development plan
   - Use of M&E by sector ministries/entities
   - M&E and results-based management
   - Types and quality of M&E conducted under SINERGIA
   - Other M&E work under the aegis of SINERGIA
   - Overall Colombian M&E strategy
   - Conclusions and summary of recommendations.

2. Preparation of the diagnostic paper is expected to involve a review of existing analyses and reports on SINERGIA and on related public sector reforms. It will also require close familiarity with the products of SINERGIA and the work of the unit in the DNP (the Directorate for the Evaluation of Public Policies) which manages the system. The current head of that unit, Sr./Sra. [insert name], will be the main government liaison point for the purposes of this diagnosis. Interviews of key informants in government, Congress, civil society, and the donor community would be expected to be involved.

3. You will complete the paper, which is to be written in English, by [insert date]. You will also be provided with tickets for business class air travel to Colombia, and will be reimbursed for hotel and incidental costs at the standard World Bank per diem rates. You will be paid $[insert amount] upon satisfactory completion of this diagnostic paper.

Diagnosis of the Colombian M&E System—Detailed Issues

Genesis of Government's Approach

What are the origins of M&E in Colombia? Who prompted this initiative and why? How has SINERGIA developed over time, and what have been the main events and circumstances underlying this evolution? What are the stated purposes of SINERGIA (for example, national or sectoral planning; budget decision making; ongoing program management or results-based management; accountability relationships to DNP and the Hacienda, to the president's office, to Congress, to sector ministries, to civil society—"social control"), and have these stated purposes changed over time? How has the priority for M&E been stated, in terms of direct and indirect links, in the context of the main public sector reforms in Colombia? What types of M&E have been emphasized as SINERGIA has evolved over the three stages in this period (that is, since 1991)?

Legal and Institutional Framework

What laws, regulations, and so forth. govern the M&E system in Colombia (for example, the constitutional requirement, the CONPES policy document, and so forth)? Who has been responsible for monitoring their application, and how closely have they been applied? What gaps and overlaps exist in them? What is the institutional framework under which M&E takes place? What are the roles of DNP, the Intersectoral Committee for Evaluation and Management for Results, CONPES, sector ministries, and so on, in commissioning evaluations? What are the other roles/responsibilities of key stakeholders in SINERGIA?—DNP, Hacienda, the president's office, the sector ministries and entities, the Contraloria, lower levels of government, and the Congress? What incentives exist for these stakeholders to take M&E seriously? How strong is demand for M&E information?

Use of M&E for Political and Social Control

How important has the current president's support for SINERGIA been? In what ways has the president used information from SINERGIA? How effective has M&E been in terms of improving the quality of public policy implementation? What have been its biggest successes/ failures so far? Does Congress demand information on public sector performance? Does it use the M&E information provided via SINERGIA? Does it have the proper incentive structure? What information is available to the public, and how is it used? How credible is SINERGIA M&E information to civil society? How can the use of M&E data be improved to promote greater accountability?

Role of M&E in the Budget

What is the actual use of M&E information from SINERGIA by DNP (DIFP) and Hacienda during the various stages of the (split) budget process—that is, to support policy advising and planning, budget decision making, performance review, and budget reporting? What are the implications of the split investment/recurrent budget and of the high degree of short-term budget rigidity? How useful has the DNP's initiative to present a supplementary document for the investment budget, reporting the government's budget outputs on a programmatic basis, been? What types of performance budgeting might be feasible in Colombia? Is there any disconnect between the M&E work of sector ministries and the use of such information in the budget process? What opportunities exist to strengthen the role of M&E in the budget?

Role of M&E in Preparing the National Development Plan

To what extent does DNP actually use M&E information from SINERGIA in the development of the 2006–2010 National Development Plan? To what extent does the plan highlight monitoring information and evaluation findings?

Use of M&E by Sector Ministries/Entities

Do sector ministries use the M&E information produced by SINERGIA? If so, how (for example, for policy development and planning, budget allocations, program management, accountability requirements within the sector or externally)? If there is little or no utilization of M&E information, why? Do there exist "islands of good practice M&E" in sector ministries/entities? Document in detail at least two successful ministry/ agency M&E systems (for example, ICBF or MEN). How persuasive are these islands for other ministries? To what extent has SINERGIA contributed to their development?

M&E and Results-Based Management

Can Colombia reasonably expect its public sector to move towards results-based management? What changes to public administration (budgeting, human resource management, auditing and control, etc.) need to take place for this to happen? Is there genuine interest in and demand from key stakeholders for results-based management?

Types and Quality of M&E Conducted under SINERGIA

Types of M&E

Which types of M&E tool are emphasized in SINERGIA—performance indicators, rapid reviews or evaluations, rigorous, in-depth impact evaluations? How much does each of these types of M&E cost? Report the total cost of each impact evaluation and of all other types of evaluation conducted so far, and provide a cost disaggregation into data collection, data analysis, management, and dissemination. What has the annual cost of SINERGIA been in recent years? What are the implications of the heavy reliance on donor funding of SINERGIA?

Performance Indicators and Data Systems

Is there a disconnect between the SIGOB focus on presidential goals and the focus of sector ministries/ agencies—are entities much more focused on micro, project-level issues? Are there multiple systems of performance indicators at the sector or agency level? To what extent are SINERGIA and ministry/entity data systems harmonized? Can they be harmonized (in terms of data definitions, periodicity, geographical coverage, and so forth), and what are the implications for M&E coordination and burden at the facility level? How are data requirements defined? What do SIGOB performance indicators focus on spending, ad-

ministrative processes, outputs and service delivery, outcomes, and national impacts? How are data collected at the entity level? Are they adequately controlled for quality and content? Have any data audits been conducted by sector ministries/entities, or by the DNP, or by others? What options exist to reduce the cost of evaluations through greater reliance on national statistical collections and less on ad hoc data surveys? Are data processed adequately by SINERGIA and presented in a useful way? How are data passed on to DNP? Is data utilization too much, too little, or just enough? What about timeliness? How can information management be improved? How are final reports prepared and presented to the president, Congress, and society?

Impact Evaluations

Who commissions and manages impact evaluations? Which stakeholders are involved in determining which programs should be evaluated and which issues investigated—are they focused on "problem programs," pilot programs, or high-expenditure or high-visibility programs, or are they based on a systematic research agenda to answer questions about program effectiveness? Who conducts the impact evaluations, and what quality assurance processes are followed? Which government programs have been subject to impact evaluation? Have any shortcomings been identified in the impact evaluations conducted so far under SINERGIA? Have these impact evaluations had any observable impact on policy decisions or program management? What sectors are good candidates for such evaluations in the future? What are the strengths and weaknesses of local supply of M&E? What are the key capacity constraints and what are the capacity-building priorities?

Other Types of Evaluation

Assess the usefulness of the pilot rapid evaluations (based on the evaluation approach of Chile's evaluations of government programs) being conducted by the Hacienda and DNP. What types of government processes—national planning, budget decision making, ministry/entity management, social control—could be supported by a broader range of evaluation types being conducted under the aegis of SINERGIA? What issues and challenges would the government face if it decided to broaden the range of types of evaluation it commissions?

Other M&E Work under the Aegis of SINERGIA

Make a rapid assessment of all other M&E capacity-building activities undertaken by DNP/DEPP, including SIGOB pilots in municipalities, performance-budgeting pilots in municipalities, "institutional incentives," and so on.

The Overall Colombian M&E Strategy

How comprehensive and appropriate is the strategy proposed by the CONPES policy document on M&E (CONPES 3294)? What are its strengths and shortcomings? How far along is its implementation? What issues need to be resolved to make it more effective? Is there adequate stake-holder buy-in? What opportunities exist for additional, lower-cost types of evaluation and review? What is the appropriate balance between independent evaluation and self-evaluation, or can the benefits of both be obtained without incurring the disadvantages of either? What are the threats to sustainability of SINERGIA?

Conclusions and Summary of Recommendations

What are the main strengths of SINERGIA and the remaining challenges it faces? What are the critical success factors and key options facing the institutionalization of SINERGIA and of M&E more broadly, in the government? How can the sustainability of SINERGIA be assured following the eventual change in administration? Briefly, what are the key lessons for other countries?

ANNEX D: EVALUATION OF IEG'S SUPPORT FOR INSTITUTIONALIZING M&E SYSTEMS

Evaluation Issues and Methodology

In 2004, IEG completed a self-evaluation of its support to governments to help them institutionalize their M&E systems (IEG 2004a). The methodology used in this evaluation, and the types of issue encountered, are likely to be of interest to other donors endeavoring to evaluate similar activities. Such activities might be conducted by donor evaluation offices or by donor operational areas. The methodological issues relate to the evaluability of efforts to institutionalize an M&E system.

Scale

One important contextual feature of the IEG evaluation was the relatively small scale of capacity-building support on which the evaluation was focused. As the World Bank's independent evaluation arm, IEG has a long-standing program of support in this area.[1] The level of resources involved has been modest, with two full-time staff and a total budget of around $1 million in recent years. These resources have been used to assist a number of countries around the world.

The scale of this support is small compared with the size of donor loans and grants to individual countries. Donor loans with components for institutionalization of M&E systems might well run to several millions of dollars, and sometimes more, depending on the specific activities being funded. Thus, the scale of activities, outputs, outcomes, and impacts from such country support could be expected to be considerably larger; there could also be strong synergies between these various activities expected.

Contribution versus Attribution

When evaluating donor support to a government, it is relatively easy to monitor the various outputs (such as country diagnoses) and intermediate outcomes (such as government establishment of a formal M&E framework) to which a donor has contributed. (See figure 13.1 for a list of possible activities, outputs, intermediate outcomes, final outcomes, and impacts.) But it is often much harder to attribute these results to an individual donor, especially when a number of donors have been involved or when donor support overall is small in comparison with the government's own efforts—such as the case of Chile. External factors, such as a change in government or the departure of a key M&E champion, can also have a significant effect on the success of donor efforts.[2]

Absence of a Standardized Approach to Institutionalizing M&E

As emphasized repeatedly in this volume, a standardized set of actions for strengthening an M&E system does not exist. Rather, the set that is appropriate for any one country will depend on that country's starting point and desired destination, in terms of the various possible uses of M&E information. As there is no standard set of actions, there can be no standard approach to evaluating them. The evaluation approach must be tailored to the specific set of actions adopted, their scale, and the country context.

Heterogeneity of Actions

Efforts to institutionalize M&E often include a long list of actions, such as those in table 13.1. Each action could be evaluated in a specific, and often different, manner. Individual activities, such as a high-level conference, might make a useful contribution to raising awareness among senior officials of the uses of M&E. But it is difficult in an evaluation to separately identify the contribution of this relatively small activity (Perrin and Mackay

1999). Training activities, which are a staple component of most efforts to institutionalize M&E, can be easier to evaluate, especially when their scale is large. And there is a well-recognized methodology for conducting such evaluations (Kirkpatrick and Kirkpatrick 2006).[3,4] Activities such as diagnoses and pilot evaluations can be evaluated in terms of their quality and depth.

Results Chain

One evaluation approach is to focus on the results chain for building or strengthening a government M&E system (figure 13.1). This comprises a set of activities, outputs, intermediate outcomes, final outcomes, and impacts. At each stage it is possible to collect performance indicators. More in-depth evaluative issues might be addressed by, for example, interviews or surveys of senior officials, detailed case studies, and so forth.

This was the approach the IEG evaluation followed. Of course, a bottom-line measure of success of all efforts to build an M&E system is the extent of utilization of the M&E information which the system produces. Such information can be obtained by means of surveys of budget officials, parliamentarians, and so on.

Diagnoses

The type of evaluation being considered here is similar in many ways to a diagnosis of a country's M&E system (chapter 12). An evaluation, of course, is usually somewhat more formal in nature, and it could encompass a baseline diagnosis and a follow-up diagnosis to measure the extent of changes over time. An evaluation can also include reviews of specific issues(see the list of in-depth diagnoses planned for Colombia, chapter 13).

The IEG Evaluation

The IEG self-evaluation provided a vehicle to clarify IEG's objectives and its eight-part strategy for helping governments (and their Bank counterparts) strengthen their M&E systems (IEG 2004a). It provided information on the amounts IEG spent in pursuing these objectives, categorized according to various types of activity such as seminars, provision of M&E training and scholarships, and country-based support work. It also mapped out a results chain for these efforts and presented performance indicators for outputs and intermediate outcomes of this work. (Most of these, of course, were only partially attributable to IEG—see preceding discussion.) These indicators included the following:

- The number of countries for which a diagnosis had been conducted
- Whether the priority for government M&E had been included in the Bank's strategy for each country assisted by IEG
- Whether the Bank had also agreed a loan for this purpose with the government
- Whether a government M&E framework had been established.

In-depth reviews of IEG's intensive efforts in two countries—Uganda and Egypt—were conducted by an external consultant. These comprised a document review, interviews of senior government officials and of senior staff of the Bank and other donors. The consultant rated IEG's work in each country against IEG's standard criteria for evaluating any Bank project: relevance, efficacy (that is, effectiveness), efficiency, outcome, sustainability, and IEG performance.

In addition, the IEG evaluation drew on a range of evaluations previously conducted on its main external training program (the International Program for Development Evaluation Training). The evaluation included performance information on the number of research papers prepared by IEG on this topic and on the level of demand for these papers.

Relying on all this M&E information, the evaluation endeavored to identify the specific outputs and outcomes corresponding to each part of IEG's eight-part strategy. It concluded with an analysis of several strategic options for IEG to consider in framing its future work in this area. This evaluation was formally presented to the Board of the World Bank and is publicly available (see http://www.worldbank.org/ieg/edc/evaluating_institutionalization_efforts.html).

IEG Evaluation: Executive Summary

Note that the following summary uses the term "evaluation capacity development" (ECD) to describe efforts to build or strengthen a government's M&E system. This term does not describe the nature of these efforts well; it emphasizes evaluation, whereas most government systems rely on both monitoring and evaluation. The use of the phrase "capacity development" suggests a supply-side approach. In fact, the demand side and issues of institutionalization are perhaps more important. The term ECD is still used by IEG and other multilateral and some bilateral aid organizations.

The development community is placing a high premium on the achievement of results, and it is committed to helping borrower countries strengthen their abilities to measure and manage for results. An important part of this entails efforts to help countries build their own monitoring and evaluation (M&E) systems. . . . Strong M&E systems can make an important contribution to sound governance in countries. And stronger country capacities for M&E would also facilitate the quality of the Bank's own M&E—both self-evaluation by Bank operations of the development interventions which they design and oversee, and IEG's own independent evaluation of them.

IEG has been a strong advocate of ECD since [IEG's] creation in 1973, and ECD has been part of its formal mandate since 1986. In pursuit of this, IEG has an ECD program, with two full-time staff, which provides ECD advice and other support to countries and to operational areas within the Bank. The purpose of this self-evaluation report is to evaluate IEG's ECD work, and thus to assess the extent to which IEG is fulfilling its ECD mandate.

This report describes and explains IEG's ECD strategy—the manner in which IEG has worked to fulfill its mandate. In pursuit of this strategy IEG has played a catalytic role intended to lead to the mainstreaming of ECD work both within the Bank and in countries, and to establish ECD good practice. The three closely related components of this strategy are the internal support it

provides to the Bank, its external support, and ECD foundation building.

IEG has successfully played a leading role in keeping M&E and ECD on the Bank's agenda, with the strong support of the Bank's Board and its Committee on Development Effectiveness. The Bank's evolving *Results Agenda*, in turn, is strengthening the focus of Bank Operations on the results of their work, and this is providing some additional focus on ECD. Since 1999, when IEG increased its resources devoted to ECD, there has been a substantial growth in the number of Bank country teams pursuing ECD with borrowers; IEG's advocacy and support for almost all of them has been a contributing factor. At least 31 of these country teams—out of the approximately 150 Bank country teams—are currently involved in ECD. This growth constitutes significant progress toward the mainstreaming of ECD within the Bank, although there is clearly a long way to go.

A number of constraints on the evaluability of IEG's ECD work are identified in this report, such as difficulties of attribution; the "upstream" nature of IEG's ECD work; lack of any standardized approach to ECD; small scale of many of IEG's ECD activities; and early-stage nature of some of this work. However, this report has also enhanced the evaluability of this work through: the mapping of ECD results chains; articulation of ECD performance indicators; and preparation of detailed criteria for rating country-level ECD. The report presents evidence on a number of outputs and outcomes of IEG's ECD work.

IEG has provided country-level ECD support to 34 countries (and their corresponding Bank country teams) since 1999: high-intensity support has been provided to 2 countries (Uganda and Egypt), medium-intensity support to 15 countries, and indirect support to another 17 countries. Such a large "footprint" of IEG's support has helped lift the profile of ECD within the

Bank, leading to the likelihood of some demonstration effect to other country teams. This country-focused work constitutes a key part of IEG's ECD strategy. An important finding of this report is that many of the countries for which IEG has provided high- and medium-intensity support have made substantive ECD progress—in terms of ECD outputs such as ECD diagnoses, identification of ECD as a priority in the Bank's country assistance strategies, and creation of Bank projects with an ECD component, and in terms of intermediate outcomes such as strengthening of country demand for M&E and of country capacities to conduct and to use M&E. While not all of this progress can be attributed to IEG, IEG has been an important contributor to these ECD results.

In-depth reviews of the two countries where IEG has provided high-intensity support—Uganda and Egypt—confirm IEG's leading role in ECD in recent years; IEG's performance in both countries is rated as satisfactory. A strength in Uganda has been the provision of sustained, high-intensity support, which achieved synergies between a range of different ECD activities and has led to some significant ECD results. The in-depth review concluded that the ECD work in Uganda represents good practice ECD. However, the situation for Egypt is somewhat different—insufficient demand from key stakeholders within the government has to some extent frustrated the work. This experience reinforces a lesson learned by a number of countries where demand has been weak: that weak demand can lead to fragile ECD efforts. For this reason, IEG needs to pay close attention to the demand side in its country ECD work, both at the initial diagnostic stage and in subsequent capacity-building work.

IEG's ECD foundation-building work has included preparation of ECD resource materials, to share lessons from ECD experience, provision of M&E and ECD training, and various cooperative initiatives such as joint evaluations and donor M&E harmonization. IEG has played a leading role in identifying and disseminating the lessons from ECD experience—in effect, ECD research—and this is reflected in the very high level of demand for its ECD resource materials. A recent IEG evaluation of the International Program for Development Evaluation Training, IEG's flagship course in M&E, found high levels of participant satisfaction with the training and also found that participants had demonstrated significant learning gains. There are also highly positive evaluation findings for the other M&E/ECD courses in which IEG has been involved. However, there are a number of gaps in IEG's evaluative information concerning the results of its ECD work, and these will need to be addressed.

There is no evidence of any conflicts of interest having arisen in relation to IEG's ECD activities. There exist important precedents inside and outside the Bank where legal or fiduciary responsibilities are reconciled with provision of capacity-building support to operational work. This reconciliation is achieved through a simple firewall approach.

This self-evaluation presents three key options for IEG management to consider in framing its future ECD strategy. These are: (1) an exit option to transfer IEG's ECD activities; (2) a scale-up option involving closer IEG collaboration with Bank central units, and a more targeted approach to ECD work with Bank country teams and with the Bank's Regional Vice Presidential Units; and (3) a renewed focus on ECD lesson-learning.

The conclusion of this report is that, given the modest level of resources committed to ECD, IEG has been highly active in ECD, and that its ECD strategy has contributed to a number of ECD results—outputs and outcomes—over the past five years. The task now facing IEG is to further strengthen its ECD work—to achieve the related objectives of mainstreaming ECD and establishing high-quality ECD more widely. There are growing opportunities for achieving a results orientation within the Bank and in countries, and the priority for ECD has never been higher.

ANNEX E: GLOSSARY OF KEY TERMS IN M&E

Source: Development Assistance Committee (DAC). 2002. *Glossary of Terms in Evaluation and Results-Based Management.* Paris: OECD. This glossary is available in English, Chinese, French, Italian, Japanese, Portuguese, Russian, and Spanish.

Further information may be obtained from OECD, Development Co-operation Directorate, 2 rue André-Pascal, 75775 Paris Cedex 16, France. Web site: www.oecd.org/dac/evaluation.

Accountability

Obligation to demonstrate that work has been conducted in compliance with agreed rules and standards or to report fairly and accurately on performance results vis a vis mandated roles and/or plans. This may require a careful, even legally defensible, demonstration that the work is consistent with the contract terms.

Note: Accountability in development may refer to the obligations of partners to act according to clearly defined responsibilities, roles and performance expectations, often with respect to the prudent use of resources. For evaluators, it connotes the responsibility to provide accurate, fair and credible monitoring reports and performance assessments. For public sector managers and policy-makers, accountability is to taxpayers/ citizens.

Activity

Actions taken or work performed through which inputs, such as funds, technical assistance and other types of resources are mobilized to produce specific outputs.

Related term: development intervention

Analytical tools

Methods used to process and interpret information during an evaluation.

Appraisal

An overall assessment of the relevance, feasibility and potential sustainability of a development intervention prior to a decision of funding.

Note: In development agencies, banks, etc., the purpose of appraisal is to enable decision-makers to decide whether the activity represents an appropriate use of corporate resources.

Related term: ex ante evaluation

Assumptions

Hypotheses about factors or risks which could affect the progress or success of a development intervention.

Note: Assumptions can also be understood as hypothesized conditions that bear on the validity of the evaluation itself, e.g., about the characteristics of the population when designing a sampling procedure for a survey. Assumptions are made explicit in theory based evaluations where evaluation tracks systematically the anticipated results chain.

Attribution

The ascription of a causal link between observed (or expected to be observed) changes and a specific intervention.

Note: Attribution refers to that which is to be credited for the observed changes or results achieved. It represents the extent to which observed development effects can be attributed to a specific intervention or to the performance of one or more partner taking account of other interventions, (anticipated or unanticipated) confounding factors, or external shocks.

Audit

An independent, objective assurance activity designed to add value and improve an organization's operations. It helps an organization accomplish its objectives by bringing a systematic, disciplined approach to assess and improve the effectiveness of risk management, control and governance processes.

Note: A distinction is made between regularity (financial) auditing, which focuses on compliance with applicable statutes and regulations; and performance auditing, which is concerned with relevance, economy, efficiency and effectiveness. Internal auditing provides an assessment of internal controls undertaken by a unit reporting to management while external auditing is conducted by an independent organization.

Base-line study

An analysis describing the situation prior to a development intervention, against which progress can be assessed or comparisons made.

Benchmark

Reference point or standard against which performance or achievements can be assessed.

Note: A benchmark refers to the performance that has been achieved in the recent past by other comparable organizations, or what can be reasonably inferred to have been achieved in the circumstances.

Beneficiaries

The individuals, groups, or organizations, whether targeted or not, that benefit, directly or indirectly, from the development intervention.

Related terms: reach, target group

Cluster evaluation

An evaluation of a set of related activities, projects and/ or programs.

Conclusions

Conclusions point out the factors of success and failure of the evaluated intervention, with special attention paid to the intended and unintended results and impacts, and more generally to any other strength or weakness. A conclusion draws on data collection and analyses undertaken, through a transparent chain of arguments.

Counterfactual

The situation or condition which hypothetically may prevail for individuals, organizations, or groups were there no development intervention.

Country program evaluation/ Country assistance evaluation

Evaluation of one or more donor's or agency's portfolio of development interventions, and the assistance strategy behind them, in a partner country.

Data collection tools

Methodologies used to identify information sources and collect information during an evaluation.

Note: Examples are informal and formal surveys, direct and participatory observation, community interviews, focus groups, expert opinion, case studies, literature search.

Development intervention

An instrument for partner (donor and non-donor) support aimed to promote development.

Note: Examples are policy advice, projects, programs.

Development objective

Intended impact contributing to physical, financial, institutional, social, environmental, or other benefits to a society, community, or group of people via one or more development interventions.

Economy

Absence of waste for a given output.

Note: An activity is economical when the costs of the scarce resources used approximate the minimum needed to achieve planned objectives.

Effect

Intended or unintended change due directly or indirectly to an intervention.

Related terms: results, outcome

Effectiveness

The extent to which the development intervention's objectives were achieved, or are expected to be achieved, taking into account their relative importance.

Note: Also used as an aggregate measure of (or judgment about) the merit or worth of an activity, i.e. the extent to which an intervention has attained, or is expected to attain, its major relevant objectives efficiently in a sustainable fashion and with a positive institutional development impact.

Related term: efficacy

Efficiency

A measure of how economically resources/inputs (funds, expertise, time, etc.) are converted to results.

Evaluability

Extent to which an activity or a program can be evaluated in a reliable and credible fashion.

Note: Evaluability assessment calls for the early review of a proposed activity in order to ascertain whether its objectives are adequately defined and its results verifiable.

Evaluation

The systematic and objective assessment of an ongoing or completed project, program or policy, its design, implementation and results. The aim is to determine the relevance and fulfillment of objectives, development efficiency, effectiveness, impact and sustainability. An evaluation should provide information that is credible and useful, enabling the incorporation of lessons learned into the decision–making process of both recipients and donors. Evaluation also refers to the process of determining the worth or significance of an activity, policy or program. An assessment, as systematic and objective as possible, of a planned, ongoing, or completed development intervention.

Note: Evaluation in some instances involves the definition of appropriate standards, the examination of performance against those standards, an assessment of actual and expected results and the identification of relevant lessons.

Related term: review

Ex ante evaluation

An evaluation that is performed before implementation of a development intervention.

Related terms: appraisal, quality at entry

Ex post evaluation

Evaluation of a development intervention after it has been completed.

Note: It may be undertaken directly after or long after completion. The intention is to identify the factors of success or failure, to assess the sustainability of results and impacts, and to draw conclusions that may inform other interventions.

Feedback

The transmission of findings generated through the evaluation process to parties for whom it is relevant and useful so as to facilitate learning. This may involve the collection and dissemination of findings, conclusions, recommendations and lessons from experience.

Finding

A finding uses evidence from one or more evaluations to allow for a factual statement.

Formative evaluation

Evaluation intended to improve performance, most often conducted during the implementation phase of projects or programs.

Note: Formative evaluations may also be conducted for other reasons such as compliance, legal requirements or as part of a larger evaluation initiative.

Related term: process evaluation

Goal

The higher-order objective to which a development intervention is intended to contribute.

Related term: development objective

Impacts

Positive and negative, primary and secondary long-term effects produced by a development intervention, directly or indirectly, intended or unintended.

Independent evaluation

An evaluation carried out by entities and persons free of the control of those responsible for the design and implementation of the development intervention.

Note: The credibility of an evaluation depends in part on how independently it has been carried out. Independence implies freedom from political influence and organizational pressure. It is characterized by full access to information and by full autonomy in carrying out investigations and reporting findings.

Indicator

Quantitative or qualitative factor or variable that provides a simple and reliable means to measure achievement, to reflect the changes connected to an intervention, or to help assess the performance of a development actor.

Inputs

The financial, human, and material resources used for the development intervention.

Institutional development impact

The extent to which an intervention improves or weakens the ability of a country or region to make more efficient, equitable, and sustainable use of its human, financial, and natural resources, for example through: (a) better definition, stability, transparency, enforceability and predictability of institutional arrangements and/or (b) better alignment of the mission and capacity of an organization with its mandate, which derives from these institutional arrangements. Such impacts can include intended and unintended effects of an action.

Internal evaluation

Evaluation of a development intervention conducted by a unit and/or individuals reporting to the management of the donor, partner, or implementing organization.

Related term: self-evaluation

Joint evaluation

An evaluation to which different donor agencies and/or partners participate.

Note: There are various degrees of "jointness" depending on the extent to which individual partners cooperate in the evaluation process, merge their evaluation resources and combine their evaluation reporting. Joint evaluations can help overcome attribution problems in assessing the effectiveness of programs and strategies, the complementarity of efforts supported by different partners, the quality of aid coordination, etc.

Lessons learned

Generalizations based on evaluation experiences with projects, programs, or policies that abstract from the specific circumstances to broader situations. Frequently, lessons highlight strengths or weaknesses in preparation, design, and implementation that affect performance, outcome, and impact.

Logical framework (Logframe)

Management tool used to improve the design of interventions, most often at the project level. It involves identifying strategic elements (inputs, outputs, outcomes, impact) and their causal relationships, indicators, and the assumptions or risks that may influence success and failure. It thus facilitates planning, execution and evaluation of a development intervention.

Related term: results-based management

Meta-evaluation

The term is used for evaluations designed to aggregate findings from a series of evaluations. It can also be used to denote the evaluation of an evaluation to judge its quality and/or assess the performance of the evaluators.

Mid-term evaluation

Evaluation performed towards the middle of the period of implementation of the intervention.

Related term: formative evaluation

Monitoring

A continuing function that uses systematic collection of data on specified indicators to provide management and the main stakeholders of an ongoing development intervention with indications of the extent of progress and achievement of objectives and progress in the use of allocated funds.

Related terms: performance monitoring, indicator

Outcome

The likely or achieved short-term and medium-term effects of an intervention's outputs.

Related terms: result, outputs, impacts, effect

Outputs

The products, capital goods and services which result from a development intervention; may also include changes resulting from the intervention which are relevant to the achievement of outcomes.

Participatory evaluation

Evaluation method in which representatives of agencies and stakeholders (including beneficiaries) work together in designing, carrying out and interpreting an evaluation.

Partners

The individuals and/or organizations that collaborate to achieve mutually agreed upon objectives.

Note: The concept of partnership connotes shared goals, common responsibility for outcomes, distinct accountabilities and reciprocal obligations. Partners may include governments, civil society, non-governmental organizations, universities, professional and business associations, multilateral organizations, private companies, etc.

Performance

The degree to which a development intervention or a development partner operates according to specific criteria/standards/guidelines or achieves results in accordance with stated goals or plans.

Performance indicator

A variable that allows the verification of changes in the development intervention or shows results relative to what was planned.

Related terms: performance monitoring, performance measurement

Performance measurement

A system for assessing performance of development interventions against stated goals.

Related terms: performance monitoring, indicator

Performance monitoring

A continuous process of collecting and analyzing data to compare how well a project, program, or policy is being implemented against expected results.

Process evaluation

An evaluation of the internal dynamics of implementing organizations, their policy instruments, their service delivery mechanisms, their management practices, and the linkages among these.

Related term: formative evaluation

Program evaluation

Evaluation of a set of interventions, marshaled to attain specific global, regional, country, or sector development objectives.

Note: A development program is a time-bound intervention involving multiple activities that may cut across sectors, themes and/or geographic areas.

Related term: country program/strategy evaluation

Project evaluation

Evaluation of an individual development intervention designed to achieve specific objectives within specified resources and implementation schedules, often within the framework of a broader program.

Note: Cost benefit analysis is a major instrument of project evaluation for projects with measurable benefits. When benefits cannot be quantified, cost effectiveness is a suitable approach.

Project or program objective

The intended physical, financial, institutional, social, environmental, or other development results to which a project or program is expected to contribute.

Purpose

The publicly stated objectives of the development program or project.

Quality assurance

Quality assurance encompasses any activity that is concerned with assessing and improving the merit or the worth of a development intervention or its compliance with given standards.

Note: Examples of quality assurance activities include appraisal, RBM, reviews during implementation, evaluations, etc. Quality assurance may also refer to the assessment of the quality of a portfolio and its development effectiveness.

Reach

The beneficiaries and other stakeholders of a development intervention.

Related term: beneficiaries

Recommendations

Proposals aimed at enhancing the effectiveness, quality, or efficiency of a development intervention; at redesigning the objectives; and/or at the reallocation of resources. Recommendations should be linked to conclusions.

Relevance

The extent to which the objectives of a development intervention are consistent with beneficiaries' requirements, country needs, global priorities and partners' and donors' policies.

Note: Retrospectively, the question of relevance often becomes a question as to whether the objectives of an intervention or its design are still appropriate given changed circumstances.

Reliability

Consistency or dependability of data and evaluation judgments, with reference to the quality of the instruments, procedures and analyses used to collect and interpret evaluation data.

Note: Evaluation information is reliable when repeated observations using similar instruments under similar conditions produce similar results.

Results

The output, outcome or impact (intended or unintended, positive and/or negative) of a development intervention.

Related terms: outcome, effect, impacts

Results chain

The causal sequence for a development intervention that stipulates the necessary sequence to achieve desired objectives beginning with inputs, moving through activities and outputs, and culminating in outcomes, impacts, and feedback. In some agencies, reach is part of the results chain.

Related terms: assumptions, results framework

Results framework

The program logic that explains how the development objective is to be achieved, including causal relationships and underlying assumptions.

Related terms: results chain, logical framework

Results-based management (RBM)

A management strategy focusing on performance and achievement of outputs, outcomes and impacts.

Related term: logical framework

Review

An assessment of the performance of an intervention, periodically or on an ad hoc basis.

Note: Frequently "evaluation" is used for a more comprehensive and/or more in-depth assessment than "review." Reviews tend to emphasize operational aspects. Sometimes the terms "review" and "evaluation" are used as synonyms.

Related term: evaluation

Risk analysis

An analysis or an assessment of factors (called assumptions in the logframe) affect or are likely to affect the successful achievement of an intervention's objectives. A detailed examination of the potential unwanted and negative consequences to human life, health, property, or the environment posed by development interventions; a systematic process to provide information regarding such undesirable consequences; the process of quantification of the probabilities and expected impacts for identified risks.

Sector program evaluation

Evaluation of a cluster of development interventions in a sector within one country or across countries, all of which contribute to the achievement of a specific development goal.

Note: A sector includes development activities commonly grouped together for the purpose of public action such as health, education, agriculture, transport etc.

Self-evaluation

An evaluation by those who are entrusted with the design and delivery of a development intervention.

Stakeholders

Agencies, organisations, groups or individuals who have a direct or indirect interest in the development intervention or its evaluation.

Summative evaluation

A study conducted at the end of an intervention (or a phase of that intervention) to determine the extent to which anticipated outcomes were produced. Summative evaluation is intended to provide information about the worth of the program.

Related term: impact evaluation

Sustainability

The continuation of benefits from a development intervention after major development assistance has been completed. The probability of continued long-term benefits. The resilience to risk of the net benefit flows over time.

Target group

The specific individuals or organizations for whose benefit the development intervention is undertaken.

Terms of reference

Written document presenting the purpose and scope of the evaluation, the methods to be used, the standard against which performance is to be assessed or analyses are to be conducted, the resources and time allocated, and reporting requirements. Two other expressions sometimes used with the same meaning are "scope of work" and "evaluation mandate."

Thematic evaluation

Evaluation of a selection of development interventions, all of which address a specific development priority that cuts across countries, regions, and sectors.

Triangulation

The use of three or more theories, sources or types of information, or types of analysis to verify and substantiate an assessment.

Note: By combining multiple data sources, methods, analyses or theories, evaluators seek to overcome the bias that comes from single informants, single methods, single observer or single theory studies.

Validity

The extent to which the data collection strategies and instruments measure what they purport to measure.

ENDNOTES

Chapter 3

1. A good practice example of a comparison of performance of the federal and state/territory levels of government in Australia is provided by the Steering Committee for the Review of Government Service Provision (2007).

2. Also known as the "new public management" (see, for example, OECD 1995).

3. Related concepts of civil society involvement in M&E are *participatory M&E*, in which ordinary citizens are active participants in M&E and not just sources of information, and *social accountability*, which includes a broad range of mechanisms, including various types of M&E by which citizens can hold the state to account. These other types of M&E include community score cards, public expenditure tracking surveys, and social audits. See World Bank (2006b).

4. http://www.bogotacomovamos.org/bogotacv/scripts/index.php. See also Sánchez (undated) and Fiszbein (2005, p. 42).

5. Chile's finance ministry, which manages the whole-of-government evaluation system, posts on-line requests for tenders to conduct the evaluations it commissions. The evaluation terms of reference, the successful tenderers (individuals or companies), and the final evaluation report are all publicly disclosed on the ministry Web site at the time of selection of tenderers. This helps reinforce the transparency of the evaluation processes and the objectivity of the evaluations themselves.

Chapter 4

1. Most government M&E systems do not *evaluate* donor projects. Two exceptions are Chile and Colombia.

2. http://www.mfdr.org/.

3. http://www.adb.org/MfDR/CoP/about.asp.

4. http://www.afrea.org/; http://www.preval.org/mapa.php?idioma=8; http://www.ideas-int.org/; http://internationalevaluation.com/index.shtml.

Chapter 5

1. For criteria for assessing the quality of performance indicators, see, for example, Hatry (2006) and Wholey (2006). For evaluation standards, see, for example, Wholey, Hatry, and Newcomer (2004).

Chapter 6

1. The MoF analyzes and seeks to verify the information contained in these reports. Some of the ministry information databases and systems are audited by the government's general internal audit committee (see Blondal and Curristine 2004).

2. These targets include outputs of goods and services, their quality, and levels of user satisfaction.

3. Reasons for not achieving the set targets include: external factors outside the control of the organization; unrealistically high targets; and poor management performance within the organization (Guzman 2006).

4. One way sector ministries use M&E information in the budget process is when they request additional resources from the MoF's *bidding fund*. This fund has been used in some—not all—recent budgets to allocate additional resources available at the end of the normal budget process. If they wish to access this fund, ministries have to submit bids using the logframe approach, showing the desired objectives of the proposed spending, the performance indicators and targets, the target population, expected results, and likely contribution to strategic goals. The MoF reviews these bids on the basis of technical criteria, especially their relevance to government priorities. Final decisions on fund allocations are made by the president (Blondal and Curristine 2004).

5. Chile's evaluations of government programs and the impact evaluations do not always report their methodology or pay sufficient attention to the program logic (the logframe). Some of the impact evaluations do not meet the MoF's own quality standards because of problems such as lack of a control group or baseline data.

These evaluations have also tended to stress quantitative methods while underutilizing qualitative information such as level of beneficiary satisfaction.

6. This figure excludes the costs borne by sector entities, which consist primarily of the cost of collecting, processing, and transmitting performance information to the MoF and the cost of preparing comprehensive management reports.

Chapter 7

1. The SIGOB systems in Guatemala and Honduras and the performance indicator system of Ceará state in Brazil are used to grade program performance, such as by using a traffic light approach to grading—green, amber, or red "grades." This approach clearly highlights the performance of each program. The Mexican government is considering the introduction of a similar system.

2. The planning department, which manages SINERGIA, has developed a rapid evaluation methodology based on a combination of that of Chile's evaluations of government programs and of the U.S. government's PART. For more details, see Mackay and others (2007). These planning department evaluations (called "executive evaluations") are expected to cost around $25,000 each. The finance ministry's rapid evaluation pilots are based on Chile's evaluations of government programs methodology and cost around $15,000 each.

3. The government is currently funding only 12 percent of the $11.1 million evaluation agenda.

4. The cost estimate for Colombia is approximate. The estimates for both Colombia and Chile do not include the costs borne by sector ministries and agencies in providing monitoring and other information for the M&E system.

Chapter 8

1. These Australian reforms included, for example, a reduction in the number of departments and provision of much greater autonomy to the consolidated departments; replacement of line-item budgeting with a system of running costs (comprising one item for salaries and another for administrative expenses), in addition to program spending; and introduction of program budgeting; introduction of a medium-term expenditure framework with three-year forward estimates.

2. The development of Australia's evaluation system is discussed by Mackay (1998a), and a comparison with the performance management system which replaced it is presented by Mackay (2004).

3. Although accountability relationships are traditionally viewed in terms of the accountability of ministers and departments to the parliament, in Australia's case another accountability relationship proved to be more powerful: accountability of departments to the DoF.

4. The annualized cost of these evaluations was equivalent, on average, to less than one percent of the government's total spending on those evaluated programs.

5. Sector ministries sometimes prepared savings options themselves, as one vehicle to help pay for new spending proposals. About one-third of all savings options were prepared by sector ministries; the remainder were prepared by the DoF.

6. There were a number of instances where line ministers' new policy proposals were not supported by evaluation findings, even though the DoF argued they could have been, and the cabinet therefore demanded that an evaluation be conducted before it would consider the proposal. And whenever there was a dispute between the DoF and a line department concerning the quality or reliability of findings of a major evaluation—an issue which proved certain to attract the ire of the Cabinet—the matter would be thrown back to officials to resolve by means of a new evaluation. This would usually take some time to complete; consequently, the line minister's proposal might have to wait another year to be reconsidered. Such delays provided line ministries with a real incentive to avoid disputes with the DoF about the quality of their evaluations.

7. See Mackay (2004) for a detailed analysis of these reforms and their impact on M&E in the federal government.

8. Examples include the departments of families; community services and indigenous affairs; employment and workplace relations; education, science, and training; and health and aging.

9. In the absence of strong accountability pressures on line departments, and in an environment in which the policy and budget processes have been weakened, any incentives for line departments to take performance M&E seriously will have to be internally generated. This in turn will depend on the priorities and commitment of the permanent secretaries of each department.

Chapter 9

1. Worldwide, about 64 countries have prepared a PRSP or Interim PRSP. See http://www.worldbank.org/prsp.

2. This section draws heavily on consultant work commissioned by IEG. See Hauge (2001, 2003), IEG (2004a, annex D), and Schiavo-Campo (2005).

3. This is known as the Joint Assistance Strategy. See World Bank and others (2006).

4. http://web.worldbank.org/external/projects/main?pagePK=64283627&piPK=73230&theSitePK=40941&menuPK=228424&Projectid=P050440.

Chapter 10

1. Note also the importance of data collected by national statistics offices, such as population censuses and household surveys. A good example of a review of existing data collected by ministries and the national statistics office in Uganda is provided by Kiryegyera, Nuwagaba, and Ochen (2005).

2. This has happened with data on hospital waiting lists in the United Kingdom, for example (Schick 2001).

3. An interesting if perhaps controversial analysis of the nature and impact of the application of Napoleonic law in developing countries is provided by Beck, Demirguc-Kunt, and Levine (2002). In contrast, countries with a Westminster system of government tend to interpret government decisions, as reflected, for example, in Cabinet decisions, in a more pragmatic manner, stressing their adaptation as circumstances evolve. A strength of Cabinet decisions is that they are collective decisions involving many government ministers; the Cabinet's collective support for the evaluation system in Australia was an important success factor in that country (Mackay 1998a).

4. There are additional advantages to having legislation for M&E in place. Legislation can ensure that central ministries have access to the data collected and maintained by sector ministries and agencies. Legislation can also ensure that evaluation reports are made publicly available, and it can ensure the confidentiality of personal data.

5. The evaluation reports are available from the ministry's Web site: http://www.dipres.cl/fr_control.html.

6. One of the first was published by the World Bank's Operations Evaluation Department (renamed the Independent Evaluation Group in 2005). See Mackay (1998b). Another distinctive example is Bedi and others (2006).

Chapter 11

1. This trichotomy—carrots, sticks, and sermons—was originally developed by Vedung (1991) in presenting a taxonomy of policy instruments (regulations, economic incentives, and information). It was not developed as a taxonomy of incentives to conduct M&E. Toulemonde (1999) has also used it to develop a taxonomy of incentives to conduct M&E.

Chapter 12

1. Compton, Baizerman, and Stockdill (2002) have characterized the building of M&E capacities as having elements of an art, a craft, and a science.

2. A detailed guide for assessing poverty monitoring systems has been prepared by Bedi and others (2006).

3. This could involve reviewing existing performance indicators against good practice criteria such as SMART—to assess whether the indicators are specific, measurable, attributable, realistic, and timely (see Australian National Audit Office 2001). Or it could involve a review of existing data collected by ministries and the national statistics office, to see what data are available concerning government priority areas (such as health or primary education) and the extent of data harmonization or overlap. (A good example for Uganda is provided by Kiryegyera, Nuwagaba, and Ochen 2005.) It could also involve a series of detailed data audits of sector ministry data systems. The International Monetary Fund's data quality assessment standards provide an illustrative diagnostic framework: http://dsbb.imf.org/Applications/web/dqrs/dqrsdqaf/.

4. Argentina, for example, has three uncoordinated national M&E systems (Zaltsman 2006a). Two are whole-of-government and the third covers all social spending.

Chapter 13

1. This is one way of achieving harmonization of the multiple and often conflicting M&E requirements of different donors. It also provides a starting point—a "bridgehead"—for future extension of an M&E system to all government activities, including all those financed by its own budget.

2. As noted in chapter 6, however, even Chile's centrally run M&E system, which is managed by the capable and powerful finance ministry, produces some evaluations that suffer from quality problems.

Chapter 14

1. The evaluation criteria applied by the World Bank to its project comprise (1) actually or likely outcome—(a) relevance of project objectives and design, (b) effectiveness (that is, achievement of objectives), and (c) efficiency; (2) risk to development outcome (that is, that the risk that actual or likely outcomes will not be maintained); (3) Bank performance; (4) borrower performance; (5) M&E design, implementation, and utilization; and (6) other issues—safeguard compliance, fiduciary compliance, and unintended positive or negative impacts.

2. One example comes from the World Bank's support of the Egyptian government's efforts to introduce performance-based budgeting. The outcome of these efforts has been rated as moderately unsatisfactory (IEG 2004a, annex G). This report lists a number of lessons from this experience.

3. See, for example, the World Bank's work on statistical capacity building, and the work of the Partnership in Statistics for Development in the 21st Century (PARIS21, a leading consortium of international donors, governments, professional bodies, and academics: http://intranet.worldbank.org/WBSITE/INTRANET/UNITS/DEC/DATA/SCBINTRANET/0,,contentMDK: 20100922~pagePK:229337~piPK:232609~theSite PK:239411,00.html http://www.paris21.org/.

4. http://www.who.int/healthmetrics/en/ The objectives of this network are relevant to other sectors, and also to national information systems: *A country health information system comprises the multiple subsystems and data sources that together contribute to generating health information, including vital registration, censuses and surveys, disease surveillance and response, service statistics and health management information, financial data, and resource tracking. The absence of consensus on the relative strengths, usefulness, feasibility, and cost-efficiency of different data collection approaches has resulted in a plethora of separate and often overlapping systems. Too often, inappropriate use is made of particular data collection methods, for example, the use of household surveys to produce information on adult mortality. HMN partners agree to align around a common framework that sets the standards for health information systems. The HMN framework will serve to define the systems needed at country and global levels, along with the standards, capacities and processes for generating, analysing, disseminating, and using health information. . . . [It] focuses the inputs of donors and technical agencies around a country-owned plan for*

health information development, thereby reducing the overlap and duplication.

5. The HMN tool for assessment and monitoring to strengthen country health information systems is available at http://www.who.int/health metrics/documents/hmn_assessment_tool_guide_english_vl_96.pdf.

6. See the OECD's DAC Evaluation Network: http://www.oecd.org/document/60/0,2340,en_21571361_3404 7972_38242748_1_1_1_1,00.html.

7. See the previous discussion on statistical capacity building (especially PARIS21) and the HMN. The criteria for assessing financial management systems were developed by the donor community to ensure the countries that were to benefit from the debt relief initiative had sufficiently reliable systems—that is, a fiduciary requirement, known as the public expenditure and financial accountability initiative. See http://web.worldbank.org/WBSITE/EXTERNAL/TOPICS/EXTPUBLICSECTORANDGOVERNANCE/ EXTPUBLIC-FINANCE/0,,contentMDK: 20687844~pagePK:148956~piPK:216618~theSite PK:1339564,00.html.

Part VI

1. In Australia, the government abolished its Bureau of Labour Market Research in 1986 after the bureau organized a high-profile media launch of its evaluation of the government's main job creation program; the evaluation was highly critical of the program. (The government abolished the program the following year.) This experience is certainly not an argument for conducting evaluations that are anything other than honest and objective. But it is an argument for handling evaluation findings with tact. If the government body conducting an evaluation has been newly established, it would be prudent to carefully select which programs are to be evaluated.

2. The extent to which an evaluation's findings are applicable or relevant to other countries—and thus do not simply reflect a special set of local circumstances—reflects its *external validity.*

3. See, for example, the articles published in the *Boston Review* in 2006 and Davidson (2006), Cook (2006), and Scriven (2006). White (2006a, 2006b) has argued that the portion of development aid that can be subject to randomized impact evaluation is severely limited.

4. The disparity of availability of M&E information is explicitly addressed in the United States through the Program Assessment Rating Tool—PART (box 3.2).

Thus, programs with poor M&E evidence concerning their performance receive a considerably lower score.

5. This is considerably easier to do within a department, compared with the situation when a program straddles several departments.

6. One very useful analytical tool to facilitate this strategic approach is logframe analysis. A more sophisticated version of this approach is provided by theory-based evaluation. An overview of these two approaches is provided in *Monitoring and Evaluation: Some Tools, Methods and Approaches* (IEG 2004b).

Annex B

1. The team that helped prepare the diagnosis included Gladys Lopez-Acevedo, Fernando Rojas, Miguel Mercado-Díaz, Wendy Cunningham, Jairo Arboleda, Tarsicio Castañeda, Rodrigo Garcia, Marcela Rubio, and Juan Manuel Quesada, with Keith Mackay as the lead author.

2. The project documents for these and some other Bank loans are listed in the bibliography.

3. Directiva Presidencial 10 de 2002.

4. Ley 819 de 2003 o Ley de Responsabilidad Fiscal.

5. This low level of permanent staff reflects the government's tight controls on the total number of civil servants.

6. Programas de Acción Gubernamental. These are reflected in the National Development Plan.

7. http://www.sigob.gov.co/ini/.

8. Colombia is a unitary republic with 32 departments (a level of subnational government) plus the district of Bogotá. Each department oversees a number of municipalities. There are about 1,100 municipalities in Colombia.

9. Evaluations are known as "strategic evaluations" or Evaluaciones Estratégicas.

10. In addition to the publicly available SIGOB database, all the SINERGIA evaluations and a range of reports on government performance are publicly available from DNP's Web site (www.dnp.gov.co). The ability of ordinary citizens to make use of this information is unclear, however, although academia and some nongovernmental organizations certainly have the potential to use such information.

11. The questionnaire is available at: http://sinergia .dnp.gov.co/sinergia/opi.

12. The results of this survey are expected to be published in 2007.

13. DEPP has supported a series of 20 radio programs on the results of the government's social policies and on ways citizens can request support from the government. The radio programs have been transmitted on 80 community radio stations across the country.

14. http://www.bogotacomovamos.org/bogotacv/ scripts/index.php.

15. However, the Hacienda reportedly applies considerable discretionary power in releasing funds to authorized expenditures. To the extent this occurs, it increases the short-term budget flexibilities.

16. An analogous approach to the setting of performance targets is the "efficiency agreements," which are meant to be agreed in the context of the Indicative Plans, which ministries and agencies have to agree with DNP and Hacienda. See CONPES (1999). It is unclear if there are any consequences for entities that fail to meet their targets.

17. The casemix method is a means of classifying hospital patients according to the nature of their diagnosis and the level of health care required. The funding provided to each hospital is based on the numbers of each category of patient who receives treatment and the average cost of providing the corresponding level of treatment. Average costs are based on the health system as a whole.

18. The evaluation work of DDTS appears to consist of assessments of municipal performance based on the performance information collected.

19. One way M&E at the subnational level has developed in other countries is by publishing benchmarking comparisons of the quantity and quality of service provision by subnational governments. This enables relatively high-performing and low-performing governments to be identified.

20. This discussion focuses on an objectives-based program structure. Alternative program structures can be built, based, for example, on type of activity (for example, hospitals) or target group (for example, the aged).

21. DEPP has estimated that SINERGIA's evaluation agenda covers about 24 percent of the investment budget. This figure relates to the government activities which have been subject to some sort of evaluation under SINERGIA. Of course, this statistic should not be interpreted to suggest that further evaluation of these activities is not warranted: it is rarely if ever the case that even an expensive impact evaluation can comprehensively evaluate all possible issues relating to a pro-

gram's implementation, outputs, service delivery, targeting effectiveness, outcomes, and impacts, and including the full geographic coverage of a program. Thus most evaluations address only a subset of these issues. Moreover, even well-established government activities require periodic, repeated evaluation.

22. There are many barriers to achieving utilization of evaluation findings. Various supply-side attributes must be achieved for utilization to occur, such as the timeliness of an evaluation and its credibility. And the demand side is key: awareness of the evaluation findings and preparedness to use them by policy analysts, decision makers, and managers of government activities (see World Bank 2005b).

23. The World Bank is providing an institutional development fund grant of $0.29 million to help DANE improve its household surveys.

24. The two conferences held in 2004 and 2006 each attracted about 800 participants, a remarkably high number, which indicates the perceived importance of monitoring and evaluating government performance.

Annex D

1. The history of IEG's involvement in the topic of building government M&E systems is discussed by Mackay (2003).

2. Donor staff often argue that for this reason they should not be held accountable for the outcomes and impacts of their efforts; rather, it would only be reasonable to hold them accountable for their own activities and outputs. This argument misses the point, however. Although donor staff typically do not have direct control of the outcomes and impacts of their work, they nevertheless do make some contribution to these results. And it is always possible to make a reasonable judgment about their contribution to such results. Such judgments can be made by their peers—other donor staff working in the same country and their government (and possibly civil society) counterparts. (An analogy is managers preparing a referee report or job evaluation of their staff.)

3. This methodology identifies four levels of evaluation of training: participant reactions and judgments on the training; extent of participant learning (measured, for example, by before-and-after testing); changes in behavior by participants (that is, changes in how they perform work); and the results on the organization in which participants are employed (that is, how the organization performs differently as a result of its staff having received the training).

4. For example, Buchanan (2004) has conducted a four-level evaluation of IEG's International Program for Development Evaluation Training.

BIBLIOGRAPHY

Adrien, Marie-Hélène. 2003. *Guide to Conducting Reviews of Organizations Supplying M&E Training.* No. 9 of *Evaluation Capacity Development Working Paper Series.* Washington, DC: World Bank. http://www.worldbank.org/ieg/ecd/.

———. 2001. "Assessment of Ghanaian Organizations Involved in the Delivery of Monitoring and Evaluation Training." Report prepared for Independent Evaluation Group. World Bank, Washington, DC. http://www.worldbank.org/ieg/ecd/.

African Development Bank and World Bank. 1998. *Evaluation Capacity Development in Africa.* Washington, DC: World Bank. http://www.worldbank.org/ieg/ecd/.

Australian National Audit Office. 2001. *Performance Information in Portfolio Budget Statements (Report No. 18, 2001-02).* Canberra: AGPS.

———. 1997. *Program Evaluation in the Australian Public Service (Report No. 3, 1997–98).* Canberra: AGPS.

Bamberger, Michael. 2006. *Conducting Quality Impact Evaluations under Budget, Time and Data Constraints.* Washington, DC: World Bank.

Bamberger, Michael, Keith Mackay, and Elaine Ooi. 2005. *Influential Evaluations: Detailed Case Studies.* Washington, DC: World Bank.

———. 2004. *Influential Evaluations: Evaluations that Improved Performance and Impacts of Development Programs.* Washington, DC: World Bank.

Barberie, Alain. 1998. *Indonesia's National Evaluation System.* No. 3 of *Evaluation Capacity Development Working Paper Series.* Washington, DC: World Bank.

Barrett, Pat. 2001. "Evaluation and Performance Auditing: Sharing the Common Ground. A Review of Developments." Address to the Australasian Evaluation Society, Canberra, 10 October. http://www.anao.gov.au/uploads/documents/Evaluation_and_Performance_Auditing_Sharing_the_Common_Ground.pdf.

Beck, Thorsten, Asli Demirguc-Kunt, and Ross Levine. 2002. *Law and Finance: Why Does Legal Origin Matter? (Paper No. 9379).* Cambridge, UK: National Bureau of Economic Research.

Bedi, Tara, Aline Coudouel, Marcus Cox, Markus Goldstein, and Nigel Thornton. 2006. *Beyond the Numbers: Understanding the Institutions for Monitoring Poverty Reduction Strategies.* Washington, DC: World Bank.

Blondal, Jon R., and Teresa Curristine. 2004. "Budgeting in Chile." *OECD Journal on Budgeting* 4 (2): 7–45.

Booth, David, and Henry Lucas. 2001a. *Desk Study of Good Practice in the Development of PRSP Indicators and Monitoring Systems: Initial Review of PRSP Documentation.* London: Overseas Development Institute.

———. 2001b. *Desk Study of Good Practice in the Development of PRSP Indicators and Monitoring Systems: Final Report.* London: Overseas Development Institute.

Boston Review. 2006. "Making Aid Work." http://bostonreview.net/BR31.4/contents.html.

Boyle, Richard. 2005. *Evaluation Capacity Development in the Republic of Ireland.* No. 14 of *Evaluation Capacity Development Working Paper Series.* Washington, DC: World Bank.

Brushett, Stephen. 1998. *Evaluation Capacity Development in Zimbabwe: Issues and Opportunities.* No. 2 of *Evaluation Capacity Development Working Paper Series.* Washington, DC: World Bank.

Buchanan, Heather. 2004. "Evaluation of the International Progam for Development Evaluation Training." Consultant report prepared for Independent Evaluation Group and Carleton University, World Bank, Washington, DC. http://www.ipdet.org/IPDET2004%20Evaluation%20Report.pdf.

Castro, Manuel Fernando. 2006a. "Colombia's National System for Evaluating Management and Results." In

Towards the Institutionalization of Monitoring and Evaluation Systems in Latin America and the Caribbean: Proceedings of a World Bank/Inter-American Development Bank Conference, ed. Ernesto May, David Shand, Keith Mackay, Fernando Rojas, and Jaime Saaverdra, 29–35. Washington, DC: World Bank.

———. 2006b. "Performance-based management of country planning and budgeting: The case of Colombia." Presentation at the International Conference on Monitoring and Evaluation of Country Planning and Politics, Beijing, October 2006.

Compton, Donald W., Michael Baizerman, and Stacey H. Stockdill, eds. 2002. *The Art, Craft, and Science of Evaluation Capacity Building.* San Francisco: Jossey-Bass.

CONPES (Consejo Nacional de Política Económica y Social). 2004. "Renovación de la administración: Gestión por resultados y reforma del sistema nacional de evaluación." CONPES 3294.

———. 2002. "Evaluación de impacto de programas sociales." CONPES 3188.

———. 1999. "Acuerdos de eficiencia: Estrategia de evaluación del plan nacional de desarrollo 'Cambio para Construir la Paz.'" CONPES 3048.

Cook, Thomas D. 2006. "Describing What Is Special about the Role of Experiments in Contemporary Educational Research: Putting the 'Gold Standard' Rhetoric into Perspective." *Journal of MultiDisciplinary Evaluation* 6 (November): 1–7.

Curristine, Teresa. 2005. "Performance Information in the Budget Process: Results of the OECD 2005 Questionnaire." *OECD Journal on Budgeting* 5 (2): 87–131.

DAC (Development Assistance Committee of the Organisation for Economic Co-operation and Development). 2006. *The Challenge of Capacity Development: Working Towards Good Practice.* Paris: OECD.

———. 2002. *Glossary of Key Terms in Evaluation and Results Based Management.* Paris: OECD.

DAC Network on Development Evaluation. 2006. *Fact-Finding Survey on Evaluation Capacity Development (ECD) in Partner Countries.* Paris: OEDC.

Davidson, E. Jane. 2006. "The RCTs-Only Doctrine: Brakes on the Acquisition of Knowledge?" *Journal of MultiDisciplinary Evaluation* 6 (November): ii–v.

Department of National Planning. 2005. "Strategic Plan for Strengthening and Consolidating Information and Performance-Based Monitoring and Evaluation 2005–2010." Discussion paper, Department of National Planning, Bogotá.

Departmento Nacional de Planeacion y Alta Conserjería Presidencial. 2005. *Presupuesto de inversión por resultados 2006.* Bogotá: Government of Colombia.

Development Bank of Southern Africa, African Development Bank, and World Bank. 2000. *Monitoring and Evaluation Capacity Development in Africa.* Johannesburg: Development Bank of Southern Africa. http://www.worldbank.org/ieg/ecd/.

Fiszbein, Ariel, ed. 2005. *Citizens, Politicians and Providers: The Latin American Experience with Service Delivery Reform.* Washington, DC: World Bank.

GAO (Government Accountability Office). 2004. "Performance Budgeting: OMB's Program Assessment Rating Tool Presents Opportunities and Challenges for Budget and Performance Integration." Highlights of GAO-04-439T, testimony before the Subcommittee on Government Efficiency and Financial Management, Committee on Government Reform, House of Representatives. http://www.gao.gov/new.items/d04439t.pdf.

———. 1987. "Federal Evaluation: Fewer Units, Reduced Resources, Different Studies from 1980." PEMD-87-9. Washington, DC: General Accounting Office.

Government of Colombia. 2006. *Visión Colombia 2019.* Bogotá: Government of Colombia.

Government of Tanzania. 2001. *Poverty Monitoring Master Plan.* Dar es Salaam: Government of Tanzania.

Government of Uganda. 2006. *The National Integrated Monitoring and Evaluation Strategy Framework.* Kampala: Office of the Prime Minister, Government of Uganda. http://www.nimes.go.ug/index.php?option=com_frontpage&Itemid=1.

———. 2004. *Poverty Eradication Action Plan (2004/5–2007/8).* Kampala: Ministry of Finance, Planning and Economic Development, Government of Uganda.

Guerrero, R. Pablo O. 1999. *Comparative Insights from Colombia, China and Indonesia.* No. 5 of *Evaluation Capacity Development Working Paper Series.* Washington, DC: World Bank.

Guzmán, Marcela S. 2007. "Monitoring and Evaluation." Presentation to a World Bank-Government of Bolivia Workshop on Managing for Results, La Paz, Bolivia, January 22–23.

———. 2006. "The Chilean Experience." In *Towards the Institutionalization of Monitoring and Evaluation Systems in Latin America and the Caribbean: Proceedings of a World Bank/Inter-American Development Bank Conference,* ed. Ernesto May, David Shand, Keith Mackay, Fernando Rojas, and Jaime Saaverdra, 11–16. Washington, DC: World Bank. http://www.worldbank.org/ieg/ecd/.

———. 2005. *Sistema de control de gestión y presupuestos por resultados: La experiencia Chilena.* Santiago: Ministry of Finance, Budget Directorate, Government of Chile. http://www.dipres.cl/control_gestion/publicaciones/Control_Gestion_Presupuestos_Exp_Chilena_Sept_2005.html.

———. 2003. *Systems of Management Control and Results-Based Budgeting: The Chilean Experience.* Santiago: Ministry of Finance, Government of Chile.

Hatry, Harry P. 2006. *Performance Measurement: Getting Results,* 2nd ed. Washington, DC: The Urban Institute Press.

Hauge, Arild. 2003. *The Development of Monitoring and Evaluation Capacities to Improve Government Performance in Uganda.* No. 10 of *Evaluation Capacity Development Working Paper Series.* Washington, DC: World Bank.

———. 2001. *Strengthening Capacity for Monitoring and Evaluation in Uganda: A Results-Based Management Perspective.* No. 8 of *Evaluation Capacity Development Working Paper Series.* Washington, DC: World Bank.

Hauge, Arild, Wenkere Kisembo, Med Makumbi, and Omiat Omongin. 2002. "Effective Implementation of Uganda's Poverty Eradication Action Plan: The Role of Monitoring and Evaluation in the Health, Education and Water Sectors." Paper prepared for the Ministry of Finance, Planning and Economic Development, Kampala.

Hentschel, Jesko. 2004. "Using Rapid City Surveys to Inform Municipal Social Policy—An Application in Cali, Colombia." World Bank Policy Research Working Paper No. 3369, World Bank, Washington, DC.

Hernandez, Gonzalo. 2007. "The Monitoring and Evaluation System in Mexico: 2007.0 Version." Presentation at World Bank, Washington, DC, March 12.

———. 2006. "M&E of Social Programs in Mexico." In *Towards the Institutionalization of Monitoring and Evaluation Systems in Latin America and the Caribbean: Proceedings of a World Bank/Inter-American Development Bank Conference,* ed.

Ernesto May, David Shand, Keith Mackay, Fernando Rojas, and Jaime Saaverdra, 47–52. Washington, DC: World Bank. http://www.worldbank.org/ieg/ecd/docs/proceedings_la_eng.pdf.

High Level Forum on Harmonisation, Alignment, Results. 2005. *Paris Declaration on Aid Effectiveness: Ownership, Harmonisation, Alignment, Results and Mutual Accountability.* Paris: High Level Forum on Harmonisation, Alignment, Results. http://www.oecd.org/document/18/0,2340,en_2649_3236398_35401554_1_1_1_1,00.html.

IEG (Independent Evaluation Group). 2006. *2006 Annual Report on Operations Evaluation.* Washington, DC: World Bank.

———. 2004a. *Evaluation Capacity Development: OED Self-Evaluation.* Washington, DC: World Bank. http://www.worldbank.org/ieg/ecd/.

———. 2004b. *Monitoring and Evaluation: Some Tools, Methods and Approaches,* 2nd ed. Washington, DC: World Bank.

———. 2004c. *The Poverty Reduction Strategy Initiative: An Independent Evaluation of the World Bank's Support through 2003.* Washington, DC: World Bank.

———. 2003a. *Toward Country-Led Development: A Multi-Partner Evaluation of the Comprehensive Development Framework.* Washington, DC: World Bank.

———. 2003b. *World Bank Operations Evaluation Department: The First 30 Years.* Washington, DC: World Bank.

———. 2002. *Annual Report on Evaluation Capacity Development.* Washington, DC: World Bank. http://www.worldbank.org/ieg/ecd/.

Joyce, Philip G. 2004. *Linking Performance and Budgeting: Opportunities in the Federal Budget Process.* Washington, DC: IBM Center for The Business of Government. http://www.businessofgovernment.com/pdfs/Joyce_Report.pdf.

Kim, Dong Yeon, William Dorotinsky, Feridoun Sarraf, and Allen Schick. 2006. "Paths toward Successful Introduction of Program Budgeting in Korea." In *From Line-Item to Program Budgeting: Global Lessons and the Korean Case*, ed. John M. Kim, 23–134. Seoul: Korea Institute of Public Finance and World Bank. http://www1.worldbank.org/publicsector/pe/bookprogrambudget.pdf.

Kirkpatrick, Donald L., and James D. Kirkpatrick. 2006. *Evaluating Training Programs: The Four Levels,* 3rd ed. San Francisco: Berrett-Koehler Publishers.

Kiryegyera, Ben, Augustus Nuwagaba, and Eric A. Ochen. 2005. "Results-Based Monitoring and Evaluation Plan for the Poverty Eradication Action Plan." Unpublished Report Prepared for the Office of the Prime Minister, Uganda, Kampala.

Lahey, Robert. 2005. "A Comparative Analysis of Monitoring and Evaluation in Four Selected Countries: Canada, United States, Australia and United Kingdom." Unpublished manuscript.

Mackay, Keith. 2004. *Two Generations of Performance Evaluation and Management Systems in Australia.* No. 11 of *Evaluation Capacity Development Working Paper Series.* Washington, DC: World Bank.

———. 2003. "Evaluation Capacity Development." In *World Bank Operations Evaluation Department: The First 30 Years,* ed. Partick G. Grasso, Sulaiman Wasty, and Rachel Weaving, 105–14. Washington, DC: World Bank.

———. 2002. *Evaluation Capacity Development (ECD) and the Poverty Reduction Strategy Initiative: Emerging Opporunities.* Proceedings of the AfrEA 2002 Conference. Nairobi: African Evaluation Association.

———. 1998a. *The Development of Australia's Evaluation System.* No. 4 of *Evaluation Capacity Development Working Paper Series.* Washington, DC: World Bank.

———. 1998b. *Evaluation Capacity Development: A Diagnostic Guide and Action Framework.* No. 6 of *Evaluation Capacity Development Working Paper Series.* Washington, DC: World Bank.

———. 1998c. *Lessons from National Experience.* No. 1 of *Evaluation Capacity Development Working Paper Series.* Washington, DC: World Bank.

———. 1998d. *Public Sector Performance—The Critical Role of Evaluation.* Washington, DC: World Bank. http://www.worldbank.org/ieg/ecd/.

Mackay, Keith, and Sulley Gariba, eds. 2000. *The Role of Civil Society in Assessing Public Sector Performance in Ghana.* Washington, DC: World Bank. http://www.worldbank.org/ieg/ecd/.

Mackay, Keith, Gladys Lopez-Acevedo, Fernando Rojas, Aline Coudouel, and others. 2007. *A Diagnosis of Colombia's National M&E System, SINERGIA.* No. 17 of *Evaluation Capacity Development Working Paper Series.* Washington, DC: World Bank.

May, Ernesto, David Shand, Keith Mackay, Fernando Rojas, and Jaime Saavedra, eds. 2006. *Towards Institutionalizing Monitoring and Evaluation Systems in Latin America and the Caribbean: Proceedings of a World Bank/Inter-American Development Bank Conference.* Washington, DC: World Bank.

Mayne, John, and Peter Wilkins. 2005. "Believe It or Not: The Emergence of Performance Information Auditing." In *Quality Matters: Seeking Confidence in Evaluating, Auditing, and Performance Reporting*, ed. Robert Schwartz and John Mayne, 237–60. Edison, NJ: Transaction Publishers.

OECD (Organisation for Economic Co-operation and Development). 2005. *Modernizing Government: The Way Forward.* Paris: OECD.

———. 2004. "Public Sector Modernisation: Governing for Performance." OECD Policy Brief, OECD, Paris.

———. 2002. "Public Sector Modernisation: A New Agenda." GOV/PUMA(2002), 2, OECD, Paris.

———. 1998a. "Best Practice Guidelines for Evaluation." PUMA Policy Brief No. 5, OECD, Paris.

———. 1998b. *Public Management Reform and Economic and Social Development.* Paris: OECD.

———. 1997a. *In Search of Results: Performance Management Practices.* Paris: OECD.

———. 1997b. *Issues and Development in Public Management: Survey 1996–1997.* Paris: OECD.

———. 1997c. *Promoting the Use of Programme Evaluation.* Paris: OECD.

———. 1995. *Governance in Transition: Public Management Reforms in OECD Countries.* Paris: OECD.

OECD and DAC. 2006. *Managing for Development Results—Principles in Action: Sourcebook on Emerging Good Practices.* Paris: OECD. http://www.mfdr.org/Sourcebook.html.

Office of the Auditor-General of Canada. 2003. "Rating Department Performance Reports." *2003 Status Report.* Office of the Auditor-General, Ottawa. http://www.oag-bvg.gc.ca/domino/reports.nsf/html/20030501ce.html.

OMB (Office of Management and Budget). 2003. *Performance Measurement Challenges and Strategies.* Washington, DC: OMB. http://www.whitehouse.gov/omb/part/index.html.

Ospina Bozzi, Sonia, and Doris Ochoa. 2003. "El sistema nacional de evaluación de resultados de la gestión pública (SINERGIA) de Colombia." In *Evaluación de resultados para una gestión pública moderna y democrática: Experiencias Latinoamericanas,* ed. Nuria Cunill Grau and Sonia Ospina Bozzi. Caracas: CLAD.

Patton, Michael Quinn. 1997. *Utilization-Focused Evaluation: The New Century Text*, 3rd ed. Thousand Oaks, CA: Sage Publications.

Perrin, Burt, and Keith Mackay. 1999. *What Makes for Successful Conferences? Lessons Learned from an Evaluation of Six Conferences Sponsored by the World Bank Institute.* Washington, DC: World Bank Institute.

Ravindra, Adikeshavalu. 2004. *An Assessment of the Impact of Bangalore Citizen Report Cards on the Performance of Public Agencies.* No. 12 of *Evaluation Capacity Development Working Paper Series.* Washington, DC: World Bank.

Roberts, John. 2003. *Managing Public Expenditure for Development Results and Poverty Reduction.* No. 203, *Overseas Development Institute Working Papers Series.* London: Overseas Development Institute. http://www.odi.org.uk/Publications/working_papers/wp203.pdf.

Rojas, Fernando, Keith Mackay, Yasuhiko Matsuda, Geoffrey Shepherd, Azul del Villar, Ariel Zaltsman, and Philipp Krause. 2005. *Chile: Study of Evaluation Program—Impact Evaluation and Evaluations of Government Programs.* Washington, DC: World Bank. http://www.worldbank.org/ieg/ecd/.

Sánchez, María Fernanda. Undated. "Evaluation of Changes in the Quality of Life in Bogotá, Colombia, from a Civil Society Perspective—*Bogotá Cómo Vamos.*" Unpublished paper.

Sandoli, Robert L. 2005. "Budgeting for Performance in the United States Using the Program Assessment Rating Tool (PART)." Presented at a World Bank-Korea Development Institute conference, "Improving the Public Expenditure Management System," December 8.

Schacter, Mark. 2000. *Sub-Saharan Africa: Lessons from Experience in Supporting Sound Governance.* No. 7 of *Evaluation Capacity Development Working Paper Series.* Washington, DC: World Bank.

Schiavo-Campo, Salvatore. 2005. *Building Country Capacity for Monitoring and Evaluation in the Public Sector: Selected Lessons of International Experience.* No. 13 of *Evaluation Capacity Development Working Paper Series.* Washington, DC: World Bank.

Schick, Allen. 2001. "Getting Performance Measures to Measure Up." In *Quicker, Better, Cheaper? Managing Performance in American Government,* ed. Dall Forsythe. Ithaca, NY: Rockefeller Institute Press.

Scriven, Michael. 2006. "Converting Perspective to Practice." *Journal of MultiDisciplinary Evaluation* 6 (November): 8–9.

Shand, David. Forthcoming. "Performance Auditing and Performance Budgeting." In *Performance Budgeting: Linking Funding and Results,* ed. Marc Robinson. Basingstoke, Hampshire: Palgrave Macmillan.

———. 2006. "Institutionalizing Monitoring and Evaluation—Issues and Experience in OECD Countries and in Latin America." In *Towards Institutionalizing Monitoring and Evaluation Systems in Latin America and the Caribbean: Proceedings of a World Bank/Inter-American Development Bank Conference,* ed. Ernesto May, David Shand, Keith Mackay, Fernando Rojas, and Jaime Saaverdra, 57–66. Washington, DC: World Bank. http://www.worldbank.org/ieg/ecd/.

Social Impact. 2006. *Monitoring, Evaluation and Learning for Fragile States and Peacebuilding Programs: Practical Tools for Improving Program Performance and Results.* Arlington, VA: Social Impact.

Ssentongo, Peter. 2004. "The National Integrated Monitoring and Evaluation Strategy." Presentation to the 2004 Conference of the African Evaluation Association, Cape Town.

Steering Committee for the Review of Government Service Provision. 2007. *Report on Government Services 2007.* Canberra: Productivity Commission. http://www.pc.gov.au/gsp/reports/rogs/2007/index.html.

Stout, Susan. 2001. "Tanzania: Rapid Assessment of Monitoring and Evaluation in the Health Sector." Draft report, World Bank, Washington, DC.

Uhr, John, and Keith Mackay. 1996. *Evaluating Policy Advice: Learning from Commonwealth Experience.* Canberra: Federalism Research Centre (Australian National University) and the Department of Finance.

Toulemonde, Jacques. 1999. "Incentives, Constraints, and Culture-Building as Instruments for the Development of Evaluation Demand." In *Building Effective Evaluation Capacity: Lessons from Practice,* ed. Richard Boyle and Donald Lemaire, 153—174. New Brunswick, NJ: Transaction Publishers.

UNDP (United Nations Development Programme). 2000. *Evaluation Capacity Development in Asia.* New York: UNDP. http://lnweb18.worldbank.org/oed/oeddoclib.nsf/DocUNIDViewForJavaSearch/C273DBBB7BC5898085256B1B005494A8/$file/ecd_china.pdf.

United Kingdom National Audit Office. 2006. "PSA Targets: Performance Information." NAO Survey Report, NAO, London. http://www.nao.org.uk/

publications/nao_reports/05-06/Acting_on_ Information.pdf.

United Kingdom Treasury. Undated. *Outcome Focused Management in the United Kingdom*. London: Treasury. http://www.hm-treasury.gov.uk/documents/ public_spending_and_services/publicservice_ performance/pss_perf_index.cfm.

Vedung, Evert. 1991. *Utvärdering i politik och förvaltning*. Lund: Studentlitteratur. (Translation: 1997. *Public Policy and Program Evaluation*. New Brunswick, NJ: Transactions Publishers).

White, Howard. 2006a. *Impact Evaluation—The Experience of the Independent Evaluation Group of the World Bank*. Washington, DC: World Bank.

———. 2006b. "Technical Rigor Must Not Take Precedence over Other Kinds of Valuable Lessons." *Boston Review*, July/August. http://bostonreview.net/BR31.4/ white.html.

Wholey, Joseph S. 2006. "Quality Control: Assessing the Accuracy and Usefulness of Performance Measurement Systems." In *Performance Measurement: Getting Results*, 2nd ed., ed. Harry P. Hatry. Washington, DC: The Urban Institute Press.

Wholey, Joseph S., Harry P. Hatry, and Kathryn E. Newcomer. 2004. *Handbook of Practical Program Evaluation*, 2nd ed. San Francisco: Jossey-Bass.

World Bank. 2007. "Colombia: Monitoring, Evaluation and Information Project." Project Appraisal Document, World Bank, Washington, DC.

———. 2006a. "Colombia: Community Works and Employment Project." Implementation Completion Report No. 37294, World Bank, Washington, DC.

———. 2006b. *Social Accountability: Strengthening the Demand Side of Governance and Service Delivery*. Washington, DC: World Bank. http://www-esd.world bank.org/sac/contact_welcome/welcome.html.

———. 2005a. *Chile: Análisis del programa de evaluación del gasto público*. Washington, DC: World Bank.

———. 2005b. "Colombia: Third Programmatic Fiscal and Institutional Structural Adjustment Loan Project." Project Appraisal Document, World Bank, Washington, DC.

———. 2005c. "Colombia: Social Safety Net Project." Project Appraisal Document, World Bank, Washington, DC.

———. 2004a. "Colombia: Proposed Second Programmatic Labor Reform and Social Structural Adjustment Loan Project." Program Document, World Bank, Washington, DC.

———. 2004b. "Colombia: Technical Assistance Loan to Support the Second Programmatic Labor Reform and Social Structural Adjustment Loan Project." Project Appraisal Document 29332, World Bank, Washington, DC.

———. 2004c. "Readiness Assessment—Toward Performance-Based Monitoring and Evaluation in Mexico: The Case of SEDESOL." Unpublished paper. World Bank, Washington, DC.

———. 2004d. *The World Bank Annual Report 2004*. Washington, DC: World Bank.

———. 2003. *World Development Report 2004: Making Services Work for Poor People*. Oxford: Oxford University Press.

———. 1998. *Public Expenditure Management Handbook*. Washington, DC: World Bank. http://site resources.worldbank.org/INTPEAM/Resources/pem9 8.pdf.

———. 1997a. *Colombia: Paving the Way for a Results-Oriented Public Sector*. Washington, DC: World Bank.

———. 1997b. *World Development Report 1997: The State in a Changing World*. New York: Oxford University Press. http://www.worldbank.org/html/extpb/ wdr97/english/wdr97con.htm.

World Bank, African Development Bank, Austria, Germany, The Netherlands, Norway, Sweden, and UK Department for International Development. 2006. Joint Assistance Strategy for the Republic of Uganda (2005–2009). http://siteresources.worldbank.org/ INTUGANDA/Resources/UJAS.pdf.

World Bank and International Monetary Fund. 2004. *Poverty Reduction Strategy Papers—Progress in Implementation*. Washington, DC: World Bank and International Monetary Fund. http://siteresources .worldbank.org/INTPRS1/Resources/prsp_progress_2 004.pdf.

Zaltsman, Ariel. 2006a. *Experience with Institutionalizing Monitoring and Evaluation Systems in Five Latin American Countries: Argentina, Chile, Colombia, Costa Rica and Uruguay*. No. 16 of *Evaluation Capacity Development Working Paper Series*. Washington, DC: World Bank.

———. 2006b. "The Monitoring and Evaluation Function in Colombia." Unpublished paper, World Bank, Washington, DC.

Useful Web sites

African Evaluation Association (AfrEA): http://www.afrea.org/

Asian Development Bank Web site on the Asian community of practice on managing for development results: http://www.adb.org/MfDR/CoP/about.asp

CLAD (Centro Latinoamericano de Administración Para el Desarrollo): http://www.clad.org.ve/siare/innotend/innotend.html

Citizen's Report Card (PAC, India): http://www.pacindia.org/

International Development Evaluation Association (IDEAS): http://www.ideas-int.org/

International Organisation for Cooperation in Evaluation (IOCE): http://internationalevaluation.com/index.shtml

Latin American evaluation associations: http://www.preval.org/mapa.php?idioma=8

Managing for Development Results initiative: http://www.mfdr.org/

U.S. PART: http://www.whitehouse.gov/omb/part/index.html

World Bank Independent Evaluation Group: http://www.worldbank.org/ieg/ecd